The three slicks came in very low, missing the rice paddies by only a foot or two. The guys and myself were standing on our helo's landing skids, grasping the sides of the doors and totally psyched to assault the enemy hootches. As the helo started flaring, we jumped out from about six feet, screaming, "Yaaaaaaoooooooohhhhhhhh!" As soon as our boots plunged into the flooded rice paddy, we began our assault with all weapons a-blazin'. Suddenly it seemed that bullets and rockets were whizzing, ricocheting, and popping all around us.

The rest of 1st Squad took the left hootch and promptly killed two VC. Trung Uy, myself, and 2nd Squad took the right hootch and bunker, hoping to shed a little blood ourselves. . . .

By Gary R. Smith
Published by Ivy Books:

MASTER CHIEF: Diary of a Navy SEAL

With Alan Maki
DEATH IN THE JUNGLE: Diary of a Navy SEAL
DEATH IN THE DELTA: Diary of a Navy SEAL

MASTER CHIEF

Diary of a Navy SEAL

Gary R. Smith

IVY BOOKS • NEW YORK

Ivy Books
Published by Ballantine Books
Copyright © 1996 by Gary R. Smith

http://www.randomhouse.com

Library of Congress Catalog Card Number: 96-94326

ISBN 0-8041-1091-3

Manufactured in the United States of America

First Edition: September 1996

10 9 8 7 6 5 4 3 2 1

This book is dedicated to my family and to Alan Maki, my friend and mentor whose previous instructions enabled me to write *Master Chief*. Moreover, this book is dedicated to my UDT/SEAL/EOD teammates of the past, present, and future.

ACKNOWLEDGMENTS

The author wishes to thank his family for their support and encouragement, Captain Robert Gormly, Lt. Comdr. Jerry Fletcher, and Comdr. Loren Decker for their introductions; Colonel Joseph Ostrowidzki for his family history in Poland and Siberia before and during World War II; Owen Lock, Editor-at-Large, Ballantine Books; Ethan Ellenberg, literary agent; Dennis Cummings's corrections and comments; Al Betters for the Golf Platoon roster; Mike Rush for various SEAL Team 1 platoon rosters and pictures; Hayes Otaupalik of Missoula, Montana; and Weaver Photography of Mineral Wells, Texas. A special thanks to my old November Platoon mates Jerry Fletcher, Layton Bassett, and Roger Hayden, who filled in a few details that I had failed to record in my diary and letters to Mom and Dad; Captain Jon Wright, for the names of the Oscar platoon personnel; BMC Joe Thrift, my UDT-12 Fourth Platoon LPO. Last but not least, a special thanks to Senior Chief Petty Officer Willie Williams of the EOD Detachment, NAS, Whidbey Island, Washington, for checking the last three chapters of this book for technical accuracy.

The "Warrior's Words" quotations at the beginning of each chapter and elsewhere were taken from *Warrior's Words a Quotation Book* (Arms and Armour Press), by Peter G. Tsouras.

Special thanks to all of Gary Smith's EOD/UDT/SEAL teammates, those still alive and those who have passed over the bar—lest we forget.

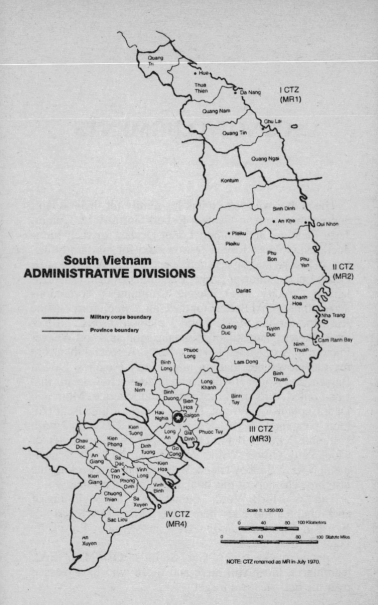

**South Vietnam
ADMINISTRATIVE DIVISIONS**

Quang
Tri

• Hue

Thua
Thien

• Da Nang   I CTZ
(MR1)

Quang Nam

Chu Lai

Quang Tin

Quang Ngai

Kontum

Binh Dinh

• An Khe   Qui Nhon

• Pleiku

Pleiku

Phu
Bon   Phu
Yen   II CTZ
(MR2)

Darlac

Khanh
Hoa

• Nha Trang

Quang
Duc   Tuyen
Duc   Cam Ranh Bay

Ninh
Thuan

Phuoc
Long   Lam Dong

Binh
Long

Tay
Ninh   Long
Khanh   Binh
Thuan

Binh
Duong   Binh
Tuy

Hau
Nghia   Bien
Hoa
Saigon

Kien
Tuong   Long
An   Gia
Dinh   Phuoc Tuy   III CTZ
(MR3)

Chau
Doc   Kien
Phong   Dinh
Tuong   Go
Cong

An
Giang   Sa
Dec   Kien
Hoa

Kien
Giang   Can
Tho   Phong
Dinh   Vinh
Long

Chuong
Thien   Sa
Xuyen   Vinh
Binh

Sac Lieu   IV CTZ
(MR4)

An
Xuyen

—— Military corps boundary

—— Province boundary

Scale 1: 1,250,000

0   40   80   100 Kilometers

0   40   80   100 Statute Miles

NOTE: CTZ renamed as MR in July 1970.

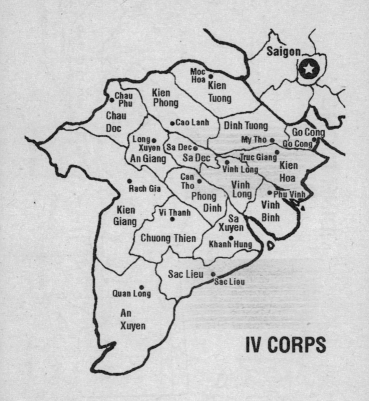

IV CORPS

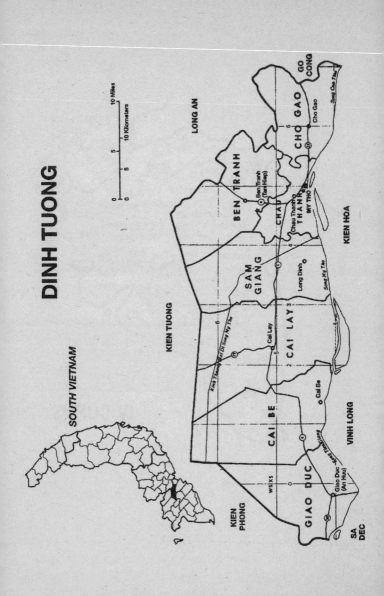

DINH TUONG

SOUTH VIETNAM

INTRODUCTION

Lieutenant Commander Jerry J. Fletcher

I count it a great honor to be asked to say a few words regarding Gary Smith's treatise about his career in the Navy SEAL team. I have many, many fond memories of the men of SEAL Team 1, November Platoon—and I hold none in higher regard than Gary R. Smith. Smitty's professionalism in every realm set the standard to which others should aspire.

There is probably no bond greater than that of men who have endured the horrors of combat together for extended periods of time, because it soon becomes evident that the reason you remain alive is the actions of your teammates. The ultimate in faith is willingly to place your life in the hands of another. I did this time and again with Smitty.

It is difficult to put these thoughts into words without it sounding like so much bullshit. But the men who have been there understand—and the others, well, they're the others.

There are many elite military organizations in the world dealing in an arena classified as "special operations." For them, violence and violent death often become a daily experience. It takes a special person to survive in such an environment, much less to excel. In the world of Special Warfare, Smitty was the warrior's warrior.

Jerry J. Fletcher
Lt. Comdr. USN
Wickenburg, Arizona
1 May 1994

Captain Robert A. Gormly

From 1979 to 1981 I had the pleasure of being professionally associated with Gary Smith. He was a highly respected leader who could do it all, and for that reason he became the Master Chief of the Command, a position reserved for only the best. It is especially significant that he has chosen to write about his life as a Navy SEAL. His experiences and insights should be heeded by all young SEALs, but more important, as society seems to be unwilling to demand personal responsibility for one's own actions, anyone can derive guidance from his words. For me personally, reading *Master Chief* evoked fond memories of the most enjoyable time of my Navy career—when I was a SEAL platoon commander in Vietnam during 1967 and 1968.

Master Chief is the chronicle of the life of a Navy SEAL. I am really impressed with the degree of detail Gary brings to his story. The journal he kept throughout his career allows him to attain a level of detail not always found in the recent works by other former SEALs. His account of off-duty SEAL platoon escapades was especially entertaining. There's a saying among SEALs that if you don't get caught, you're doing a good job. Gary always did a good job.

Of particular interest to me is his account of the successes, the frustrations, and the eventual boredom of one of the last SEAL combat platoons in Vietnam trying to "wind down" operations in accordance with the policy of the Nixon administration. He shows quite well the inability of "higher authority" to understand how SEALs should be employed. From the beginning of SEAL combat platoon involvement in Vietnam in 1966 to the bitter end, there was no strategy for the SEALs' employment. In more than five years of dangerous and successful SEAL operations, each platoon commander determined the quantity and quality of his platoon's efforts. Gary brings this out loud and clear.

He also describes well the relationship that normally exists between SEALs and staffs. SEALs tend to fall into two categories: operators or "ticket punchers"—the latter are disliked, disrespected, and distrusted. During the Vietnam era the operators sought combat and the "ticket punchers" sought other jobs. This is not to say that operators don't ever find themselves on staffs, but when they do, they are usually good staff officers who abide by the notion that they ought to be influencing higher authority and supporting subordinate units. Gary shows this was the case when he describes the personalities of the fledgling Naval Special Warfare Unit Vietnam staff.

SEALs made their mark in Vietnam, but after the war there was a feeling among some senior officers in the Navy that SEALs ought to be put back in their cages until the next war. Frankly, these officers didn't see what SEALs could do for the Navy, and for a time we didn't do a very good job explaining it. So from 1972 to the beginning of the Reagan presidency we scrambled for recognition and money. Most of the post-Vietnam training evolutions described in *Master Chief* were done on what the Navy called "No Cost Orders." Technically, the men had to volunteer for such orders, because it was against Navy policy to order someone anywhere without paying travel and per diem expenses. During much of the 1970s there was not enough money in the SEAL teams to pay for all the required training. SEALs accepted the fact that to keep themselves qualified they would often have to pay their own way. As highly motivated as the men were, self-financed training was a poor substitute for combat, particularly for the combat veterans. Some sought challenge elsewhere.

For Gary Smith, it was Explosive Ordnance Disposal (EOD). As he recounts his experiences, I am reminded of an old "axiom"—the only thing crazier than a Navy SEAL is a Navy EOD man.

Today all the special operations forces of the Army, Navy, and Air Force are funded and prepared for combat under the U.S. Special Operations Command, an organization headed by a four-star general. SEALs are a firmly entrenched, well-respected, well-funded, and properly employed part of that command, as demonstrated by their recent successes in Desert Storm and Somalia. SEALs have reached that point because of superb men like Gary Smith. *Master Chief* is a SEALs book that will be enjoyed by all.

Robert A. Gormly
Capt. USN
Chula Vista, California
16 August 1994

Commander Loren E. Decker

Graduating from Basic Underwater Demolition/SEAL training in the 1960s was a heady experience, and receiving one's first orders to SEAL Team 1 only added to the swelling pride and excitement. Life as a new SEAL soon became a never-ending cycle of days and nights of intense training punctuated by long periods of profound intoxication and brief periods of slumber. It was in that tumultuous atmosphere of excellence and expectation that I first met Radioman Second Class Gary Smith.

I don't believe that Gary remembers our first meeting, since he was acting leading petty officer of the electronics shop and I was just an FNG seaman assigned for field day. (The NG in FNG stands for "new guy.") I remember our brief meeting because even then I had been told that Smitty knew what he was doing and did not suffer fools gladly. I kept my mouth shut and cleaned the ET space the best way I knew how, because I wanted the respect of men like Smith.

There was no way that either of us could have known then how our lives would subsequently touch, nor the heights of pleasure and depths of pain that we were to share.

Our paths briefly crossed during my first commissioned tour at SEAL Team 1, and it was then that I first recognized just how valuable a good chief could be to a young ensign. Our commanding officer at the time was, to put it charitably, not operationally oriented. As the team ordnance officer, I had been directed to conduct a type of demolition training for the team that I felt was unsafe (because of the close proximity of a naval-dependent housing area to our practice range). Smitty had just reported to the ordnance department as our chief petty officer, and I was discussing my concerns with him when he gave me kind of a disgusted look and said "OP [Ordnance Publication] Five, Volume Two." I eventually got him to explain that that publication lists minimum safe distances for explosive detonations, and even to show me where to find them. My concerns were well-founded, and while the CO wasn't very happy, at least we didn't kill any dependents.

Smitty served me well in two other tours. First as my

assistant training officer at Underwater Demolition Team 12, and again when I was air operations officer at Naval Special Warfare Group 1. For some three years we ran platoons through weapons, tactics, diving, and parachuting courses, enjoying life to the fullest. A winter exercise in Alaska gave us the opportunity to ski and snowshoe. Designations as range officers gave us weekend access to the Special Warfare rifle range where we spent most Sunday mornings. Hunting seasons found us with rifles and rucksacks, heading into some of the best wilderness areas in southern California.

As I look back on twenty-seven years of naval service, I can count on one hand the number of men who have impressed me as much as Smitty, and there were none who impressed me in the same way. He was a consummate technician in every field of Special Warfare expertise, a strong leader, a loyal subordinate, and one of the best friends a man could ever have. I can personally attest to the truth of what he says in *Master Chief*, although I can also attest to the fact that he left out much of the bad that happened. Perhaps that is as it should be, and it's definitely Gary Smith.

Loren E. Decker
Comdr. USNR
Waco, Texas
27 October 1994

Author's Note

Master Chief covers some of my experiences as the LPO (Leading Petty Officer—E-6) of SEAL Team 1's November Platoon in Dinh Tuong province, Vietnam, 1971. It was my fifth and last tour in Vietnam.

My remaining years with SEAL Team 1 and Underwater Demolition Team 12 were spent deploying twice more to WESTPAC (Western Pacific) and attending many schools; that is, EOD (Explosive Ordnance Disposal) School, U.S. Army Sergeants Major Academy, Radioman B School, and Instructor School. My responsibilities varied from CMAA (Chief Master at Arms), Assistant Training Officer, Acting Command Master Chief, Ordnance Chief, Air Department Chief, and Cadre Inspector. In November '81 I was assigned to EOD Detachment Whidbey Island, Washington, until my retirement in '84.

I consider it a privilege and honor to pass on a small portion of the history of the U.S. Navy and my experiences as a Special Warfare and EOD technician. Admittedly, many of my opinions are biased in one form or another; however, my goal has been to tell the story of how I perceived issues at that time. All of my SpecWar and EOD mates and myself were arrogant to one degree or another and were fond of saying, "It's hard to be humble when you know you're the best." Many of my perceptions, however, have changed over the years—for the better, I hope. I've tried to accurately describe the good and the bad and to be subjective or objective at the appropriate times. Toward the end of my Navy career I began to understand that many times the worst enemy I had to face was myself, as we *all* are our worst enemy at one time or another. Some folks call that the beginning of maturity and wisdom. There were several times that I felt the need for a wise SpecWar/EOD friend/counselor/mentor, but for whatever reasons, they were rare or simply not available. I would like to recommend to today's SpecWar and EOD Groups to be more sensitive to these needs in the future, if they haven't already.

I'm very thankful for having had the privilege and honor of serving with some of the best-trained and most highly motivated personnel in the world. If you're sick and tired of living a tax-burdened, besotted, proletarian or bourgeois lifestyle, I highly recommend a career in Special Warfare and/or EOD—*if* you can qualify and *if* you can survive the training. You'll never regret it. However, be advised, I spent approximately seventy percent of my career away from home. This is a very difficult career for a married man and a Christian! Frankly, a career in Special Warfare may be, over the long haul, counterproductive and inadvisable for a married man or a Christian, as this book in some ways proves.

Some of the names have been left incomplete and/or changed to protect those who are still living or serving with civilian or military intelligence information-collection agencies or units.

The missions and events of my fifth and last tour in Vietnam in '71 with SEAL Team 1's November Platoon are true. I kept a detailed diary throughout my '71 tour in preparation for this book, and had the benefit of letters that my mom and dad saved. The conversations are not always verbatim, but represent the typical dialogue and interaction between me and my teammates, friends, and others who were an important part of my naval career.

The second portion of this book continues chronologically and highlights specific accounts that I have chosen to record and pass on to the past, present, and future generations of all branches of EOD and Special Warfare warriors.

My name is Gary R. Smith. This is my first book as the sole author.

PROLOGUE

A lot of water had gone under the bridge since I graduated from high school in 1960. My short stint in college taught me the value of diligent study, even though I hadn't done much of it. Working in North Texas in construction, oil fields, and ranching before I enlisted in the Navy taught me that I wanted something more out of life—I wanted adventure, not drudgery.

In 1964 Navy boot camp taught me responsibility, discipline, and a combination of respect for and fear of authority. UDT Training the following year gave me confidence in my virtually unlimited physical and mental capabilities and taught me the necessity of teamwork and the rewards of hard work and commitment. I also began to understand the power of encouragement and loyalty—two of the foundation stones of motivation and camaraderie.

My first tour to Vietnam, in 1966–67, with the UDT-12's 4th Platoon, introduced me to combat, tested my resolve, and gave me experience with and appreciation for my teammates, as well as a stronger love for and allegiance to my great country. I learned that courage is the will to control my fear regardless of the circumstances and the act of faithfully obeying my orders.

My second tour to Vietnam, in 1967–68, seasoned me with the exhilaration, disappointments, and tragedies of combat, and the sorrow of losing a close friend. I began to understand the wisdom of listening carefully; in silence, understanding comes.

My third tour to Vietnam, in '69 as a PRU (Provincial Reconnaissance Unit) adviser, taught me how to be a better follower and introduced me to the administrative and operational responsibilities of leadership—through advising and leading combat-hardened Vietnamese, Cambodian, and Chinese PRUs without offending, and in organizing and executing helicopter assault operations. As I began to understand the differences between political conservatives and liberals, it didn't take me long to deduce that I was a conservative, spiritually and politically. I proudly voted for Mr. Nixon to be the next President of my great country. It was also during those times when the team personnel's families began receiving threatening and harassing phone calls from the antiwar, anti-God, anti-family, pro-drug, and pro-Communist traitors. Those phone calls to our families continued throughout the war.

My fourth tour to Vietnam, in 1970, awakened my anger toward the liberal news media's lies, half-truths, and innuendos against the war in Vietnam and toward the liberal politicians who supported them. I simply couldn't understand their beguiling and treasonous attitudes. I especially hated their use of the power of innuendo—there was little chance of defense, vindication, or justice for the falsely impugned. Because I was a conservative, I despised the liberal long-haired college students, draft dodgers, and hippies for what they stood for and for who they were—knowingly or unknowingly—serving, and for their lack of patriotism, and their outright sabotage of the war effort.

The political left's hidden agendas and the liberal student demonstrations *against* democracy and freedom and proclamations *for* Marxist tyranny and encouragement *to* the North Vietnamese military and political machines sickened me. I especially felt betrayed when they carried the Viet Cong and North Vietnamese flags during their demonstrations. Sadly, during those years, men in uniform were not safe on the streets or highways of America.

By the time I began my fifth tour in Vietnam, in 1971, I found it difficult to deal with the politics that were thrust upon the military in Vietnam and the political and social situation in my country. The news media continued to insist that we were losing the war, when in fact we had been kicking the hell out of the Viet Cong and the North Vietnamese war machines all along, and with one hand tied behind our backs. In spite of President Johnson's having forbidden U.S. forces to seek and destroy the VC/NVA main force divisions decisively beyond the borders of South Vietnam to Laos, Cambodia, and North Vietnam, and limiting our tactical objectives within South Vietnam (to my knowledge there has never been a war won by defensive tactics and with limited objectives), we managed to inflict such heavy casualties on the Communist forces during their Tet and other offensives that they were forced to withdraw to lick their wounds time and again.

Sadly, in October 1968 President Johnson stopped all bombing against North Vietnam. His decision opened the door for the infiltration of several divisions of North Vietnamese combat troops and massive supplies into the South Vietnamese highlands and remote delta areas, eventually resulting in some of the war's worst battles within South Vietnam. The consequences were dreadful increases of U.S., Allied, and South Vietnamese civilian and military dead and wounded. Interestingly, President Johnson and his Democratic Congress initiated their massive Great Society social welfare programs during that same year.

That the soldier is but the servant of the statesman, as war is but the instrument of diplomacy, no educated soldier will deny. Politics must always exercise an extreme influence on strategy; but it cannot be gainsaid that interference with the commanders in the field is fraught with the gravest danger.

—Colonel George F. R. Henderson, "Stonewall Jackson," 1898

On January 20, 1969, Mr. Nixon became President. He wisely listened to the advice of the Joint Chiefs of Staff, Dr. Henry Kissinger, MACV (U.S. Military Assistance Command Vietnam), the CIA, and others, and soon ordered U.S. forces to go on the offensive outside the boundaries of South Vietnam in accordance with the established political and military objectives.

On May 1, 1970, MACV executed a raid that penetrated nineteen miles inside Cambodia. The military objective was to attack and destroy the North Vietnamese COSVN (Central Office for South Vietnam), divisional base areas, and immense supply depots that had historically supported all VC/NVA strikes on Saigon and surrounding areas. The political objective was to support Cambodia's prime minister, Lon Nol, and the National Assembly that had overthrown Prince Sihanouk on March 18, 1970. Because of President Nixon's decisive leadership, it was not surprising that the offensive had a psychological effect on both sides of the fence. The morale of the U.S., South Vietnamese, and Allied armed forces skyrocketed (especially mine) during that invasion, resulting in increased confidence in the military and political objectives.

In spite of the liberals', leftists', and draft-dodging students' antiwar movement at home, President Nixon performed well as commander in chief of the armed forces. Lest it be forgotten, President Nixon honorably served his country during the Second World War as a naval officer. Because of his loyalty and service to his country, he'll always be one of my American heroes. Unfortunately, according to Phillip B. Davidson in *Vietnam at War*, "Hanoi's *dich van* program [action among the enemy people] was working well in the United States." In other words, the North Vietnamese were winning their Marxist war through turncoat professors in our universities, leftists, draft dodgers, and self-serving politicians and media.

There was the treasonous ilk of "Hanoi Jane," whose hypocritical Marxist aspirations and arrogance supported the North Vietnamese political and military machines and Russian and Chinese advisers. When "Hanoi Jane" and her husband, our liberal media and their Communist partners, failed to win in Vietnam, they increased their vocal and financial support of open Marxism on our campuses and congressional hallways.

> Once initiated there were but few public men who would have the courage to oppose it. Experience proves that the man who obstructs a war in which his nation is engaged, no matter whether right or wrong, occupies no enviable place in life or history. Better for him, individually, to advocate "war, pestilence, and famine" than to act as obstructionist to a war already begun. The history of the defeated rebel will be honorable hereafter, compared with that of the northern man who aided him by conspiring against his government while protected by it. The most favorable posthumous history the stay-at-home traitor can hope for is—oblivion.
>
> —General of the Army Ulysses S. Grant, *Personal Memoirs of U. S. Grant*, 1885

> In late March, 1971, House Democrats approved a resolution calling for the termination of the United States involvement in Indochina by 1 January 1973.
>
> —Phillip B. Davidson *Vietnam at War*

After the war ended April 30, 1975, I tried to suppress my memories of how the liberal politicians had progressively decreased military aid to the South Vietnamese war effort. Many of those same liberals had vigorously supported the Vietnam War under Presidents Kennedy and Johnson. By 1975 the South Vietnamese military was forced to issue small quantities of first-aid equipment, ammunition, and ordnance to their combat infantrymen; two rounds of 40mm HE per grenadier (M-79), forty rounds of 5.56mm ammo, and one hand grenade to face the well-equipped North Vietnamese Communists. In effect, American liberals sold out our South Vietnamese allies to a Marxist police state whose citizens had few if any judicial rights. I tried to forget about my Vietnamese, Cambodian, and Chinese friends and their families, whom U.S. liberal politicians had left behind. However, I failed miserably and often thought about my PRU friends Sao Lam, Ba To, the courageous Hoa Hao and his small village. If they were captured (and I doubt that they were—they would have fought to the death), they would have been considered guilty until proven innocent. If they didn't have a politically powerful advocate (they wouldn't have), they and their families were most certainly executed.

CHAPTER ONE

People are afraid of a leader who has no sense
of humor. They think that he is not capable of relaxing, and as a result of this there is a tendency
for that leader to have a reputation for pomposity,
which may not be the case at all. Humor has a tendency to relax people in times of stress.
—Louis H. Wilson

I was waiting at the HAL-3/VAL-4 (Helicopter Attack,
Light, 3/Light Attack Squadron 4) hangar until the duty
driver came to take me and the Black Pony pilots to a
bunker near the parked OV-10 aircraft where the briefing
room was located. I had been assigned to ride with a Lieutenant (jg) called Sam (I forgot his last name) who flew
Bronco number 113. I had occasionally seen the Black
Ponies from a distance during my '69 and '70 tours, but I
had never inspected one up close. The Rockwell OV-10A
fixed-wing Bronco was beautiful to look at, had twin engines that were propeller-powered and controlled by a pilot and copilot. It looked somewhat like the old WWII
Lockheed P-38 Lightning. Its armament was impressive.
It had four internal M-60 machine guns, a 20mm cannon,
a 7.62mm GAU-2 minigun, and could carry 2.75-inch
and five-inch Zuni rockets. There was nothing second-
rate about the outfit whose aircraft were referred to as the
"Black Ponies."

The previous day, June 4, 1971, Lieutenant Fletcher, or Dai Uy—Vietnamese for navy lieutenant or army captain—and I were given permission to ride a Black Pony on an actual strike so that we would be familiar with the Bronco's capabilities. We were especially interested in finding out just how close we could call in AW (automatic weapons) and rocket strikes to our position on the ground. Assuming we were in contact with the enemy and there were only thirty meters between us, could we call in five-inch Zuni rockets with impact-detonating warheads and expect to survive the explosions? That was the question.

Before our briefing, Sam helped me put on the parachute and harness, survival kit, and so on, and instructed me in the use of them. After the briefing, Sam and I went to his Bronco, where he taught me which knobs to pull and not to pull, as well as the basics of how to fly the craft. In short order we were taking off with another Bronco.

We flew past Vi Thanh, the capital of Chuong Thien province, and close to Song Ong Duc, a river, where a convoy of boats was proceeding upstream. We remained on station for approximately thirty minutes until Ca Mau's sector TOC (Tactical Operations Center) of An Xuyen province requested Sam to make a rocket run on a Green Hornet target. "Green Hornet" was a code name for known locations of VC/NVA radio or communication bunkers that were transmitting messages. They were located by our ELINT (Electronic Intelligence) folks with their direction-finding equipment and were generally accurate to within at least four-digit, or one-thousand-meter, coordinates.

Sam peeled off to our left and said, "Hang on, Smitty. We've got ourselves a target that we'll soften up with our rockets." We headed directly for the clandestine radio station located in the center of the U Minh forest.

The delta is considered to be the rice bowl of Asia and

can supposedly raise enough rice to support all of it. I was always amazed at the beauty of the Vietnamese delta—especially from the air. The rivers, streams, and canals were a deep blue, while the ride paddies reflected a light blue hue. The jungles, however, were a deep and ominous green and reminded me of a time past, about 1950, when a battalion of French Foreign Legionnaires were parachuted into the U Minh forest. After a couple of days of futile requests for unavailable reinforcements and support, none of them were ever heard from again. Leon Rauch and I had operated in the U Minh forest on one occasion in '69 with the PRU. We had intel/info of a VC/NVA POW camp and its location. We inserted by helicopter slicks and managed to rescue a few Vietnamese POWs and capture some communications equipment. Still, it was no surprise to me that the U.S. and South Vietnamese military generally avoided the U Minh forest.

Upon arrival, Sam and I didn't spot anything other than a man-made structure and a sampan. However, that was all the evidence we needed, since they were located in a free-fire zone.

Sam put the Bronco into a shallow dive, then said, "We'll send a couple of twenty-pound Zuni warhead messages into their communications center and see how they like it."

"Sounds great to me, Lieutenant," I replied.

"Call me Sam, Smitty."

"Okay, Sam," I replied while chuckling. "I haven't had so much fun since last winter when I was hunting Gambel's quail in the Chocolate Mountains near our SEAL training camp."

Sam made two strikes. He fired all four of his M-60s and launched two Zuni rockets that completely destroyed the small radio shack and a nearby sampan.

"Hoo-Yah!" I yelled as the rockets hit their intended target. "You guys are really good with these rockets. Just how close would you dare place a Zuni to a SEAL squad that's pinned down by the VC?" I asked.

"I wouldn't want to place a Zuni any closer to you guys than fifty meters," he said pointedly. "However, I wouldn't hesitate placing 2.75-inch rockets to within thirty meters of you. Is that good enough?" Sam asked.

"Yessir!" I exclaimed. "That's just what we're looking for when we get into trouble—good, reliable, and accurate fire support."

Immediately after Sam destroyed the comm shack, we were called to a point near the coast between Ca Mau and Rach Gia where a U.S. Army adviser and his counterparts from the Army of the Republic of Vietnam were in contact with the VC and had one ARVN casualty. Because there were helo gunboats already on station when we arrived, Sam decided that we should head for home before our fuel got too low.

"How would you like to fly this ship, Smitty?" Sam asked over the intercom.

"I'm used to jumping out of airplanes, not flying them," I teased. "However, I would love to give it a try."

"Okay, grab the stick between your legs and place your feet on the left and right pedal. Now pay close attention to what I do," Sam instructed. It was surprisingly easy. Sam dodged a few small clouds by going over, under, left, and right of them, then stated, "Okay, you've got it."

I thought I had died and gone to heaven. It was great! I dodged clouds with total aplomb. Just as I was beginning to spout a light case of braggadocio, Sam said, "Take her into a roll."

Suddenly, my stomach felt as if it were filled with a brood of vipers. "I respectfully decline, Sam," I replied meekly.

"Here, I'll show you. It's a piece of cake," Sam said as he pulled her up, then down, and rolled her completely over and to the right. "Okay, you've got her."

Oh shit! I thought. I didn't say a word as I pulled her up and started a roll to the right. Once we were in an upside-down position, I simply didn't know what to do with the stick. Sam, no doubt, continued us through the roll, for it certainly wasn't me.

As Sam was dodging another cloud, I stupidly asked, "How many g's does it take before a fellow blacks out, Sam?"

Sam chuckled ominously, then answered, "Between six and seven. Here, I'll show you." Sam put the ol' gal into a steep dive, then pulled all the way back on the stick.

In a heartbeat I was already regretting my curiosity. This is definitely a white-knuckle experience, I kept thinking as my vision narrowed to the size of a pencil. Damn! I thought. He's continuing into a barrel roll! "Shiiiiiiiit!" I shrieked over the intercom between belches. Suddenly, I felt a pressure in my stomach that was simultaneously pushing upward and downward. I began to panic when I realized that I could potentially puke on the back of Sam's helmet, piss in my pants, and fill my jungle-green bottoms to boot! This is not good! I thought as I held my left hand under my crotch and my right hand over my mouth.

"How did you like that, Smitty? Wasn't that fun?" Sam asked, snickering.

"Somehow, I bet you like pulling wings off butterflies, huh, Lieutenant?" I replied sarcastically. "For a minute there I thought I had died and gone to hell." We both laughed until our arrival at Binh Thuy, which was located a few miles upstream of Can Tho.

"Sam," I said as we shook hands on the ground, "I want to thank you for a great experience today. I hope that when we do call for VAL-4 support, you'll be one of the pilots laying those five-inch Zunis and 2.75-inch rockets in there for us."

Sam nodded and replied, "However, on the other side of the coin, if I ever have to make a crash landing in the midst of Indian country, I hope you'll be one of the guys to come to my rescue."

"You can count on it, sir," I concluded.

I caught a ride to the SpecWar Det (i.e., Special Warfare Detachment) Golf office, where I found out from Lieutenant B. that Dai Uy Fletcher, my November Platoon OIC, had already gotten a flight back to Dong Tam. Not to worry, I was told. And sure enough I caught a ride on an Air America plane to My Tho with the Dinh Tuong province chief, Colonel Dao, and Dr. Evans, the province senior adviser. Colonel Dao didn't recognize me from my previous tours in '69 and '70, but, frankly, I was glad neither one of them knew who I was. Anonymity is generally preferred in this business, especially in a hostile environment.

CHAPTER TWO

The more intimately it [the staff] comes into
contact with the troops, the more useful and valuable it becomes. The almost entire separation of
the staff from the line, as now practiced by us, and
hitherto by the French, has proved mischievous,
and the great retinues of staff-officers with which
some of our earlier generals began the war were
simply ridiculous.

—William T. Sherman
Army General

Lieutenant Fletcher and I departed CONUS for Vietnam on the twenty-third of May, 1971, and arrived at the
Tan Son Nhut airport on the twenty-sixth at 2220 hours.
The airport was located approximately five miles west of
the center of Saigon, adjacent to the South Vietnamese
and U.S. Air Force bases. VC/NVA rocket squads, sapper, and occasional infantry units were frequently rocket-
ing, probing, and harassing the huge complex and its
security forces.

Dai Uy Fletcher and I had been given special permission to come to Vietnam, specifically Dinh Tuong
province, one month earlier than the departure of the remainder of November Platoon. That gave both of us a
little extra time to observe protocol and establish rapport
with the U.S. and Vietnamese military units and civilian

agencies at Sector and Subsectors (province and districts). It would also give Dai Uy time to gain knowledge and insight into the intelligence community's modus operandi.

Lt. Jerry J. Fletcher was born in Muleshoe, Texas, on September 1, 1937. J.J. stood five feet nine inches tall, and was lean and mean in build, weighing in at 170 pounds. Fletcher's hair was brown, his eyes were blue, his right bicep had a professional tattoo of the Texas flag with the words "Texas Germ," and his left forearm had a homemade tattoo that said "Germ."

Dai Uy started riding in rodeos at the young age of fourteen and graduated from high school in Ropesville, Texas, in 1955. Jerry attended college for two years at Texas Tech, then enlisted in the Navy for a two-year tour as an aviation electronics technician. Following Dai Uy's stint in the Navy, he returned to college to complete his degree in agricultural economics and became the Director of Agriculture at Lubbock's Chamber of Commerce. After a bad marriage, Lieutenant Fletcher returned to the Navy, was commissioned as a lieutenant (jg), went to BUDS (Basic Underwater Demolition/SEAL school) and graduated with Class 56. Lieutenant Fletcher was assigned to UDT-13 and deployed to WESTPAC in 1970. In early 1971 Dai Uy went through SBI (SEAL Basic Instructions) with November Platoon of SEAL Team 1, and at the ripe old age of thirty-four he was November Platoon's OIC. One uninformed individual stated that my lieutenant was a half bubble off plumb, but I knew better. I had no doubt that Dai Uy just didn't want to live a bourgeois lifestyle, and neither did I. There was no doubt in my mind that the lives of Dai Uy and all of us in November Platoon would never be the same after our tour together in Vietnam.

Later, after I had reached the Plaza Hotel, I went up to

the roof and watched the continual mortar and aircraft-dropped para flares float softly to the ground. Some oscillated wildly and several descended in a clockwise fashion similar to a parachutist circling his ground target. Occasionally, red tracers streaked upward on various tangents, leaving their phosphorous traces behind as they continued their parabolic trajectory back to the war-torn jungles and rice paddies below. Welcome back to Vietnam, I thought.

The next day, Dai Uy Fletcher and I reported to the SpecWar offices, located within the NavForV (Naval Forces Vietnam) building and compound. I had first met Lieutenant Fletcher the previous August when I was returning to CONUS after my LDNN (the South Vietnamese equivalent to SEALs) advisory tour. Dai Uy was a member of UDT-13 then, and we were riding a Navy CH-46 helo from Clark Air Force Base near Manila to Cubi Point Naval Air Station located at Subic Bay, Philippines.

I knew November Platoon was in good hands (I say sarcastically) when it was brought to my attention that Lieutenant Commander Worthington, better known to the graduates of UDT Training Class 36 as "Lord George Worthingstone," was the operations officer, and that Lieutenant Van Heertum's primary responsibility was the rewriting of Staff, UDT/SEAL, and MST/BSU (Mobile Support Team/Boat Support Unit) personnel award submissions. When I reflected on my experiences and encounters with Lieutenant Van Heertum during my last three tours in 'Nam, I realized that Dai Uy and November Platoon would have to be very careful about covering our back end and accept the fact that most of our platoon awards submitted to staff would be downgraded or filed in a trash can.

While Dai Uy was being briefed by Commander Del Guidice (SpecWar Detachment CO), I spent most of the morning with Lieutenant Commander M., who was the SpecWar intelligence officer. Some of the information he gave me was very disturbing.

"Unfortunately, it won't be long before your platoon and all other SEAL platoons will be forbidden to target VCI [Viet Cong Infrastructure]," Mr. M. stated with disgust. "I spent several hours trying to convince the CO the other day that SEAL platoons should not generally target VC sapper units or chase guerrilla mortar tubes hither and yon. I also explained to him that there were well-trained Vietnamese infantry divisions with units available for such conventional tasks," Mr. M. recounted as he raised his hands in frustration. "I carefully explained to him that SEAL platoons should be guardedly utilized for unconventional tasks; i.e., Bright Light operations"—code name for U.S. POW rescue—"pilot rescue missions, and the capturing of high-level VCI/NVA that are listed on the Phuong Huang committee's blacklist in conjunction with Vietnamese units and/or agencies."

"I assume you're about to hit me with the punch line," I interjected with a sinking feeling in my stomach.

"Yes!" the lieutenant commander said, filled with frustration. "With that, he ran me out of his office. . . . However, Admiral Salzer, whose office is located downstairs, has apparently made this decision. Whether it was a unilateral or bilateral decision, I don't know."

After lunch, Dai Uy and I spent the afternoon with Mr. M. and discussed November Platoon's basic agenda and modus operandi within Dinh Tuong and Kien Hoa provinces and our sources of intelligence information. Afterward, Lieutenant Commander M. issued us NILO (Naval Intelligence Liaison Officer) ID and travel cards that authorized us to travel anywhere without restriction.

Finally, on the morning of May thirtieth, Dai Uy and I departed Saigon and headed west on highway QL-4 for

Dong Tam. Originally, the Dong Tam operations base was constructed in '66 for the 2nd Brigade and later the 3rd Brigade of the U.S. Army 9th Infantry Division (Old Reliable) that was home-based at Fort Lewis, Washington. The 2nd and 3rd brigades remained at the operations base until late '69 or early '70, when they turned it over to the ARVN 7th Infantry Division. SEAL Team 1's Victor Platoon barracks was located within the Vietnamese navy compound. Between the Vietnamese compound and the My Tho River was the U.S. Navy's compound, which consisted of admin spaces, barracks, clubs, and the PBR repair shops, docks, and boats. I had lived in the same two-story open barracks in July and August 1970, as an adviser to the Vietnamese SEALs, with Tu Uy Son's LDNN Platoon and SEAL 2's 5th Platoon.

We pulled up to the SEAL barracks about 1700 hours as most of the Victor Platoon guys were heading for the chow hall. They had all been busy cleaning equipment and packing their gear for their return to SEAL team and the beautiful Silver Strand of San Diego County. Victor Platoon personnel was as follows: 1st Squad: LT Roger Clapp (OIC), EN1 Bill Doyle, PT2 Michael Jerry Walsh, GMG3 Marshall Daugherty, GMG3 Barry Schreckengost, EN3 Donald Barnes; 2nd Squad: LT(jg) Jim Young (AOIC), BMC Bruce Russell, HM1 Terril Bryant, EM2 Frank Richard, ANT3 Elwood Shoemaker, RM2 Tipton Ammen, and BT3 Shawn Cymbal.

Lieutenant Clapp (OIC) and Lieutenant (jg) Young (AOIC) were anxious to talk to Dai Uy and get all of the latest scuttlebutt from the Strand and Saigon, while Chief Russel, Doc Bryant, Mike Walsh, and I decided to converse over a couple of beers at the platoon's makeshift bar in the front end of the barracks. After several beers each, Mike Walsh recounted what happened in early March when X-ray Platoon was ambushed for the third and final time. The end result was that Lieutenant Collins was killed, Lou DiCroce received a severe head wound, and everyone else was wounded to one degree or another. We didn't stop talking until 2200, when I turned in.

Lieutenants Clapp and Fletcher spent the next couple of days traveling to the districts of Dinh Tuong and Kien Hoa provinces saying "soo-long" and "howdy" to the province chiefs, PSAs (Province Senior Advisers), district chiefs and the U.S. Army DSAs (District Senior Advisers), and ARVN 7th Infantry Division's U.S. Army advisers, among others.

Doc Bryant took me to My Tho and dropped me off at the Embassy House. I was sorry to find out that John T. and Ian S. had returned to CONUS and were relieved by Al S. and Jake B. However, Al and Jake were very receptive and appeared inclined to help November Platoon as needed. I went to the 525 house and was delighted to find that Larry hadn't returned to CONUS yet. We had been visiting for a short while when Lieutenant John W., who was the NILO for this area, stopped by. After the introductions, John became very interested in November Platoon and Dai Uy Fletcher. He began by asking a few questions about Dai Uy's operational goals. I was amused at his straightforward elicitation and impressed by his credentials. He was a graduate of the much respected Fort Holabird intelligence collection and tradecraft school. In that light, John was surprisingly open, and later told me that Mr. Bai, who worked for the Embassy House, was an MSS (Vietnamese Military Security Service) penetrant within the PSB (Police Special Branch) and OSA (Company—office of the Special Assistant to the Ambassador).

I shook my head, saying, "Well, there's no doubt that Mr. Bai has natural placement and access within the Embassy House. In '69, when I was a PRU adviser here, I had perceived that Bai was highly trusted and probably used as an agent handler."

Lieutenant W. didn't respond to my leading statement about Bai being an agent handler. However, he did go on to tell about CIA officer John T.'s past clandestine meetings with a province-level VCI late at night before his return to the States. Apparently, their rendezvous took place in the middle of the My Tho River, in a sampan. No wonder John wanted a stubby Uzi submachine gun that would conveniently fit snugly into his attaché case! I thought.

Later that afternoon, Doc Bryant and I stopped by the PRU office to see my PRU friends of '69 and '70 once again. I was very eager to visit with my very good friend Sao Lam, who, I had heard, was still the deputy PRU chief and a continuing thorn in Province Chief Colonel Dao's side. Unfortunately, Sao Lam wasn't there. I left word with Hung, my old interpreter, that I was back in-country again and that I was looking forward to sharing a bottle of American whiskey with my old friend. Afterward, Doc and I returned to Dong Tam in time for supper at the Navy mess.

I was beginning to really like Doc Bryant. He was an amiable fellow, clean-cut in appearance, about six feet tall and approximately 180 pounds. Doc was a very good worker, innovative, conscientious in all that he did, and always ready to go the extra mile. Lieutenant Commander M. and Lieutenant Clapp had encouraged Doc to establish and run a bilateral intelligence net with a supposedly ex-Hoi Chanh (alias Oscar), who lived across the street from the Chieu Hoi Center, as his principal agent. Doc and the platoon interpreter were the agent handlers. Oscar, in turn, notified Doc, through the interpreter, when he knew of a motivated Hoi Chanh that had timely, firsthand information of a good target, and, more important, was willing and available to guide Victor Platoon to the target. With the information from Doc and Oscar, Victor Platoon was successful in capturing several VCI and weapons caches. I was sorry that I wouldn't have the opportunity to operate with Doc Bryant—he was fast becoming my friend.

On the morning of June first, I went to the Embassy House to talk with Jake B. while Dai Uy, Lieutenant Clapp, and Son, the interpreter, went to Ham Long and Truc Giang districts in Kien Hoa province. I explained to Jake that we needed to get a few BIs (background investigation) run on several potential agents who had natural placement and access to very lucrative targets. Jake was only too glad to take care of our BIs and also stated he could run a BI on any Vietnamese without MSS or PSB awareness. I explained to him that Dai Uy, Lieutenant W., and I had thought this would be the best approach to getting BIs of potential agents and would protect us from inadvertently employing double or dual agents. Dai Uy and I eventually discovered that it was virtually impossible to establish and maintain a truly unilateral intelligence information net in Vietnam.

Again, I heard from a second source that Mr. Bai was an MSS double agent. He and Colonel Dao, the province chief, had determined that Bai would work covertly for MSS as a penetrant within the PSB (Police Special Branch) of the National Police, and the Embassy House. Overtly, Bai's loyalty lay with the National Police, PSB, and the Company, in that order. His wife, also, conveniently worked in the Embassy House's document interpretation office. Bai obediently passed all information received from his sources within the Embassy House to National Police Chief Muoi and Chief Hue of the PSB, and, secretly, to Dao and MSS. Evidently this served as a way for Colonel Dao and MSS to monitor all that PSB and the Company were trying to accomplish clandestinely. Vietnam, it seemed, had hidden agendas in every nook and cranny. It was no wonder that Sao Lam, as deputy PRU chief, was always a thorn in the side of Colonel Dao.

The next day, June second, Dai Uy, PO3 Wood, Hoan—our interpreter—and I drove to Sam Giang sub-sector at Vinh Kim village, where we met Capt. Dave Campbell, the DIOCC adviser. The captain had previously told Dai Uy about a Hoa Hao hamlet (Vietnamese for village) chief by the name of Ba To who hated the VC. His small hamlet had been established in the midst of a VC-controlled area of undeveloped brush and jungle. We had planned to visit Ba To's village until Campbell told us that it was located approximately two and one half miles from a Regional Force outpost at the end of a road.

While we were debating whether we should hike to Ba To's village without a radio, Captain Campbell commented, "Two nights ago elements of 261B Main Force Infantry Battalion, the 267B Sapper MF Battalion, and 269B Infantry Battalion of Dong Thap One Regiment overran and destroyed the outpost where you'll have to leave your jeep before your hike to Ba To's village."

I looked at Dai Uy and he looked at me, then both of us started laughing. "Well, Lieutenant, I think it's time to call in the dogs, piss on the fire, and head for the house," I suggested.

"Sound wisdom, Smitty. Load up boys. We'll return another day with better provisions," Dai Uy said, chuckling.

After Dai Uy had dropped off Wood and Hoan at Dong Tam, we went to My Tho to visit NILO John W. and OSA Jake B. at the Embassy House. We soon found out that John, Jake, and 525 Larry had been very worried about our future operations. In the past, SEAL platoons had inadvertently greased several of 525's turnarounds and defection-in-place agents. John, Jake, and Larry complained that it took years and millions of dollars to develop unilateral intel info nets within targeted areas.

John led off with their pitch: "Jake and I will work out an agreement with PSB whereby they will furnish you with all the targets that your platoon could possibly want as long as you go on combined operations with three or four PSB agents and their guide. They'll also legalize any complications as to any inadvertent killing of legal, card-carrying VCI. What do you think?"

"I'm still listening," Dai Uy said, grinning from ear to ear.

Jake spoke up and said, "We've received many reports and documents that the Communist high command are creating special district, mang, village, and hamlet political indoctrination committees to undermine the GVN's [Government Vietnam] pacification program and cause an upset this fall during the South Vietnamese national elections." We nodded as Jake continued, "There are approximately seventy of these VC committees in Dinh Tuong province. If you guys and PSB can eliminate fifteen of them between now and the elections, we'll be able to confuse their supporters, weaken their power base, destroy their image, and neutralize their objectives."

Dai Uy finally stood up, saying, "I accept your proposal. Let's shake on it!"

"Damn!" I exclaimed. "It would be downright un-American not to accept y'all's offer."

John and Jake were delighted and so were we. I think we all breathed a sigh of relief.

June third found Dai Uy and me in Binh Thuy visiting HAL-3's executive officer, Lieutenant Commander White. Dai Uy requested that we be granted permission to utilize the new "Black Bomb," the CBU-55B (Cluster Bomb Unit fuel/air bomb), on a future mission to create a helicopter LZ in a double- or triple-canopy jungle and neutralize enemy-held bunker complexes. White seemed interested and stated that he would do everything that he could to support us.

Later I ran into Lieutenant Boyhan at SpecWar's Det Golf office. The lieutenant was Romeo Platoon's OIC, and his platoon was located in a village called Rach Soi in Kien Giang province. Boyhan was one of the best officers SEAL Team 1 ever had, simply because he took very good care of his men. His platoon was, in return, very loyal and dedicated to him. Romeo Platoon was an effective, professional platoon in spite of occasional micro-management by the SpecWar staff in Saigon and the gross corruption and interference by Kien Giang's province chief.

On the morning of June seventh I arrived at the Embassy House by 0745. Al S. had previously invited me to attend a week of "Case Officer's Tradecraft" classes that he was to teach to PSB's district case officers. Al had encouraged me to explain to the classes Lieutenant Fletcher's ideas about desirable and undesirable targets. The class was attended by fifteen of PSB's case officers from all seven districts of the province. After Al's introduction, Chief Muoi entered the classroom and began shaming the case officers. He reminded them that the VC had been living under appalling conditions and, in spite of those circumstances, had successfully accomplished their duties and responsibilities, regardless of the risk. Muoi continued to rebuke the case officers and compared their lack of motivation and professionalism to their much harried adversaries' successes.

After Al started the rather long process of establishing the level of ability of his new students, I noticed a pretty Vietnamese woman dressed in black slacks and the traditional *ao dai*, a white, full-length tunic that was split on the sides from bottom to the waistline. I'd seen her in the past, but couldn't remember the time or place. During a class break, I asked Al who she was.

Al grinned. "Don't you remember, Smitty?" he said. "She used to be Trung Uy Loc's number-two wife. Her name is Pham Thi Ly."

Loc had been the PRU team chief from early summer of '69 until midsummer of '70, when he was killed while assaulting a VC bunker. Al went on to say that Miss Ly had been left out in the cold after Loc's death because she was his concubine. At that time she had started living with a Vietnamese air force pilot.

The next day, Al stressed AO (Area of Operation) and target analyses. Later, I had the opportunity to talk to Miss Ly. She recognized me when I told her that I had been Trung Uy's *co van*, or adviser, in '69.

"Loc said that you were a good adviser and that you had tears in your eyes when the PRU gave you a going-away party," she recounted.

Surprisingly, I had a sudden surge of emotion well up within me. I thanked her for her kindness and excused myself.

After Al finished the morning classes, he invited me to eat lunch at the Embassy House with the rest of the crew and General Timmings, who had arrived earlier from Region. Following lunch, I chatted with Mr. Ha, who was the maitre d' of the Embassy House. He told me that his wife, Ann, was pregnant again and was still working in the Embassy House's radio and reception room. Ha was a large, rotund Chinese fellow who had a great personality and a jovial countenance. Ha also spoke good English. We had been fast friends since '69.

Later, I was fortunate to catch a ride with 525 Larry to Dong Tam in time for PT and a run with Dai Uy, Lieutenant Clapp, and Lieutenant (jg) Young. Afterward, Victor Platoon gave a wild going-away party that the Seawolf crews and our MST/BSU buddies attended. Truly, SEAL team guys are perfect representations of the total depravity of mankind, myself included, I thought as I drifted off to sleep that night.

The next day Al taught "Penetration and Infiltration Operations" against targeted organizations. It was a great class. Al was an excellent teacher. Unfortunately, he and Bai had to secure the classes for that day and attend a briefing at the National Police's compound at 1010 hours. Chief Muoi, the Province National Police chief, had briefed the Directorate General of the National Police about the successes and problems of the provincial police forces, which included the PRU and PSB.

After lunch, I was finally able to locate Sao Lam at the PRU office. After our initial handshaking and mutual compliments, I explained to him that I was not a *co van* anymore, that I had been assigned to a SEAL platoon and was living at Dong Tam. Sao Lam was very pleased and suggested that we get together at his home soon to celebrate our reunion. When I assured him that I would also bring a couple bottles of special American liquor, his face really lit up.

I hitchhiked back to Dong Tam with a couple of Army guys who were traveling to Can Tho. They weren't sure of the route, so I gave them a 1:50,000 scale map covering parts of Dinh Tuong and Kien Hoa provinces and directions to Giao Duc district—the westernmost district in the province—where they would have to cross Tien Giang River on a ferry to Vinh Long.

"As long as you stay on highway QL-4, you won't have any problems," I told them. "However, drive fast and watch out for ambushes."

They assured me that they would.

June eleventh was a day of mixed blessings. Al's excellent case officer classes were completed that afternoon. Al was a creative instructor; he maintained interest and curiosity by mixing a variety of humorous satire in his lesson applications and explanations. That was the good blessing.

"You are the most gifted instructor that I've ever sat under to date," I respectfully told Al before I caught a ride back to Dong Tam. "Thank you for inviting me to attend this course." Al was very pleased.

Later, after Dai Uy had returned from SpecWar staff in Saigon, he explained to me that NavForV was limiting all in-country SEAL platoons to VC military targets only. In other words, we would not be allowed to target civilian VCI. We were both very upset. That was the bad blessing delivered by our SpecWar staff.

Dai Uy decided that we had best go to My Tho immediately to notify NILO John, OSA Al at the Embassy House, and 525 Larry as to NavForV and SpecWar's newest policy.

"The new policy won't really affect your future missions," John reasoned, "simply because you'll be accompanying PSB operatives and their guide."

Larry jumped in and said, "That's right! Many of PSB's targets are military in nature, and nearly all of mine are."

"Well, Jerry," Al said, "I'm certain the three of us will be able to offer you and your platoon enough legal operations to keep you busy until your departure in December."

Dai Uy laughed. "Well, I certainly thank y'all, John, Larry, and Al," he said. "All I have to do is somehow keep Staff from micromanaging myself and my platoon to death."

June thirteenth found Dai Uy and me back in Saigon. While he was taking care of platoon responsibilities at Staff, I went to the marketplace with PO2 Van Flagg, the SEAL LDNN adviser, PO3 Gerson, and PO3 McGready and looked at the snakes, ocelots, quail, finches, parrots, banana cats, dogs, and so on. One Vietnamese vendor wanted 20,000 piasters for an ocelot, which translated into one hundred bucks. Later, I was surprised to find a cobra for sale. The hair stood up on the back of my neck when I remembered my experiences with two cobras I'd seen in the Nam Can swamp last year with the Biet Hai. However, I did consider buying a five-foot rock (reticulated) python for about 3,000 Ps, or fifteen dollars, until I recalled what happened to Bolivar, my pet boa constrictor in Nha Be, back in 1967–68, and how Randy Sheridan killed his pet python and then tried to bite its head off in '69. I even considered buying a monkey until I remembered Demo Dick Marcinko's platoon giving their monkey a hand grenade and locking him in a safe constructed of steel and cement.

The morning of June fourteenth Lieutenant Clapp and his platoon pulled out for Saigon. All of Victor Platoon were excited and anxious to board a Navy C118 at Tan Son Nhut Air Base and return to their families and SEAL Team 1 near San Diego. The platoon conex boxes were forwarded to San Diego by ship after they had been cleared by customs.

The lieutenant (jg), Washburn, and his boat crew, along with Dai Uy and I, had spent the day preparing our gear for that night's interdiction operation by MSSC (Medium SEAL Support Craft) at the mouth of the My Tho River between the provinces of Go Cong and Kien Hoa. Dai Uy and I had been in that area previously to meet with Major Bigelow, the district senior adviser of Binh Dai district's subsector. He was an interesting fellow and highly motivated. As the DSA, he took his responsibilities seriously and did all that he could to help and advise his counterpart, the district chief.

Bigelow had briefed Dai Uy and me about sightings of

large Chinese trawlers and junks and one sighting of a submarine. Whoever had seen that submarine was besotted from *ba xi de*, Vietnamese rice whiskey, and/or La Rue "Tiger" beer, I thought, as I did my best to keep a straight face. When I was with UDT-12 in '66, we had performed a hydrographic reconnaissance off the tip of the Thanh Phu peninsula, in Kien Hoa province, out to five hundred yards prior to the Deckhouse V amphibious operation. The gradient was so gradual that the man on the end of the flutter-board line, five hundred yards out, didn't have to swim at all. The most distant source of the Mekong and Bassac rivers begins in China's South Tsinghai province and travels for 2,600 miles to the South China Sea. Its many rivers and tributaries progressively washed soil into the South China Sea and gradually formed South Vietnam's delta. I doubted that a Chinese or Russian submarine could safely navigate any closer than three or four miles from the coast, and even then the maneuver would have had to take place only during the night.

Regardless, Major Bigelow had notified Dai Uy that there would be several trawlers that night at the mouth of the My Tho River to unload medical supplies, weapons, and ammunition, and he requested that we interdict the Chinese Communists' distribution to the local junks and sampans.

Considering that we and MST had little else to do, we departed Dong Tam by MSSC at 1915. It was an awful night in which to operate; we began the trip in a thunderstorm that rained sheets of water upon us constantly. Mr. Washburn and his crew doggedly guided the MSSC through the storm as it plunged, plodded, and bounced its way downriver to the Binh Dai pier, where we picked up two miserable National Policemen, Major Bigelow, and his Vietnamese counterpart. We continued downstream to Ilo Ilo Island, where Demo Dick Marcinko's SEAL squad spent hours crawling through the tidal flat's deep mud early one morning in late '67. We located and searched two junks but found only one fellow with no ID papers. Shortly afterward, Lieutenant (jg) Washburn turned the MSSC north for Go Cong province through the heavy rain and rough seas. We searched several large covered sampans without a sign of contraband. Undaunted, we returned to Binh Dai district's coastline and searched more sampans and junks without results. It was an all-too-familiar wet, dark, and disappointing night.

"Major, I'm afraid that your counterpart's informant had been soused on *ba xi de* and stoned on betel nut [opiate]," I teased while we were returning to the Binh Dai pier to drop the men off.

With his right eyebrow raised, Bigelow grinned, then replied, "Well, whoever he is, he's got it all in a nutshell!"

We finally returned to Dong Tam by 0230, put away all of our gear, and crawled into wonderfully warm, dry, and secure sacks. After I snuggled into my bed, it struck me that happiness, after a bone-chilling and wet night on rough seas, is having warm, dry clothes, a hot meal, and a warm, dry bed.

June seventeenth was a very busy and exciting day. At 1000, Dai Uy, interpreter Son, Same Tam—the Kit Carson scout assigned to November Platoon—and I boarded the sector helo, a Huey slick, at the Seawolves' helo pad and were dropped off at Ba To's Hoa Hao hamlet. It was located, as a crow flies, four kilometers and due west of Vinh Kim village, in Sam Giang district and Kien Tuong province. Ba To and his hamlet were all members of the Hoa Hao "Reformed" Buddhist military and political sect, which was ideologically, politically, and militarily opposed to the North Vietnamese Communists in general and to the Communist-backed National Front for the Liberation of South Vietnam (NFLSV) specifically. To put it bluntly, the Hoa Hao and VC/NVA bitterly hated each other, and for good reason.

Huynh Phu So founded the Hoa Hao religion in 1939 and named it after his hometown in Chau Doc province, located in the northwestern corner of the delta. He became the sect's preacher, faith healer, and prophet by stressing elements of Taoist mythology and Confucian ethics. However, So longed for national independence from the French and the Viet Minh and became militarily and politically active by establishing his three instruments of revolution: religious fervor, a political party based on the principles of democratic and socialistic systems, and overt and covert armies. In 1946 the Hoa Haos refused to accept the Viet Minh's totalitarian leadership. So was ambushed and killed by the Viet Minh on the Plain of Reeds in 1947. The French then armed approximately eight to ten thousand Hoa Haos and operated jointly with them against the Viet Minh until the French withdrawal in 1954. After South Vietnam's independence in '54, some of the Hoa Haos pledged support to the Emperor Bao Dai. This placed them at odds with the new national leader, Ngo Dinh Diem. However, these Hoa Hao units eventually rallied to Diem's government under the Chieu Hoi program in 1967 and loyally resisted the Communist insurgency in the delta.

After the sector helo departed, the four of us started walking toward a prominent, open-sided hootch located about fifty meters from the hamlet's large community bunker. Ba To was sitting in his wheelchair, in the shade of the hootch. His legs were gone; and only short stubs protruded from his hips.

Dai Uy and I walked up, bowed slightly, greeted him in Vietnamese and shook hands Vietnamese style, with both hands. Ba To was pleased. He welcomed us to his humble village and invited us to sit down at his small table for warm tea. He quickly ordered his wife to heat water for fresh tea and to bring four clean teacups and snacks for his guests. After the initial amenities of tea drinking and snacks, Dai Uy opened the conversation through our interpreter, Son.

"Mr. Ba To, Captain Campbell at Vinh Kim has told us that you need help to fight against the VC and that you were severely attacked just four weeks ago by forty men."

Ba To nodded his head in acknowledgment as Son translated. "Yes, we fought bravely. There were only myself and six other men to fight them and protect our families. One of my men was killed. I personally killed three VC with hand grenades when they tried to kill me. We have few weapons—a few M-16s and M-1 carbines—and little ammunition to protect ourselves. The district chief refuses to give us weapons or ammunition to fight the VC. We have no machine guns or mortars. We have no recoilless rifles or grenade launchers. We have no more grenades. We are very poor. Yes, we need help. Can you help us?" Ba To asked.

Dai Uy and I were both touched by his plea.

"We will be very happy to help you protect your village," Dai Uy promised. "We also need your help. Will you tell us where the VC units are located and where their families live?"

"Yes," Ba To said, "my men know where many VC live near here. We will show you where they live and where they operate during the day and the night. I know where the VC District Security section's sabotage subsection chief lives."

"Good!" Dai Uy replied with a big grin. "We will pay you rewards for all VC we kill or capture, and for weapons and caches too. Smith will be contacting you in the future," Dai Uy said as he placed his hand on my shoulder. "He has worked here in Dinh Tuong as *co van* of the PRU in 'sixty-nine and the Vietnamese SEALs in 'seventy. He will be returning to your village soon with supplies," Dai Uy promised.

Afterward, Ba To opened up and told us about his past. He had lost both of his legs in 1962 when he was working for the Company as a member of the predecessors of the PRU called CTs, for counterterrorists. Ba To had been with a small group of CTs patrolling toward their target when a VC unit ambushed them, detonating an antipersonnel claymore mine. Ba To was severely wounded from his thighs to his feet. The CTs managed to drive the VC away and were able to carry Ba To to the hospital, where the doctor amputated his legs.

I believed that Ba To was a sincere and honest man. He had to be a good leader, I thought, or the Hoa Haos of this hamlet wouldn't follow him. Ba To reminded me of the ancient military maxim that "a man must become a good follower before he can be a good leader." I also believed that he and his hamlet sincerely hated the VC. Sadly, all that they had wanted was to be left alone to build their homes, to farm and fish and raise their families in peace. Unfortunately, there are always those who seek power over others through dishonorable forms of control and manipulation, I thought as I reflected on what Ba To said about the district chief's lack of support.

After our visit, we returned to Dong Tam by sector helo. Shortly after our return, we were heavily mortared for about two minutes, with most of the rounds landing near the Navy Seawolves' helicopters. No doubt, the VC mortar squad were members of the 309F Main Force HW Battalion, which wasn't far from Ba To's hamlet. Fortunately, the 82 mm HE (High Explosive) mortar rounds had done little damage.

Dai Uy and I had little time to concern ourselves with the

aftermath of the VC mortar rounds. Fletcher had received a message over our KY-8/VRC-46 secure voice radio from NILO John that PSB had an informant who would guide us to the location of ten VC guerrillas and several weapons caches located in Binh Phuoc district of Long An province, north of Dinh Tuong province. We wasted no time in driving to My Tho and the National Police compound, where we talked to Hai Binh, the informant, for an hour. Dai Uy and I decided that Mr. Binh's information was good enough for a helo op the next afternoon.

After our return to Dong Tam, Lieutenant Fletcher contacted SEAL Team 1's Quebec Platoon OIC, Lieutenant Taylor, at Ben Luc, located in the northern part of Long An province, and asked for volunteers to go on our op the following day. Chief Marriott, Doc Johnson, and two other SEALs, plus two SAS Aussies and two LDNNs, arrived in time for lunch.

On the morning of June eighteenth Dai Uy called Lieutenant B., of SEAL Team 1's Detachment Golf OIC at Binh Thuy, and asked him to request two Huey Sea Lord slicks from HAL-3 and two OV-10 Black Ponies from VAL-4, and asked that the pilots arrive at our location early enough to attend Lieutenant Fletcher's briefing at 1530. Dai Uy Fletcher also requested two CBU-55B fuel/air bombs to be used to soften up the VC bunker complex before our insertion, in order to reduce our casualties. Fletcher also described to him how we were going to mark the bunker complex with smoke grenades and/or 2.75-inch and five-inch Zuni rockets to insure that the bombs would land exactly on target. Dai Uy assured Mr. B. that he had previously arranged to use the bombs on a mission with the executive officer of VAL-4, Lieutenant Commander White, on June third. Fletcher's primary reasons for utilizing the CBU-55B were to clear a small area of brush and trees for a helicopter LZ, if needed, clear the target area of booby traps, and neutralize any VC resistance to our insertion by helicopters and our capture of the weapons caches. Lieutenant B. assured Dai Uy of his assistance and that he would attend Dai Uy's briefing at 1530.

In the meantime, I had run over to the ARVN 7th Division's G-2 for a 1:4,000 split vertical mosaic of the op area for our study and for Dai Uy's briefing. It was particularly useful for Mr. Binh's aerial orientation and recognition of the target before our VR (visual reconnaissance) and insertion by the Navy Sea Lord slicks. When Mr. Binh and the two PSB operatives arrived, they, Dai Uy, Son, and I boarded a Seawolf and flew to the target area for a VR. The target was located within very thick vegetation and under double-canopy forest. However, Binh was able to recognize the landmarks and had no difficulty pointing to the VC bunker complex. Dai Uy and I were confident that the CBU-55B bombs would be dropped exactly on target. Upon our return to Dong Tam, Dai Uy requested and received clearance of several AOs (Areas of Operation) within Long An province. Only one of them would contain our target, which was located in Binh Phuoc district.

All went well until Dai Uy's PLO (patrol leader's order) briefing at the Seawolves' hootch with the Seawolf and Black Pony pilots, two PSB operatives, Mr. Binh, our interpreter Son, Lieutenant B., and me. In the middle of his thorough briefing, Fletcher explained that the twelve of us were to insert approximately five minutes after the CBU-55B was dropped.

Then Lieutenant B. spoke up, saying, "There won't be any CBU-55B bombs dropped today because there are no fuses."

Poor Dai Uy! I thought. I bit my tongue. Why didn't Lieutenant B. tell Dai Uy before the briefing? I wondered. Amazingly, Dai Uy handled it without any sign of anger.

"Very well," he replied coolly. "We'll go ahead and give it a try anyway. Mike, Jim Bob"—senior Seawolf and Black Pony pilots—"I would like y'all to work out your own plan to prep the target for a few minutes until you give me the word that you're ready for us to insert. I'll be in the lead helo with Smitty, Son, and the three VNs. The second slick will come in close behind and insert Chief Marriott and his men approximately fifty meters to my right flank. We'll set up a simple skirmish line until Mr. Binh and the two PSB men are ready to move in toward the bunker complex. At that time the line of march will be Mr. Binh as the point, followed by the two PSB fellows, myself, then Smitty with the radio, and Son. Chief Marriott, you and your men will fall in behind us as we work our way toward the caches. Let's grab our gear and load up."

After the Seawolves and Black Ponies took turns raking the bunker complex with 2.75 and five-inch rockets, 20mm cannons, .50-caliber machine guns, 7.62mm GAU-2 miniguns, and M-60 machine guns, we headed in toward the target. I was the first off the starboard side of my slick. I took about four steps, tried to jump over a large puddle, and went in up to my neck. Out of the corner of my right eye I watched Dai Uy try his luck at getting over a similarly deceptive puddle. He failed miserably and went completely under and out of sight. It was embarrassing! I bet the pilots are getting a good laugh at our predicament, I thought.

Mr. Binh and the PSB lads also fared poorly, falling flat on their buns in another seemingly innocuous mud puddle. To make matters worse, we were receiving AK-47 rifle fire at two o'clock from our position and at a range of one hundred meters. That just happened to be where our target lay.

Dai Uy instructed me to call for 7.62mm minigun and 2.75-and five-inch rocket fire. Afterward we moved toward the cache until we came to a heavily booby-trapped area with signs saying *min*, or mines. Mr. Binh began having nervous stomach problems and started complaining that the VC had changed the booby traps' locations and that he didn't want to guide us to the caches anymore.

"Okay, Smitty. Call in the Sea Lord slicks for extraction," Dai Uy ordered. "It's time to go to the house, boys."

After we returned to Dong Tam, Lieutenant B. turned to Dai Uy and said, "Jerry, be sure my name is on your SpotRep," or after-action report.

After Lieutenant B. left, I went over to Fletcher, put my hand on his shoulder and said, "Well, there's always another day, Dai Uy, huh?"

"You can count on it, Smitty," he replied emphatically.

"Well, on the bright side, the Seawolf guys have just invited us over to their hootch to eat a couple of juicy steaks and chase it down with free beer. I don't know about you, but I like the thought of a steak so thick that I'd have to flip it with a pitchfork," I teased.

"I agree!" Dai Uy replied with a giant grin on his face. "However, I think I'll start off with a six-pack of beer before I dive into a large, rare steak."

CHAPTER THREE

The typical staff officer is the man past middle life, spare, unwrinkled, intelligent, cold, passive, noncommittal; with eyes like a codfish, polite in contact but at the same time unresponsive, cool, calm, and as damnably composed as a concrete post or a plaster-of-paris cast; a human petrification with a heart of feldspar and without charm or the friendly germ; minus bowels, passion, or a sense of humour. Happily they never reproduce and all of them finally go to hell.

—Anonymous

The next few days were an enormous pain in the butt. On the morning of June twentieth, Dai Uy and I, along with Son and Juan, our interpreters, headed for Saigon in a dilapidated jeep to pick up our platoon, which was supposed to arrive that afternoon. We got as far as Cholon when we had a flat tire. Fortunately, there was a Vietnamese sidewalk tire shop nearby. An old Vietnamese man fixed the tire within an hour.

When we reached SpecWar, we did a little research on the CBU-55B cluster bomb, which seemed to irritate some folks at Staff. Strangely, initiative seemed to threaten a couple of them. From there we went to Tan Son Nhut Air Base to pick up the platoon at 1600.

About 1700 hours, Dai Uy called Guam by autovon to

check on the whereabouts of the platoon and was told that
the aircraft had just departed Midway and wasn't due to
arrive until the morning of the twenty-second. Unfortunately, we were unable to locate Lieutenant Clapp's platoon; however, Dai Uy called Staff and notified them of
the delay.

On our return to SpecWar, we had another flat. We
called the MACV motor pool approximately fifteen times
over the next three hours before they brought us another
tire. We finally made it back to SpecWar at 2030, where
we met up with Lieutenant Clapp and Lieutenant (jg)
Young. They had just returned from Tan Son Nhut after
having received the bad news that their plane had only recently left Midway Island with November Platoon.

The next day, Staff told us that our platoon would be
delayed in Subic Bay for an additional two days while
VR-21 was tasked to ferry chickens to Vietnam for the
Vietnamese Accelerated Turnover Plan.

"In other words, the chickens have a higher priority
than our combat troops," I remarked to Dai Uy.

Dai Uy shook his head, saying, "I'm afraid so, Smitty."

"It's no wonder we're losing this war," I muttered to
myself. I looked at Dai Uy and started laughing, "Well, at
least the guys will have a ball in Olongapo during their
stay at Subic Bay."

"I'm sure Chief Bassett will take good care of Mr.
Kleehammer," Dai Uy replied, laughing.

Dai Uy decided that it was time we headed back to
Dong Tam. We certainly didn't want to stay anywhere
near Staff any longer than we had to. It was just too easy
to get into trouble.

It wasn't until June twenty-fifth that the rest of November Platoon arrived at Tan Son Nhut and Lieutenant
Clapp's Victor Platoon departed for CONUS. It was
sure good to see and be with the guys again. The slightly

hungover scandalmongers were full of hilarious tales of their four-day stay at Barbers Point, Hawaii, and five-day stay in Olongapo. As Dai Uy had previously inferred, Chief Layton Bassett had indeed taken good care of ENS Kleehammer. EN1 Gary "Chambo" Chamberlain and HM1 Tom "Doc" Holmes were the senior petty officers and had their hands full while trying to keep track of BM2 Rick Knepper, RM2 Roger Hayden, BM2 Ron Quear, RM3 Gordon Compton, RM3 Dave Eberle, EM3 Leonard Same, ET3 Terrence Waneous, and ETSN Timmy "Bear" Barron.

Once the rowdy lot of us arrived at the SpecWar staff offices, we learned that some folk on the staff didn't feel that they were responsible for making arrangements for the platoon's berthing and messing that night and the next day. I had a few words with the staff's commander and Lieutenant Van Heertum about the issue and was quickly shouted down. In deference to their rank I said nothing more. I had never seen such arrogance and gross disregard for the welfare of the men as I did that day. There is no doubt that authority improves some men and ruins others, I thought to myself.

With that in mind, Dai Uy and I started looking for beds. I contacted the NavForV photographers' mates that I had known from '70 and was offered three spare bunks in their hotel rooms for the night. Dai Uy managed to locate eight bunks elsewhere. By the afternoon of June twenty-sixth we had loaded our gear and were headed for Dong Tam. It was like a breath of fresh air to depart Saigon.

On the morning of June twenty-eighth I drove with Doc Holmes, Barron, and our Kit Carson scouts Hoan and Kiem to Vinh Kim village and left our jeep there. It was a beautiful day for a two-mile walk to Ba To's hamlet. We were heavily loaded with all of the extra 5.56mm ball ammo, M-26 frag grenades, M-72 LAAWs (Light Anti-Armor Weapon), an M-79 40mm grenade launcher that I had traded for with a PBR sailor, 40mm HE rounds and pop parachute flares that we carried in addition to our regular field gear.

While Doc Holmes was holding unofficial sick call for the families of the hamlet—officially called MEDCAP, for Medical Civic Action Program—Hoan and I were able to get away from the crowd and alone with Ba To. I presented the M-79 and the rest of the ordnance to Ba To as bona fides for November Platoon's commitment to help his hamlet, and I assured him that there would be more. After the stage had been set, I asked Ba To to be my agent handler and offered to pay him 8,000 piasters a month and his agents 5,000 piasters a month in cash—at that time the exchange rate was 275 piasters for one dollar—plus cash rewards according to results. Ba To was very pleased and immediately gave me information on two potential targets. I then gave him history statements to be filled out so that OSA Al and naval intelligence could prepare BIs for each agent's dossier. I warned Ba To that his agent net was not to know about our agreement and that his agents were to report only to him. We further agreed that I would visit Ba To's village weekly, using Doc Holmes's medical care of the villagers as a cover. During each visit, Ba To would inform me of enemy locations and activities, plus any logistical support that he might need for the protection of his hamlet. After Doc's sickcall was completed, the five of us returned to Dong Tam in the midst of a heavy rainstorm.

Shortly after our return to Dong Tam, Lieutenant Fletcher handed me an immediate priority Air Force message that reported two special forces and one ARVN personnel's death and burial by VC forces in Tay Ninh province, South Vietnam, in 1969. It read as follows:

26/0100Z June 71

CONFIDENTIAL/[illegible]

The following is raw and unevaluated information and has received no substantial [1 word illegible] or evaluation by intelligence production analysts.

Message in four parts

Part 1

25 June 1971

1. Country: South Vietnam
2. U.S. ??? in Tay Ninh Province RVN

        SIGNED: [illegible]
                              Gerald [illegible]
                              Chief, AFX ? Team?

                              CONFIDENTIAL

3. ISC Number:
4. Date of Info: Late April 1969
5. Date of Acquisition: 24 June 1971
6. Evaluation: F-6
7. Source: Returnee LUU HOANG TIEN (LUWU HOANGS TIEENS) aka LE HOANG PHONG (LEE HOANGS PHONG) aka LUU MINH PHUC (LUWU MINH PHUCS)
8. Report Number: D-0513-118-71
9. Date of Report: 25 June 1971
10. Number of Pages:
11. References:
12. Originator: Hq. 1021 USAF FLDACTYSQ
13. Prepared By: Gerald J. Kreiger, AFE Team D Det 6 1021 USAF FLDACTYSQ

14. Approving Authority: RUDOLPH C. KOLLER, Col USAF

15. Summary: This report contains information concerning the location of the graves of two U.S. personnel KIA in late April 1969 in an operation against COSVN headquarters. The graves are in the vic of 113842N/1061856E, XT434875 (Sheet 6232II), TAN HOI Village, Phu Khuong District, Tay Ninh Province, RVN.

PART II SOURCE DESCRIPTION

1. This report is the result of a HOI CHANH interview by a USAF interrogator. Source was born in 1940 in CAY DIEU Hamlet, TAN LOC Village, Thoi Binh District, An Xuyen Province, RVN. He received no formal education and no special military training. Source joined the VC on 19 September 1959 and was assigned as a guerrilla to TAN LOC Village, Thoi Binh District, An Xuyen Province, RVN. The following are his assignments until he rallied on 5 February 1971 at the Ha Tiem Chieu Hoi Center:

21 July 61—soldier, 2nd sq, 3rd plt, 1st co, 330th bn, the protection bn for MR-3 Current Affairs Org.

28 June 62—promoted to assistant sq ldr same unit.

June 63—bodyguard for doctor in civilian hospital in MR-3.

Sept 65—assist sq ldr, 1st sq, 27th plt, 3rd co, 3173rd bn (formerly 330th bn).

Sept 67—assigned to ATK Grp to protect South Liberation Front.

Oct 67—soldier, 1st sq, 1st plt, 1st co, 1st bn, 180th grp (protection of Current Affairs Org of COSVN).

Apr 69—remains in same unit at old site of COSVN as COSVN moves.

9 Sept 70—assist sq ldr, 1st sq, 4th escort team, Security Section, COSVN.

11 Nov 70—caught malaria, released from duties, started home, rallied 5 Feb 71.

PART III U.S. BURIAL SITE IN TAY NINH PROVINCE, RVN

2. Circumstances of Knowledgeability: In April 1969 Source was a member of the 1st sq, 1plt, 1st co, 1st bn, 180th Armed Public Security Grp, responsible for the protection of the political half of COSVN hq. In late April 1969 he witnessed an attack on COSVN hq. He saw the bodies of the two U.S. personnel and watched their burial. The information in this report is the result of personal observation and hearsay.

3. Attack on COSVN: Approx 0600 hours on an unrecalled date in late April 1969 two helicopters landed on unknown amount of ARVN troops in the vic of 113852N/1061725E, XT406877 (Sheet 6232II). The ARVN proceeded Eastward approx 3000 meters to a clearing where they made contact with the VC. The VC were patients of a COSVN military hospital located on the Eastern side of the clearing. The ARVN point man and two U.S. personnel were killed in the action, which took place approx 0900 hours. The remaining ARVN troops placed a cloth, half yellow, half red, approx 80X60 centimeters, on the ground and threw an unknown number of yellow and black smoke grenades. Two helicopters strafed the area for approx ten minutes and withdrew. The ARVN troops withdrew Westward across the clearing. The VC had no more contact with the ARVN that day. The following day the VC lost two men in a skirmish with the ARVN in the vic of 113820N/1061740E, XT412868. (The preceeding information was told to the Source by the VC personnel who engaged the ARVN. Source saw the two-colored cloth after the contact as it lay on the ground. Source observed the yellow and black smoke from his posi-

tion near COSVN political hq in the vic of
113915N/1062005E, XT455885.)

4. Burial Site: Source first observed the one ARVN and
two U.S. dead approx 1500 hours the day of the attack.
His unit came to the VC hospital to reinforce the de-
fenders about that time. The bodies were left where
they fell in the hope that an attempt would be made to
retrieve them and an ambush could be made. No such
attempt was made and the bodies were buried at approx
1800 hours. Source saw the VC carry the bodies from
the clearing and bury them in a bunker in the vic of
113842N/1061856E, XT434875, on the Eastern edge
of the clearing, approx 1500 meters South of MONG
stream, approx 4500 meters Northeast of BO TUC
Hamlet, TAN HOI Village, Phu Khuong District, Tay
Ninh Province, RVN. The bodies were stripped of their
uniforms and footgear and were buried in their under-
shorts. Source did not see any rank, unit insignia or
name tags on the green fatigues worn by the one
ARVN and two U.S. He did not see any dogtags on any
of the bodies. Source was told by other VC that the at-
tacking force was Special Forces because that was the
type of operation that they usually performed.

5. Bunker: The three bodies were buried in a bunker
shaped like the letter "Z". The middle part of the "Z"
was 3 meters long; each end of the "Z" was 1.5 meters
long. The bunker was 80 centimeters wide throughout
and 1.2 meters deep. The bunker had a roof 1.2 meters
thick made of logs covered with earth. The bunker had
an opening at each end of the "Z." The three bodies
were buried by removing the earth covering the
bunker, caving in one side of the log roof, placing the
bodies inside and covering them with earth. The two
entranceways were filled with earth.

6. Buried Personnel: The dead ARVN troop was approx

1.6 meters tall and weighed approx 52 kg. He had been killed by a single round passing through his throat and out the back of his neck. One of the Americans was Negro and the other was Caucasian. The Negro was approx 1.67 meters tall and weighed about 65 kg. He had been killed by one round through his stomach and out his back and he also had one round in his right thigh. The Caucasian was approx 1.7 meters tall and weighed about 68 kg. He had been killed by three rounds in the chest.

7. Miscellaneous: Source stated that a few days after the attack the area was hit by B-52 strikes until September 1969. Source claims the area has bomb craters too numerous to count. (Craters measure 9 to 15 meters in diameter and 3 meters deep.) Source is willing to lead an operation to the area to recover the bodies, but fears the site may have been obliterated by the bombing.

PART IV COMMENTS OF THE COLLECTOR

8. Source Credibility: Source is above average intelligence despite his lack of formal education. Source was cooperative about furnishing information and control questions indicated no apparent attempts to deceive the interrogator. Source has been offered and accepted the promise of remuneration if he leads an operation to the burial site and the bodies are found and identified as U.S.

9. Map References: AMS Series L7014, Sheet 6232II, First Edition, dated 1965.

10. Source Disposition: Source has furnished information concerning COSVN hq in Kampong Cham Province, Cambodia and two commo-liaison stations in Kandal Province, Cambodia. Source has no further information of air intelligence interest. Exploitation has been terminated. Source is presently in the MR IV Regional Chieu Hoi Center, CAN THO City, RVN.Gp3

On July 30th, four Australian SAS lads named Ray, Jim, Terry, and Bill arrived from Nui Dat. At 1730 hours we dutifully did our daily PT (physical training) and a three-mile run. Afterward, it was time to wet our whistles and to party with our newfound SAS mates.

The following day, Doc, Ray, and I went via sector slick to Vinh Kim subsector, picked up Captain Campbell, then proceeded to Ba To's hamlet. I had managed to bum a case of 40mm HE and pop flares from the PBR sailors in My Tho for Ba To and his men. As expected, they were very thankful for the ordnance. It was only a matter of time until units of the 309F MF HW Battalion attacked Ba To's tiny hamlet again.

Ba To gave me information on the activities of the VC village security subsection and a twenty-bed VC hospital that was located in the midst of a large bunker complex. Doc and I spent the afternoon back in Dong Tam making a 1:4,000 scale mosaic from split vertical photos for future enemy targets. We also replaced the malfunctioning KY-8 crypto unit in our FM, AN/VRC-46 radio.

Later that afternoon, Dai Uy and NILO John went on a VR near one of the cache sites that Ba To had told us about. After they returned to Subsector, Dai Uy gathered all information about the cache site from Captain Campbell. Fletcher had learned that approximately one month earlier a VC/NVA sapper school with nineteen instructors had educated fifty students in the arts of assaulting and destroying government outposts and hamlets such as Ba To's. The school had been located in the immediate vicinity of two tombs and the cache. There was also a possibility that a seventy-man VC unit was located near the cache. Regardless, Dai Uy gave the warning order at 2130. There was no party with our SAS buddies that night.

On the morning of July second SAS Ray and I drove to Vinh Kim subsector to pick up two guides from Ba To's hamlet. Unfortunately, the guides didn't show and we were forced to return to Dong Tam empty-handed, but Lieutenant Fletcher and I decided that the guides weren't really that important.

Dai Uy gave his patrol leader's order at 1000. By 1200 we had inserted in a rice paddy and were covered by Seawolf gunships. The line of march was the three Kit Carson scouts, me, Dai Uy, Doc Holmes with the radio, Barron, Waneous, Chief Bassett, Chamberlain, Eberle, Mr. Kleehammer, and others.

I was carrying my favorite weapon, my M-16 with an XM-148 40mm grenade launcher that was attached to the rifle's barrel. I had an added gadget secured to the carrying handle of my M-16's upper receiver. The "Singlepoint" gun sight produced a red dot that was radioactively illuminated day or night. Both of the shooter's eyes were kept open while pointing and firing the weapon. The trick was to learn to point, not aim, in a manner similar to trap or skeet shooting. I especially liked it for night operations. While my right eye focused on the red dot, my left eye focused on the target. If I could make out a human silhouette or see muzzle flashes, I would simply place the dot on the enemy and fire with deadly accuracy. I wouldn't have been able to do that at night very well, if at all, with peep sights. My weapon was great for applying the principles of "quick kill" out to two hundred yards.

I started the day's op with sixty-three 40mm HE rounds, four 40mm para flares, four hand-initiated pop flares, two MK-13 day/night flares, two minifrag grenades, two mini-CS grenades, two M-26 frag grenades, six thirty-round M-16 magazines, three thirty-round M-16 magazines taped together and carried with one magazine inserted into the rifle, first-aid kit, two LRP meals, two to four quarts of water, strobe light with extra infrared, blue and red lenses, survival gear, and one

M-18A1 claymore antipersonnel mine. It was a heavy but ideal load for our short-duration operations, during which we inserted by helo and captured, killed, or liberated our targets and extracted within a couple of hours.

After we patrolled to the edge of the jungle near the reported location of the two tombs and cache, Dai Uy had me set up and command detonate one claymore mine at a time until I had blown a safe path through the booby traps and entangled jungle to the tombs. It was a trick that I had learned from the PRU in '69.

The day was very hot and humid, the marshy terrain had deep bog holes of mud and slime, and worst of all, there wasn't even a slight breeze to dry the sweat beads that kept flowing into my eyes and smearing my cammi paint. After several miserable hours of crawling through the muck and bramble, some of the guys were beginning to suffer from heat exhaustion.

Seaman Barron was our M-60 machine gunner and stood six feet two inches and weighed about 225 pounds. This was Barron's first tour in Vietnam. He was a strong man and very fast with his hands and feet. Despite good motives, Barron had decided to carry twelve hundred rounds of 7.62mm bandoleers crossed around his chest plus all of the rest of his basic field gear. By 1400 hours one of his bandoleers had been dropped into the deep mud. In between the sucking noises of bodies being pulled out of the muddy pitfalls, I heard sniggering to the rear of our file. Later, I found out that poor Barron's ammo dumping hadn't gone unnoticed by the men behind him.

We progressed slowly toward the tombs until we came upon a lean-to and a bunker. There were cooking utensils, a box of radio batteries, and two twenty-round M-16 magazines lying under the lean-to. The bunker was located approximately fifteen meters forward of a well-camouflaged camp. Dai Uy had me shoot two 40mm HEs at the bunker to liven things up a bit and get everyone's adrenaline flowing—we had all become a bit weary and needed bracing. Due to the HE rounds' noisy detonation at a range of only fifteen meters, all hands were totally rejuvenated. Once the dust had settled, the scouts and I went forward to the bunker and threw an M-26 frag grenade inside it.

"No one home," I told Mr. Fletcher disgustedly.

Dai Uy had us search the immediate area very carefully for the huge cache, while remaining watchful for booby traps. There were no booby traps, however, and no huge cache either. We considered trying to enter the Vietnamese tombs but decided against it because of the potential political consequences and certain wrath from Staff. Before we departed, Lieutenant Fletcher had me crawl into the bunker and leave a 2½-pound M-5 block of C-4 plastic explosive with an eight-minute time fuse as our calling card.

While we were hurriedly patrolling out to the rice paddy, PO3 Waneous teased Barron by pointing to his discarded bandoleer, which was lying in the mud. Barron only smiled and remained silent.

After the C-4 detonated, we had to move into the rice paddy and set up for our H formations for extraction. Doc was then ordered to notify the slicks to extract us. All of us, plus our weapons and gear, were almost totally covered with mud.

Upon our return to the barracks at Dong Tam, over twenty guys and guns headed directly for the roofless, three-spigot, outside shower adjacent to the barracks. The shower area had sides constructed of three sheets of plywood placed end to end, a door at the entrance, and wooden pallets for its floor.

In the midst of the pandemonium and anarchic methods of trying to clean fermenting bodies, untidy weapons, and entangled gear, Ray, one of our SAS mates, proclaimed, "You bloody blokes can shove this bloody mud up your bloody arses and piss off! We don't have mud like this at Nui Det, and it's a bloody good thing. And furthermore . . ."

Ray's humorous tirade had everyone in stitches. While he continued his condemnation of the delta's mud, Chief Bassett was impelled to yell, "We had better hurry up and start the debriefing, sir, *if* we're going to have one."

Dai Uy had already discerned the mood of the rabble and hurriedly replied, "Ray has just completed the debriefing—have at it boys!"

Eberle, who was the epitome of a gaffer, initiated the row by letting go at the down-under guttersnipe with a handful of dunghill mud that was scraped from off his web gear. His aim was perfect, and he hit Ray right on his snot locker (nose). From that point on it was every man for himself until all hands were finally motivated to properly clean up the weapons, gear, and their bodies, in that order, and take the party to the bar.

On the morning of July seventh Bear, Hoan, and I had been tasked to drive to Sam Giang subsector and pick up Tinh and Nghieu, of the Popular Forces, and return to Dong Tam. Tinh and Nghieu were residents of Ba To's hamlet and were assigned to be our guides for that night's operation.

At 1230 Dai Uy gave the PLO, followed by all hands gear inspection at 1530. By 1730 we had inserted in the midst of a heavily populated farming area that was near Ap Dong hamlet and approximately two klicks north of Ba To's hamlet. Tinh, the PF guide, went with Dai Uy's squad, while Nghieu went with ENS Kleehammer and my squad.

We split up, maintaining visual contact, and quickly searched hootch after hootch, finding only women and children. Dai Uy and Tu Uy Kleehammer gained valuable experience in command and control of their squads and especially calling in accurate fire support. When we received occasional fire from the VC hidden in the tree lines, Dai Uy or Tu Uy kept the Seawolves busy suppressing the enemy fire with 2.75-inch rockets, 7.62mm M-60 machine gun fire, and minigun fire.

At 1830 Dai Uy called in both of the Sea Lord slicks to extract Kleehammer and half of the guys and return to Dong Tam. The two PFs, Dai Uy, myself, and six others set up a clandestine "stay behind" L ambush between two hootches. Same Tam and I were inside one hootch on the right flank while Dai Uy and others were located near another hootch that was approximately fifty meters away on the left flank. I set out two M-18A1 claymore antipersonnel mines to cover the right flank.

At last light a woman walked toward the hootch in which Same and I were hidden and stopped at about twenty-five meters. She may have seen my claymore mine or noticed me sitting just inside the doorway of the hootch. Regardless, she coolly turned around and slowly returned to where she had come from. Unfortunately, she never got close enough for me to chase her down and capture her. Shortly afterward another woman came from the opposite direction, took a good look, then turned around and left the area.

At 1945 Tinh, a PF guide, spotted a man carrying an AK-47 Russian assault rifle at a range of fifty meters. Tinh opened up full automatic with his M-16 and shot the VC. It was then that Same and I began receiving fire at our end of the L ambush. Those VC women must have done a thorough recon of our positions, I thought. Same rushed out the door and fired his Stoner machine gun toward the muzzle flashes, while I concentrated on firing 40mm HE into their midst.

Shortly afterward, Dai Uy and his crew started receiving fire from left flank. While we continued a steady rate of fire, the Seawolf gunships were called in to wreak havoc on the VC. It was a bit tricky because of the darkness; however, the VC's positions were easily pinpointed by the green and red tracers—from their AK-47s—which were streaking toward our position. It was very exciting to watch the enemy's green and red messengers of death rip toward Same and I and hear the pop of the projectiles as they sailed over our heads.

After the Seawolves had suppressed most of the VC fire, Dai Uy had half of our guys extract by the one remaining slick. While the slick was returning to Dong Tam, Dai Uy had me detonate all three claymore mines, then return to his location, where the rest of the men had set up a small five-man defensive H formation in preparation for our extraction. Because it was a very dark night, four of us—the corner men—held strobe lights with blue lens covers high above our heads to mark our positions for the Sea Lord slick to use as a guide for landing safely between us. However, the helo pilot wasn't able to see the blue strobe-light flashes, so Dai Uy had us use our flashlights to mark the corners, which worked well.

After our extraction and return to Dong Tam, the whole Navy team of SEALs, Seawolves, and Sea Lord pilots and crews debriefed by brainstorming the operation's insertion and extraction and fire-support procedures. There were always lessons to be learned and SOPs to be adjusted for a new Navy team. We needed flexibility and the willingness to adapt those lessons to future operations. The pilots mentioned to us that at one point we had received fire from 270 degrees, or three points of the compass, but all in all it was a good op—we got two VC KIAs and the Seawolves got five KBAs (killed by air). None of our guys had gotten hurt, and we learned from our mistakes, I thought as I started replenishing my gear's ordnance and cleaning my beloved combination weapon before I showered and hit the sack.

The morning of July tenth began with November Platoon making final preparations for a helo insertion and extraction operation that afternoon in Cai Be district. Just before I was to drive to My Tho to pick up a PSB operative to accompany us on the op, Dai Uy decided to call Lieutenant B. at the SpecWar Det office in Binh Thuy. Lieutenant Fletcher wanted to confirm his arrangements for Sea Lord and Seawolf helos and OV-10 Black Pony support for the day's op. However, Lieutenant B. told him that November Platoon wouldn't be going on an op because Fletcher had to be at Binh Thuy no later than 1300 for a meeting with the commodore of CTF 116.

Lieutenant Fletcher was pissed, and rightly so. He had to hurriedly notify HAL-3 and VAL-4 at Binh Thuy, Dinh Tuong sector and subsector TOCs, and our PSB counterparts in My Tho, that the operation had been cancelled. And, to add insult to injury, Dai Uy had to arrange a flight to Binh Thuy in time for the meeting with the commodore. I had begun to understand the difference between administrators and operators. I was later to learn that it was mainly a matter of power—true power was held by the administrators. They controlled the agendas but never had to operate!

At Dai Uy's meeting at Binh Thuy, he learned that the commodore only wanted to discuss the SEAL platoon messages called UNODIR—unless otherwise directed. Lieutenant Fletcher explained to Lieutenant B. and the commodore the procedures for sending UNODIR messages during SEAL platoon operations. It was disgusting that November Platoon's op had been halted for such a frivolous meeting.

July eleventh, on the other hand, was a fruitful day for

November Platoon. Waneous, our expert vehicle thief, managed to steal a good 2½-ton Army truck at Tan Son Nhut Air Base by hot-wiring the switch. From that point on, we didn't have any problems hauling Chief Bassett's cumshaw gear from Saigon to Dong Tam. Chief Bassett managed to get sheets of plywood, wiring, refrigerated air conditioners, refrigerators, steaks, and booze, among other things.

Later that day, we gave our old jeep to our three Vietnamese Kit Carson scouts and two interpreters. The five of them were tickled to death and promptly headed to My Tho on liberty with their prized possession. After their glorious entry into town, the jeep's rear end suddenly went out. The only way they could get the temperamental beast to move was to engage the front axle by placing it in four-wheel drive. Much to our amusement, the jeep would only move in reverse and at a very slow pace. Our scouts had a long, humbling ride back to Dong Tam.

On the morning of July twelfth, November Platoon was preparing for another operation with Navy Seawolves, Sea Lord slicks, and Black Pony OV-10s that afternoon. We had good, hard operational intelligence information from the Cai Lay district PSB subsection chief Muoi—not the Provincial National Police chief Muoi in My Tho—that a VC District Military Proselytizing Section chief's home was located in the village of Tan Hoi approximately four klicks north of highway QL-4. There were reports that units of the VC 269B Main Force Infantry Battalion were also located in the nearby tree line. Chief Muoi and another of his operatives were to be our guides.

Dai Uy had given all hands the warning order that morning, followed by his PLO at 1600, inspection at 1630, and rehearsal until 1745. The basic idea was that the slicks would swoop in side by side at treetop level, flare the two helo slicks near the hootches, and hover six feet from the ground. Each SEAL squad was to exit the helos, Dai Uy's 1st Squad taking right flank and ENS Kleehammer's 2nd Squad taking the left flank. One fire team from each squad was to set up skirmish lines while the other two fire teams assaulted the hootches immediately after insertion—John Wayne style. The Seawolves and Black Ponies would take care of the enemy fire from the tree line.

At approximately 1830 our slicks popped up over the tree line and hovered near the targeted hootches long enough for both squads to jump from the helos. Our setup and assault went as planned. The nearest huts were quickly searched, with negative results.

Shortly afterward, Lieutenant Fletcher was notified by the helo pilots that they had inadvertently inserted us in the wrong location. Dai Uy immediately had us extracted and inserted near our targets, but there wasn't a man in the area—only women and children. We had begun to learn that the VC/NVA had a variety of ingenious escape routes and techniques to evade surprise helo ground-troop assaults. In spite of our best efforts, we were forced to extract empty-handed and return to Dong Tam for the debriefing.

Our primary problem was that we needed timely guidance and direction from above. For tactical reasons, our Sea Lord slicks were forced to skim the treetops at a good rate of speed to ensure surprise. This SOP was based on several requirements: low visibility, especially when there were several helos; reduction of the Huey rotor's unique whump-whump-whump sound (the trees and vegetation absorbed much of the helo's noise); security from enemy ground fire; and once seen by the enemy, speed to the insertion point. We then defined what was needed: an aircraft on station at a much higher elevation, good communications with the helos and ground troops, and most important, natural placement and access—that is, aircraft that wouldn't arouse too much suspicion from VC/NVA units on the ground prior to our insertion. The solution was obvious—we would utilize the Forward Air Controller pilot. The Army's FAC pilots usually flew the Cessna O-1 fixed-wing observation plane in the delta.

"That's a great idea, Dai Uy!" I exclaimed. "All the FAC pilot would have to do is vector the slicks on specific avenues to the target/insertion point by radio."

Then Mr. Kleehammer opined, "All you have to do, Jerry, is coordinate with the Army and convince them of our need for a FAC pilot and aircraft for all of our helo ops."

"That's true," Dai Uy replied. "I've got to somehow get the time to visit several Army units and work out the details with them." Fletcher took a deep breath, looked at his Rolex watch, grinned, and yelled, "It's time for a beer! I'll buy the first round for everybody. Hoo-Yah!"

CHAPTER FOUR

For an officer to be overbearing and insulting in the treatment of enlisted men is the act of a coward. He ties the man to a tree with ropes of discipline and then strikes him in the face, knowing full well that the man cannot strike back.

—Major C. A. Bach, 1917

On the morning of July thirteenth I spent several hours cleaning and repairing a rusty 7.62mm M-60 machine gun that SEAL Team 2's 8th Platoon had left behind. I had decided to give it to Ba To. It was to be his hamlet's only machine gun. Shortly afterward, Dai Uy gave the platoon a warning order for a helo op the following morning. Cai Lay district's Vietnamese ARVN S-2, a trung uy, or first lieutenant, and six of his men were to combine forces with November Platoon to assault two enemy-bunkered hootches. There were supposedly more than fifteen VC in the immediate area. The Vietnamese trung uy told Dai Uy that we were to take no prisoners—we were to exit the helos with all guns a-blazin' and blow holes into the bunkers with M-72 LAAWs. It certainly sounded like fun.

Reveille was at 0400. At 0530 I was sitting on the edge of a Navy Sea Lord slick's starboard door with my legs hanging out and my boots just touching the skids. We were flying at about one hundred feet altitude and ninety knots airspeed.

I loved to look down and watch the moon's reflections on the many canals, streams, and rice paddies and inhale the strangely aromatic smells of the Vietnamese delta. The cool, moist morning air was, on occasion, the cause of chill bumps that started at the crown of my head, prickling their way down my body to the tips of my toes. There was always something timeless, mystifying, and exhilarating about those experiences. No doubt, much of it was nothing more than youthful exuberance, love of living life to its fullest and absolute confidence in my infallibility.

We eventually crossed the QL-4 highway, headed north for a few kilometers and started circling. Because the Black Ponies couldn't see the targets to begin prepping the tree lines, Dai Uy agreed that it was necessary for one of the Seawolves to drop two one-million-candlelight para flares. Four flares later the Seawolves led the aerial assault.

After the last para flares started sputtering down, we inserted by Sea Lord slicks near the bunkered hootches. While our Navy buddies in the air continued blasting the nearby tree line about two hundred meters west of our insertion point with rockets and minigun fire, we exited our slicks blazing away at the two bunkered hootches and their immediate area.

Initially, I had a hard time judging the distance to the bunkers—approximately two hundred meters—because it was so dark. However, I soon got the range and lay the 40mm HE rounds right on target. Most of the red tracers from our Stoners, M-60s, and M-16s were ricocheting in an inverted dovetail wedge until they were dispersed by brilliant flashes from our detonating 40mm HE rounds.

Lieutenant Fletcher's 1st Squad and Vietnamese were on right flank, while ENS Kleehammer's 2nd Squad, my Vietnamese, and I were on left flank. The VC bunkers were at twelve o'clock, or straight ahead. Basically, Dai Uy had set a frontal skirmish line for maximum firepower and command and control. I was lobbing 40mm HE rounds directly into the bunkers with my XM-148 while everyone else was doing the same with their weapons. Dai Uy fired several M-72 LAAWs at one of the bunkers with deadly effect.

After we reached the two bunkers, the Vietnamese trung uy and his six men coaxed an old man and two small boys from a nearby bunker before they threw hand grenades into it. When things had settled down a bit the trung uy and his men interrogated the old man and learned that six VC had run for the tree line shortly after the first para flares had been dropped.

The Seawolves continued to drop para flares while we searched the area hootches for bodies and VC. I almost stepped directly on a very large water buffalo bull that was lying in his favorite mud hole. He snorted and jumped up and I jumped back. My trigger finger had squeezed back about four of the five-pound trigger pull. It's a Mexican standoff! I thought. However, when Brutus violently shook his horns at a range of four feet, I decided to retreat.

"I hope you realize just how lucky your are, you ugly SOB," I told the old bull while I slowly retreated around the corner of a flimsy hootch.

We searched other hootches and bunkers in the area, with negative results. However, we did find the fleeing VC's personal gear in plastic bags that they had abandoned when they were heading for the tree line. Interestingly, I had three 40mm HE dud rounds, the Vietnamese had five dud hand grenades, and Dai Uy had one dud M-72 LAAW. Apparently, "Hanoi Jane" and her Communist henchmen were very successful in their sabotage of U.S. ordnance at the ordnance factories. Someday, Jane, I muttered to myself as we prepared to extract, you'll reap your rewards for all of the American blood you've shed and the misery you've caused through your treasonous works.

On July sixteenth Dai Uy got the platoon together and told us that NavForV and our SpecWar command didn't really want us operating in Vietnam anymore. They wanted to ensure that we left Vietnam with a good record. The next day, Dai Uy received a message from CTF 116 canceling all SEAL ops until further notice. The only exceptions were Bright Light ops—the rescue of U.S. POWs. All hands were disappointed, frustrated, and pissed.

"Dai Uy, that's what I call pulling out your six-gun and shootin' yourself in the foot," I said. "It'll be difficult for us to maintain our operational readiness without continuing to operate."

"We can't just sit around here sucking suds and playing volleyball either. Why don't they—" Chambo began before Fletcher cut him off.

"I understand all of this, guys," he said as he stood up and stretched his back. "However, when the commodore tells us we have to squat, then we'll squat. But I think we'll be allowed to operate within a few days. In that light, let's continue to plan and prepare for future operations."

On July twentieth Doc Holmes, NavForV combat photographers PO1 Shiplette and Chief Rainwater, interpreter Hoan, and I drove to the Sam Giang subsector to notify Captain Campbell that we were going to Ba To's hamlet for MEDCAPs. From Subsector we drove one and a half klicks west on the remains of a country road to a bridge that was located near an ARVN outpost and parked our jeep. It was a beautiful day for a two-and-a-half-mile patrol to Ba To's hamlet. After we had reached the hamlet, I debriefed Ba To while Shiplette and Chief Rainwater took pictures and wrote notes about the medical needs of the villagers for an article in "The Jackstaff News."

When we returned to Dong Tam later that afternoon,

Dai Uy got the good news from SpecWar staff that we would be operating again soon.

Dai Uy went on to explain, "The rules of engagement haven't changed; however, SpecWar staff is just letting us know that if we get into any political trouble, we can't look to them for any help. Be advised boys, we must keep our noses clean at all costs."

Chambo had about all he could take. He stood up and angrily exclaimed, "What a bunch of assholes, man! Is there any possible way we can get those guys out into the field with us, Dai Uy?"

"Yeah, Dai Uy! Let's use them as ammo bearers for Little Bear's M-60 bandoleers," Waneous teased.

Barron was totally unimpressed with his new sobriquet. He smiled, then said, "I don't get mad, you bunch of wimps—"

Everyone replied in unison with, "Oooooohhhhhhh."

Not to be outdone, Little Bear continued, "I just get even."

Dai Uy had sensed that the Yahoos were about to start a rout and managed to interject, "I have a message from the comm center that says Chief Bassett, here, is now a senior chief petty officer and Mr. Kleehammer is now a lieutenant (jg)! Hoo-Yah! Have at it, boys!"

Bassett, knowing he was going to get it, tried to save himself by shouting, "I'm throwing twenty dollars on the bar. The drinks are on me!"

The twenty-first to the twenty-fourth of July were spent taking care of the many administrative details for Kit Carson scout discharge and recruitment, administrative and operational organization of intel/info nets, and preparing for our next operation once we got the go-ahead from NavForV via SpecWar staff.

On the afternoon of the twenty-fourth, Dai Uy returned from Binh Thuy and briefed the platoon about the new rules of engagement: the enemy had to initiate a firefight before we were allowed to return fire. Fortunately, the new rules didn't restrict us any more than before in our combined ops with PSB operatives. If there was an inadvertent killing of a legal VCI—a VC Communist who had acquired a South Vietnamese ID card illegally and whose name wasn't on the provincial Phuong Hoang committee's blacklist—PSB's chief Hue would have taken care of the details because he was administratively in charge of our combined ops with his PSB operatives. In other words, we were supporting *his* operations. We also had the blessings of the province chief, Colonel Dao, the Provincial National Police Chief Muoi, and our U.S. intelligence collection agency friends. The more VC/VCI killed or captured, the better the Vietnamese provincial Phoenix program looked.

After Dai Uy had briefed everyone, Mr. Kleehammer and I went to My Tho and picked up a PSB operative to accompany him on that night's river interdiction of a small civilian ship that was distributing heroin. It seemed strange to me, at that time, that the province chief, the province's National Police, and the Police Special Branch chiefs were committing only one operative to the op. Even the U.S. Navy had committed two Customs agents to the operation. Because I had a very bad head and chest cold, Ensign Kleehammer took the rest of 2nd Squad and accompanied Lieutenant (jg) Washburn, his crew, and the two Customs lads aboard the Mobile Support Team's MSSC and LSSC boats to interdict the drug runners. According to intelligence, the drug-laden ship was proceeding upstream toward Cambodia and would off-load heroin near Dong Tam that night. Tu Uy's plan was for the MST/BSU (Mobile Support Team/Boat Support Unit) boats to locate the ship using starlight scopes as the MSSC and LSSC cruised quietly up and down the My Tho River on planned avenues of surveillance. Once the ship was located, the MSSC would lead the way at low speed until they reached the ship or were compromised. If the element of surprise was blown, they would simply make a frontal assault and continue the operation.

The LSSC would follow in the MSSC's wake until the action began, maintain control of river traffic, and suppress any small arms or recoilless rifle fire from the beach with its three M-60 7.62mm machine guns, one M-2 .50-caliber machine gun, one MK-19 40mm automatic grenade launcher, and one six-barreled minigun, which fired up to six thousand 7.62mm rounds per minute.

The boarding party was to consist of Trung Uy, 2nd Squad—nine men total—and a couple of our SAS mates with their Stoners, M-60s and SLRs, and Knepper's M-16/XM-148 40mm grenade launcher. The tricky part of the plan required climbing over the gunwale—the upper edge or rail of a ship's or boat's side—by means of a Jacob's ladder or gangway, quickly neutralizing the security forces and taking control of the bridge without receiving too many casualties. After the ship was under control, the PSB operative and the two U.S. Customs agents would board and officially seize the contraband.

Kleehammer, Washburn, and crews returned to Dong Tam about 2300. They had been unable to locate the merchant ship. The ship's first mate must have had friends in high places.

While Mr. Kleehammer and our MST mates were having fun on the river, the rest of us watched the movie *Kelly's Heroes*. It was an interesting WWII vintage story of a few deceitful and unscrupulous individuals totally obsessed with the desire for wealth. All of us were delighted with Donald Sutherland's humor as a Sherman tank commander. We cheered his disdain for any form of negative thoughts or words by saying, "No negative waves, maaaan." Each time he commanded his tanks to advance or assault the enemy, he waved his arm forward and yelled, "Yaaaaooooooooohhhh," like the calvary commander in the John Wayne movies. We swore that on all of our future helo ops we would exit the Sea Lord slicks screaming "Yaaaaoooooooooohhhhhhh" as we assaulted the VC targets. It was easy to have fun with highly motivated teammates.

On the morning of July twenty-fifth at 0900, Dai Uy gave us our warning order for that evening's helo op. All hands spent the remainder of the morning carefully preparing their gear. At about 1100 Dai Uy was notified that elements of the ARVN 7th Division were within one klick (one kilometer) of our target area. It seemed that whenever we cleared AOs in Cai Lai or Cai Be districts, the ARVN 7th directed units to move near the edge of our AOs and set up blocking elements. It was unfortunate for us because after units of the 7th moved into place, the VC/NVA became suspicious and vacated the immediate area.

After lunch, Dai Uy and I drove to Cai Be subsector (Camp Schraeder) and discussed the problem with the Army advisers and district PSB chief Muoi. The consensus was to wait another twenty-four hours and hope that the ARVN 7th units would withdraw, thinking we weren't going into the area. We also learned that the day before, a company of RFs (Regional Force ARVNs) were nearly annihilated. They had been patrolling approximately two klicks above our next target, just above Snoopy's nose—a hairpin curve in a stream that separated Cai Lai and Cai Be districts—and were within one hundred meters of a PF outpost when they were ambushed at 1700 by a large enemy unit suspected of being the VC 261B MF Battalion. The RFs had twenty-four KIA, eighteen MIA, and fifteen WIA. The VC's element of surprise was so complete that the surviving remnant threw down their weapons and fled. All of their weapons and three hard-to-get PRC-25 radios had been lost. Because of their panic, they had also failed to call for air and/or artillery support.

After our return to Dong Tam, Doc got word from MARS—radio communications to CONUS—that his wife had had a baby boy who weighed six pounds fourteen ounces. The joyful Doc brought out champagne and beer to commemorate the birth of his son. The refreshments were shared as thanksgiving for the divine gifts that his wife and son were in good health. It was a night filled with goodwill, merriment, and fraternal brotherhood.

After breakfast on the morning of July twenty-seventh, we were again very busy preparing our gear for that afternoon's helo op. Dai Uy had had to delay the op for an additional day until the ARVN 7th unit departed from the edge of our AO and Sea Lord slicks from HAL-3 became available. Later, at 1000, Fletcher gave the warning order followed by the patrol leader's order at 1530. Our targets were several Communist Mang political indoctrination committee members. They were a newly created North Vietnamese administrative level of political control that was established between the district and village levels of government in contested areas. One source of information reported that replacement units of the NVA's 111th Infantry Regiment, which supported the local VC company-sized units, was in the area of the Mang committee cadre's hootches.

After we had driven to the helo pad at 1700, we rehearsed assault formations, hootch search and seizure, prisoner handling, squad formations, and other SOPs.

We lifted off at 1745, flew aboard three UH-1 Sea Lord slicks to Cai Be, and picked up Chief Muoi and his four men. From there we flew to the Plain of Reeds, where we rendezvoused with the UH-1 Seawolf gunships and OV-10 Black Ponies. Once our Navy, Aussie, and Vietnamese team was complete, we headed south toward our targets. Not counting our Navy HAL-3 and VAL-4 buddies, there were fourteen SEALs, three Kit Carson scouts, five SAS mates, and five PSB operatives headed for the targets and looking for trouble. We had carefully studied our 1:4,000 scale split vertical photographic mosaic of the VC/NVA targets, rehearsed the assault, and were ready to engage our enemy face-to-face.

The three Sea Lord slicks came in so low that the slicks' skids couldn't have missed the rice paddy dikes by more than a foot or two, with the target at twelve o'clock. Before the slicks began to flare, we were standing on our helo's landing skids, grasping the sides of the doors and totally psyched to assault the enemy hootches. As the helo started flaring, we jumped from about six feet, screaming "Yaaaaaaooooooooohhhhhhhh!" As soon as our boots plunged into the flooded rice paddy, we began our assault with all weapons a-blazin'.

Dai Uy, Senior Chief Bassett, and the rest of the 1st Squad took the left hootch and promptly killed two VC. Trung Uy, the 2nd Squad, and I took the right hootch and bunker, hoping to shed a little blood ourselves. Our communist adversaries had wisely turned chicken and were heading toward the tree line on the opposite side of our hootch, with a blaze of our tracers hot on their tails. One of the Seawolf pilots, who had seen our small group of VC running toward the tree line, requested permission to make a firing run on them.

Mr. Kleehammer yelled, "Get your heads down. The Seawolves are going to make a minigun run over our position."

There really wasn't much cover to be had, so I continued clearing the hootch's mats and palm fronds from its framework with 40mm HE rounds and I placed a couple rounds in the mouth of the large bunker to take care of any remaining VC who might be in there. I later tossed a mini-CS grenade into the bunker for good measure. We were receiving some .51-caliber and a lot of small arms fire from the tree line, which was approximately three to four hundred meters at ten to two o'clock from our positions.

"There must be a fairly large VC/NVA unit in there somewhere," I told Trung Uy as the Seawolves swooped over our heads and started returning the stubborn VC fire with their miniguns spitting out six thousand rounds per minute and a half-dozen 2.75-inch rockets. It seemed that bullets and rockets were whizzing, ricocheting, and popping all around us.

"Damn, we couldn't ask for better support than that!" I yelled to the guys who could hear. I sure was glad the Seawolves and Black Ponies were on our side as I watched a large fireball erupt from the tree line after one of the Black Ponies had taken its dive with a couple of five-inch Zuni rockets.

After we had searched the hootch and the bunker and collected all documents and souvenirs, Chambo and Barron destroyed the remnants of another hootch near the tree line, reconning by fire for hidden VC that might still be lurking in the general area. When Barron and Chambo got bored with the hootch, they turned their M-60s on the tree line and concentrated on accurate short bursts at the sources of the green and red VC tracers. Barron had brought along enough ammo to shoot to his heart's content.

Same and Tam were carrying as many 5.56mm rounds as Barron was 7.62mm, but without much of the weight. Same's Stoner was set to fire belted 5.56mm at a rate of 850 rounds per minute. While Same let off a short burst with his Stoner, Waneous and Compton would cease fire, and vice versa. Like all well-trained combat troops, we always tried to maintain a steady rate of fire without lulls.

A couple of the SAS mates had concentrated their semiautomatic fire on the VC muzzle flashes from the tree line with their version of the 7.62mm FN light auto rifles referred to as SLRs. The two PSB operatives were squatted down behind the remnants of the hootch jabbering as they went through the VC Mang documents. Our scouts were busy firing their M-16s toward the tree line where a secondary explosion had erupted. Poor Mr. Kleehammer was too busy observing the operation and coordinating with Dai Uy and the Seawolves and Black Ponies to have any fun destroying things.

It wasn't long before Dai Uy radioed Trung Uy, telling him to move his squad south toward first squad's position to link up for extraction. Apparently, Dai Uy was satisfied that we had gotten all of the documents that PSB Chief Muoi needed from the Mang cadre's bodies and hootches and had determined that it was time to get out of Dodge and let the Seawolves and Black Ponies really go to it.

After we had split up into three H groups and were being extracted from the open rice paddies by the Sea Lords, the Huey gunships and OV-10s continued to strafe and rocket the tree line. We circled nearby and watched while the Seawolves and Black Ponies took turns diving into the thick of the fray until they had expended most of their ordnance on the VC/NVA positions in the tree line. After I had watched them for a while, I began to realize that our Seawolf and Black Pony buddies also knew a little about tactics. It appeared that, when they could, they made their approach by hugging the line of trees to reduce their time of exposure to the VC/NVA ground gunners.

"Give 'em hell, Sam," I yelled out the starboard door of our slick as I watched a Black Pony take its dive toward the source of the green and red tracers that were streaking toward him. For a time, as I had watched the HAL-3 and VAL-4 guys systematically destroy the enemy positions in the tree line, I was caught up in the emotional exhilaration and privilege of being a member of a great team of Navy guys. For some reason, tears welled up in my eyes when I remembered what some fellow had yelled: "Let slip the dogs of war; cry havoc."

We were fortunate that only one of the Seawolves had received a few VC rounds through the helo's instrument panel. However, the crew managed to return to Dong Tam safely.

After our own return, I inventoried my gear and found that I had expended forty-seven 40mm HE rounds, fifty rounds of 5.56mm ball ammo, and one CS grenade. Some of the other platoon guys had expended more than I. After we had finished the debriefing, everyone was famished and decided to celebrate by heading for the chow hall and getting a good, hot meal.

Later that evening our little bar's bulkheads occasionally rattled violently between Barron and Knepper's nipping on their favorite bottles of solace. They were taking turns trading blows with each other to see who would show or grunt any signs of pain first. Unfortunately, neither one did—hence the rattling of the bulkheads till midnight and taps.

The morning of July twenty-eighth was a spit-and-polish day. After we had finished with our barracks, the outside area, and the hot vehicles, all of us got dressed in our best set of jungle greens and stood for inspection by Admirals Salzer and Clarey. Shortly after the admirals had visited and inspected our regular Navy mates next door, they arrived aboard their beautifully waxed Saigon jeep. They were impressed with our cleanliness and the organization of our living quarters, intel room, and operational gear and spaces, while we were eyeing their beautiful jeep.

Senior Chief Bassett noticed our covetous looks and quickly said, "No way, guys! I'm already in hot water enough as it is."

I spent much of July twenty-ninth trying to get Tuoi, one of our action agents, released from the Cai Lai district's subsector National Police. Tuoi was one of the agents we had hired on the recommendation of an ex-PRU agent. It turned out that Tuoi was a draft dodger, among other things, and didn't have an ID card. I had not yet gotten a completed name trace from Saigon.

I went to 525 and discussed my problem with Al. He'd just received a written report on Tuoi, and gave me a brief rundown of Tuoi's activities since his initial contact with the Vietnamese military. In 1964 Tuoi was an ARVN trainee in Kien Phong province's Tran Quoc Toan Regional Force Training Center. During his stay he reportedly killed several of his fellow soldiers, took their weapons, and fled to the VC Y-4 HQ located in the Cai Lay district of Dinh Tuong province. In March of '65 Tuoi joined the Popular Forces at the Tan Hoi outpost. During that period, a VC unit attempted to overrun the outpost and failed. Shortly afterward Tuoi took his weapon and disappeared.

In early '68 Tuoi volunteered for service with the ARVN 11th Regiment, 7th Infantry Division. While he was serving as an ARVN, he was arrested by the upper-delta MSS. He had been uncovered as a VC penetrant. In April of '68 MSS used Tuoi as an action agent within the VC Y-4 HQ unit. However, Tuoi passed only small amounts of general information for a short time before he again disappeared.

In '70 Tuoi decided to take advantage of the Chieu Hoi amnesty program and change sides. At that time, MSS reported that Tuoi was deeply in debt to the VC and several South Vietnamese government organizations. Supposedly, he had stolen three ammo cans full of VC finance and economy tax money. Tuoi, not to be discouraged by his past reputation and to establish his bona fides, then led an ARVN unit to three caches that contained 82mm HE and 61mm HE mortar rounds, B-40 rocket rounds and

7.62×39mm ball and tracer ammo. He had been working for us for several weeks. Not surprisingly, his information reports were general in nature. Fortunately, I had submitted all required forms through our chain of command for a background investigation. Nothing was lost or compromised and a valuable lesson was learned.

The next two days were spent working on intel files, OB (Order of Battle) maps and overlays, barracks improvements, future op planning and coordination, and so on. The five SAS Aussies, Hayden, Waneous, and Compton, left for Nui Det, where the Aussie Diggers (regular army) and the SAS unit was headquartered. Hayden, Waneous, and Compton were planning a ten-day LRP (Long Range Patrol) with the SAS folks during their stay.

While I was at the Embassy House visiting Jake B., Dan, the Company PIC (Provincial Interrogation Center) adviser and Chieu Hoi Center observer, asked me if we had any agent reports or other information about sightings of U.S. POWs near the infamous Route 66 canal in the northwestern portion of Sam Giang district. He also asked if we or any SEAL platoons had operated in that area. Sadly, I had to tell Dan that November Platoon hadn't operated in that area and we didn't have information about any POW camp in that area, nor did I have access to our Barndance cards of past operations. However, I did assure him that we would be very interested in such information. Dan made no comment and left the room.

I looked at Jake, shrugged my shoulders, and said, *"C'est la vie."*

CHAPTER FIVE

He who does not carefully compare his own
forces with those of the enemy will come to a
disastrous end. Things which are unexpected or
sudden frighten the enemy, but they pay little
attention to things to which they are accustomed.
It is better to avoid a tricky opponent than one
who never lets up. The latter makes no secret of
what he is doing, whereas it is difficult to find out
what the other is up to.

—Emperor Maurice,
The Strategikon, ca. A.D. 600

Shortly after breakfast on August second November Platoon was given its warning order. I was to carry sixty-three 40mm HE rounds, two concussion grenades, 145 5.56mm ball ammo, two quarts of water, four minifrag grenades, three mini-CS grenades, two mini-smoke grenades, one survival radio, pencil flares, a T panel, a strobe light with a blue lens, mosquito repellent, a first-aid kit, a Swiss seat, an M-16/XM-148 with Singlepoint, a penlite, a flashlight, two MK-13 day/night flares, four pop flares, a 1:50,000 scale map of our op area, a Silva compass, and a knife.

At 1500 Dai Uy gave his PLO. Our op was to insert by Sea Lord slicks and assault two hootches with Seawolves overhead for support. Interestingly, that day's targets were near the hootches we had assaulted in Cai Be district on our two previous missions. Inspection was at 1700, followed by rehearsal until 1800, when we loaded the slicks and flew to Cai Be subsector to pick up Chief Muoi and his two male operatives. Chief Muoi also brought along a very pretty and well-built Vietnamese woman of about nineteen years of age. She was originally from the area of that op and had recently Chieu Hoied. Some of her family members had been tortured and killed by power-hungry Communists. There was no doubt in my mind that her primary motivation for coming along as our guide was to settle a few scores. A few weeks later she was ambushed and killed while riding her motorbike on QL-4.

At 1835 the two Sea Lord slicks swooped in low, side by side, with the targets at twelve o'clock, and flared within fifty meters of the hootches. While our helo was still moving forward at about ten knots, all of us jumped out the side doors, screaming "Yaaaaaooooohhhhhh," à la *Kelly's Heroes*.

As soon as my boots hit the deck I sprinted into one of the hootches and had an old man and a young boy out before most of the guys had a chance to offload. We carefully searched the area and nearby hootches for the enemy and found nothing. Surprisingly, we didn't receive any enemy fire from the tree line. We threw concussion grenades into the canals to force any hidden VC who were underwater and breathing through air tubes to the surface, but had no results.

It wasn't long before we learned from our Seawolf buddies that there were friendlies in the tree line. We knew that a unit of the ARVN 7th had an AO adjacent to ours cleared. However, they had strayed into our AO and were within six to seven hundred meters of our location. Needless to say, there were no VC/VCI in the area. We extracted before zero dark thirty and returned to Dong Tam. After our debriefing, we sat around and discussed the problems we were having with some of our Vietnamese allies.

The next two days were spent working on agent dossiers, information reports, plotting VC/NVA Order of Battle on our 1:50,000 scale situation map overlays, OB organization charts, agent handling and recruitment, and piecing together mosaics.

August sixth was a fun day. Lieutenant Fletcher, Same, interpreter Hoan, and I went to the Seawolf helo pad with one case—72 rounds—of 40mm HE, fifty 40mm para flares, fifteen M-18A1 claymore mines, hand grenades, pop flares, smoke grenades, and two M-72 LAAWs. A Navy Sea Lord picked us up at Dong Tam and dropped the four of us off near Ba To's hamlet at 1300.

After the usual courtesies and respectful bowing, Ba To and his hamlet defense personnel were absolutely ecstatic about the ordnance that we had brought him and his men. Their hamlet was overdue for an attack from the VC; Ba To knew it, and so did we.

Later, Ba To told us that the local VC District Civilian Proselytizing section had been telling the nearby Vietnamese people how to corrupt the upcoming government elections in October. They must have been trained by the Democrats back home, I thought. I later wrote a SEAL intelligence report on Ba To's information.

When the Sea Lord returned to pick us up at 1345, I slipped Ba To his last month's pay as an agent handler—8,000 piasters—in a sealed envelope and handed him a bottle of French cognac. That day was a good one for Ba To and his clan. They had enough ammunition to fight off a VC attack for at least one night and a bottle of encouragement for the twilight hours.

The Navy slick dropped Same and me off at Dong Tam while Dai Uy and Hoan went on a VR of the upper Cai Be district. I spent the rest of that afternoon and evening working on intel reports, OB card files, and so on, before I called it quits.

During the morning of August seventh, I worked on intel files, took pictures of our Kit Carson scouts for their dossiers, and later drove to My Tho to visit with Al and Jake at the Embassy House. There, I inquired about Tuoi's imprisonment and status with MSS. Afterward, I stopped by PSB to see Chief Hue. I passed him some information that we had received from one of our agents about the exact location of a VC My Tho sapper. I also requested one PSB operative to accompany Mr. Kleehammer on his river op that night. Chief Hue was very happy to support us and handed me the name-trace results of our two hootch maids. As it turned out, one of the hootch maids had been arrested in May of '68 and imprisoned for six months for working with and for the VC. I later approached her and asked her why she hadn't mentioned this in her past-history statement. She gave me a confusing story about how the VC had killed her husband and then coerced her into serving the Marxist cause. In that light, I didn't bother to question her any further. I later briefed the platoon to be very careful in all that we said in the presence of the hootch maids or the Kit Carson scouts and never to allow any Vietnamese in our intelligence room.

After lunch, Commander Del Guidice, Lieutenant Morrow, and Lieutenant (jg) Antrim of the SpecWar staff spent the afternoon inspecting and quizzing November Platoon. I briefed Commander Del Guidice and Lieutenant Morrow on *all* of our intelligence activities. They seemed properly impressed. Lieutenant Morrow was especially thoughtful and encouraging.

The next morning, August eighth, Dai Uy received word that our CBU-55B FAE (Fuel Air Explosive) bomb op for that afternoon and the following day had been canceled because we had no fuses. However, Fletcher wasn't easily discouraged.

Later, Eberle, Tam, the PSB operative, and I drove to My Tho to take care of myriad administrative details. After we had dropped off the PSB fellow, Eberle, Tam, and I drove down to the My Tho riverfront and bought fresh papaya and coconut drinks mixed with raw sugar. I also ate a large papaya. All three items cost me 250 P, or less than a dollar. We returned to Dong Tam by the river road, which was a little more dangerous but much shorter than the roundabout route.

The rest of the afternoon I piddled with my field gear, worked out with weights, and played horseshoes with the guys until we were rained out. After supper, at 1945, Dai Uy gave the warning order for the next day's helo operations. We were to utilize one Sea Lord for insertions and extractions and two Seawolves for gunship support. The Seawolves would be guiding us to numerous VC/NVA targets that were located in the southern edges of the Plain of Reeds—the NVA's major infiltration route from North Vietnam into the South Vietnamese III and IV Corps Tactical Zones. We were to fly to the northwestern half of Cai Lay district, near the abandoned My Phuoc Tay strategic village that was south of the King Tong Doc Loc canal and west of the Kinh Cai Chuoi canal. Once enemy locations were identified, the Seawolves would prep the enemy's position if needed and the Sea Lord slick would insert us. Depending on the enemy's reaction, we would either assault or patrol to the target to begin our pillaging and burning. Those types of off-the-cuff missions were called "Parakeet" ops, or targets of opportunity. Parakeet ops were a lot of fun but were very risky because we were not always certain of our enemy's strength or reactionary capabilities.

In 1970 a SEAL 1 squad was having great fun working with the Seawolves and Sea Lords on Parakeet ops near Sea

Float. On their last insertion of the day, the SEAL squad was inserted into a fairly large opening and were immediately taken under heavy small arms fire by a company-size VC unit that was not expected to be in the area. Worst of all, the enemy unit was well-hidden and camouflaged within a heavily fortified jungle area. One of the men in the SEAL squad took an AK-47 round (7.62×39mm) in the chest. The projectile entered one side of his chest, traveled all the way around the inside of the rib cage and exited on the opposite side. Amazingly, the fellow survived the terrible wound, but no doubt his recovery was long and painful. It was also incredible that all members of the SEAL squad were eventually rescued, thanks to our airdale buddies of the Navy Seawolves, Black Ponies, and Sea Lords.

On the morning of August ninth, Fletcher gave us a warning order and I worked on field expedient antennas for our PRC-77 radios until lunch. At 1300 Dai Uy gave his PLO. Afterward the eight of us went to the helo pad and rehearsed until 1400 when our Navy slick arrived. All eight of us loaded our slicks, and I took my favorite spot on starboard side just aft of the pilot. I held onto the edge of the door and looked closely for enemy bunker complexes while we were flying over the Route 66 canal— Kinh Thuong Mai Di Song My Tho—to the northwestern corner of Cai Lay district, near the borders of Kien Phong and Kien Tuong provinces. We were only thirty to forty klicks south of the infamous "Parrot's Beak" of Cambodia that stuck its nose into the interior of South Vietnam. The U.S. Army's 25th Infantry Division, 196th Infantry Brigade, 1st Infantry Division, 173d Airborne Brigade, 11th Armored Cavalry Regiment, and others had shed a lot of blood fighting the infiltrating NVA in that area since '65.

The Seawolves, who were leading the way, soon identified five hootch and bunker complexes. After Dai Uy chose our first target, we inserted within fifty meters of the complex while the Seawolves circled overhead. Kit Carson scout Same Tam and I were points, and we moved into the hootches and bunkers once Dai Uy had the rest of the squad set on a frontal skirmish line for security and maximum firepower. The gunships also circled overhead as observers.

Tam led the way because he was an ex-VC sapper—he knew all of the VC's tricks of the trade. I was amazed at how fast he moved toward the hootches and bunkers. He seemed to know just how fast to go and where he was going. In some ways he had a lot in common with some of my PRU buddies, who were ex-VC also. When we reached a bunker, Tam went past it and I threw a grenade into it. When we reached a hootch, I set it afire after Tam and I had gathered VC AK-47 magazines and other ammo. At times the going was very slow because of thick brush and potholes of water.

Those potholes of water were heavily polluted. If I drank any of it, I probably would be in the hospital within a few days. For the VC, however, it was only a small part of their occupational hazards. During my previous tours, it was common to see babies who were heavily infested with internal parasites and suffering from malnutrition. The hair on their heads was sparse, their stomachs were swollen, and their eyes were listless. Sometimes they were too weak to cry.

We extracted and inserted into a new area. However, that area was also very brushy, and it was hard to maneuver. Tam and I waded chest-deep in a small canal trying to find a trail leading to the hootches and bunkers, but we failed.

After Tam and I hooked up with Dai Uy and the rest of our squad again, we patrolled one hundred meters west to another hootch and bunker complex. We hadn't gotten very far into the tree line when we saw VC signs saying

Bay no, or booby trap. Lieutenant Fletcher decided it
would be best to call in the Seawolves to clear the area of
booby traps with miniguns and 2.75-inch rockets.

After the Seawolves made their strafing and rocket run,
Tam and I went back in, crawling on our hands and knees.
We hadn't gotten far when we came upon one of the Sea-
wolves 2.75 rockets that was still spewing and smoking.
We moved by it very carefully, not knowing the condition
of the warhead.

When we reached our first bunker, Tam just crawled by
it without checking it. Once I got to it, I tossed in a minifrag grenade. Apparently, no one was home. I didn't hear
any screams or grunts, or smell blood.

We then came to a hootch that had Chinese and North
Vietnamese grenades, AK-47 magazines, web gear, and
cooking utensils lying around in disarray. I wondered where
the little weasels were hiding and if they were watching us.
Both of us then patrolled farther to two more hootches,
where we found one dead VC, his AK-47 rifle and miscellaneous personal gear. I threw a CS grenade into another
bunker. No one came out. Once Tam and I had burned the
hootches, we patrolled out past the dud 2.75-inch rocket and
back to 1st Squad. Dai Uy called for extraction.

We inserted twice more near hootch complexes. After
we collected loot, threw grenades in the bunkers, and
burned the hootches, Dai Uy called for extractions.

After he called for our last extraction, Dai Uy prepared
to throw a smoke grenade to mark our position and give
the Sea Lord pilot an indication of the wind direction. As
he was throwing the grenade, it blew up in his hand, causing flesh damage and second-degree burns. His hand was
a mess. Someone had installed an instantaneous explosive cap in the smoke grenade. We had taken that grenade
out of a sealed container that had been packaged at the
munitions factory.

"Thanks, Hanoi Jane," I yelled in my frustration. I respected my VC and NVA adversaries; they were straightforward in carrying out a ruthless seizure of power and, as I saw it, enslavement. However, I had only contempt for those who worked deceitfully against my country at our expense; we were fighting against Marxism and for the freedom of the South Vietnamese people.

We finally returned to Dong Tam at 1830. There would be little partying that night. Everyone was tired, and Dai Uy's hand was causing him a lot of pain and had to be cleaned and bandaged at the dispensary. It had been a good day, however. No one was badly hurt, the Seawolves had killed one VC that we knew of, and we had learned a few tricks of the trade and reinforced our ability in others. We were all ready for a hot meal, a shower, and a good night's rest.

During the morning of August tenth, Hayden, Waneous, and Compton returned to Dong Tam from Nui Det. They brought with them five SAS mates to spend the next few weeks partying and operating with us. They were Sgt. Graham Brammer, L. Cpl. Dennis McCarthy, and troopers Bob Kilsby, Ian Lawrence, and Hartley Smithwick. We all spent the afternoon getting to know each other by telling war stories over a few beers. Unfortunately, Doc and I had to take the chief's exam the following day so we didn't get too carried away with our newfound mates.

The following morning, Senior Chief Bassett, Doc, and I caught a Sea Lord to Binh Thuy. After lunch we visited the EOD detachment and caught up on the latest scuttlebutt. PO1 Waterbury had an extra bunk in his room and suggested that I spend the night there. Doc and I spent most of the evening studying for the chief's exam.

On the morning of August twelfth both of us took our exams. At 1300 Lieutenants Fletcher and Morrow arrived from Dong Tam to check on the possibility of using the

CBU-55B FAE bomb during the next few days. Dai Uy also said that we had been promised Sea Lords and Seawolves for the next day's Parakeet ops.

At 1350 Lieutenant B. drove Doc, Dai Uy, and me to the Air America terminal near Can Tho. Our flight was very enjoyable and we arrived at the Binh Duc air field just west of My Tho in a little over a half hour. From there we bummed a ride to Dong Tam with an Aussie adviser.

At 2015 Tu Uy gave us our warning order for the next day's Parakeet ops, which were to take place in the same area as on August ninth. I suggested that the Seawolves try to maintain the element of surprise by changing their initial tactics, swooping in low and fast to prep the targets as quickly as possible prior to our insertion. I explained that because we were striking VC positions near the same area as before, the VC would be wise to our tactics and have time to set up claymore mines and booby traps before our ground assault, if they hadn't already. We already knew that the VC had a 2.75-inch rocket warhead to use as a booby trap or mine. I also suggested that if we went on any more Parakeet ops, we should operate in a different area and not set patterns. Dai Uy and Tu Uy thought that these were good ideas.

The dawn of August thirteenth was beautiful. I loved sunrises and sunsets. They were timeless and, somehow, always comforted me. Trung Uy and 2nd Squad were to go on morning Parakeet ops, and Chief Bassett and 1st Squad were to go on Parakeet ops later that afternoon.

Mr. Kleehammer was the patrol leader, and gave the PLO at 0715. Our SAS mates Sergeant Brammer, troopers Kilsby and Smithwick, came along with 2nd Squad—Chambo, Same, Waneous, Compton, Little Bear, and myself. We were at the helo pad by 0800, where we rehearsed basic SOPs until our Sea Lord slick arrived. By 0900 hours the slick was stuffed with ten happy, weak-in-the-upper-story imbeciles, and headed for the infamous Plain of Reeds in northern Cai Lay district looking for trouble.

Our first insertion was adjacent to a canal and near a group of hootches and bunkers. Trung Uy was carrying the PRC-77 radio and concentrated on communicating with the Seawolf gunships. It was a nice arrangement for both of us—Mr. Kleehammer monitored the radio and requested strafing and rocket runs when warranted, while I directed the men. As usual, the VC had made tracks for the tree line before we could intercept them by air or on the ground. While Trung Uy called in helo strikes, the rest of the squad maintained security by advancing in a wedge formation and returned the sporadic VC fire from the tree line. Tam and I were kept busy laying waste to hootches, blasting bunkers, and scuttling a sampan during our march of at least five hundred meters alongside the small, brushy canal.

Our second insertion was made near another group of hootches and bunkers that had been abandoned for some time. We took great delight in setting fire to anything that would burn, so as to deprive the VC and NVA of future shelter. We had been burning and pillaging for over three hours when the helos notified Trung Uy that they were getting low on fuel. Also Chief Bassett and 1st Squad was supposed to use our slick later that afternoon. Considering that 2nd Squad and our three Aussie mates had missed breakfast, and all of us had developed a powerful hunger while ravaging the area with fire and sword, we decided it was time for a hot meal. Why not? I thought. The mess hall would be open at 1130.

I looked at Mr. K., then looked down at my watch and said, "What do you think, Trung Uy?"

Kleehammer glanced at his watch, grinned, and yelled, "Chow time!"

Later that afternoon, Chief Bassett's Parakeet op was canceled because only one Seawolf helo was available.

Second Squad and our Aussie mates spent the rest of the afternoon faithfully cleaning weapons, gear, and filthy bodies, and replenishing our basic field gear load of ordnance in case of a call for an unexpected immediate-action mission.

All went well until 1900 hours, when the base electrical power went off. In short order all of the guys began to get rowdy. The nervous Vietnamese base security personnel began shooting para flares occasionally for illumination. They must have heard the hootin' and hollerin' emanating from our den of iniquity and thought that we were a company of suicidal VC sappers headed for their position.

In that light, Same got the idea that all nineteen of us should simultaneously shoot two para flares each to celebrate the next year's July fourth. Our Aussie buddies thought it was a great idea too; they had little love for their limey mates.

Trung Uy spoke up and said, "What if we catch our barracks on fire?"

Chambo, an ex–Hell's Angel, yelled, "Why, hell, all we have to do is aim them over toward the Vietnamese area. Who gives a damn if the VN hootches burn down as long as it isn't ours!"

Trooper Smithwick commented, "That's right, mates! No guts, no glory!"

Most of us felt that we weren't appreciated anyway, and worse yet, one lieutenant staff admin'er judged us as nothing more than a necessary evil to be tolerated only for a short time. In that light, the vote was unanimous— onward to infamy.

After everyone had an M-82 para flare in each hand and we were all a safe distance from each other, we lay on the ground as Dai Uy gave the command, "Ready, aim, fire!"

Upon the command to fire, we slammed our pop flares hard against the ground and watched the finned flare assemblies rocket upward approximately 150 feet, where the parachutes deployed and the incendiary charges were ignited. It was deafening, and the whole world seemed to light up as the flares slowly descended toward the Vietnamese quarters across the road. As expected, all of the flares burned out well before their landing near the Vietnamese barracks. Unfortunately, the sons of Gomer had illuminated themselves for what they had done. Righteousness loves light. Considering that "there is none righteous, no, not one," all of us scurried back to our darkened tavern, where we continued to scheme and kept watch for any Navy admin'ers/staffers or revengeful Vietnamese who might have been snooping around prior to taps. The next morning, Dai Uy said the base commander called him on the carpet about the flares—but his innocent "Who me?" carried the day.

After a day of rest and replenishment, Dai Uy gave us our warning order on the morning of August fifteenth. At 1230 Fletcher gave his PLO to November Platoon, our SAS mates, MST folks, VAL-3 and VAL-4 comrades. After the briefing we cammied up, held inspection, and rehearsed emergency SOPs and immediate-action drills.

We had previously received intelligence information from 525, NILO, and the Binh Dai DSA Major Bigelow that units of the VC 263 Main Force Infantry Battalion and 516A Local Force Infantry Battalion were supposedly located in an area that was approximately ten klicks south of the Binh Dai subsector and near the Song Ba Lai, a river, for R&R, replenishment, and training. Our adversaries had picked a good area for their safe haven. It was almost impenetrable in places, and, after the French withdrawal, was and had always been totally controlled by VC/NVA units.

Because the fuses for the new CBU-55B FAE bomb had been made available, Dai Uy decided that it was time to test and evaluate the cluster bomb against jungle canopies and entrenched enemy forces and for creating helo LZs. Hopefully we wouldn't have to insert into a hot LZ. We were also tasked to recon the area for enemy activities and to leave behind a few booby-trapped calling cards and psyops documents. The Army's 10th Psyop Battalion, 4th Psyops Group, in Can Tho, had previously dropped a new batch of Chieu Hoi leaflets throughout the area to win over the VC/NVA units' hearts and minds.

Initially, the cluster bombs were to be dropped from an OV-10 Black Pony. Once the dispenser was released from the Bronco and had sufficient separation from the aircraft, it would release the bomblets. The individual bomblets would, in turn, descend to the ground by parachute with six-foot-fused probes extended. When the long shaft contacted the ground, the bomblet's liquid fuel would be dispersed into the air until the delayed detonation of an incendiary charge ignited the fuel. In theory, the ensuing overpressure blast would violently create an opening through double- and triple-canopy jungle large enough for a UH1 Huey LZ. It was believed that the overpressure would also neutralize or kill all VC/NVA troops within the immediate area by destroying the alveoli (air sacks) within their lungs. The idea sounded great, but would it work? We intended to find out.

By 1440 hours we had loaded our two Sea Lord slicks and followed the Seawolves south, across the My Tho River and over Binh Dai district's dense jungle. The two Black Ponies had flown ahead of us to the targeted area and dropped the cluster bomb units just prior to our insertion.

While the Black Ponies and Seawolves were circling overhead, our slicks wasted no time in getting us to the newly created LZs that had penetrated the thick jungle canopies. There were tall coconut trees that sporadically spiked their way into the deep blue sky from the double canopy below. Surprisingly, we didn't initially receive any ground fire. Dai Uy and 1st Squad's slick started its descent into a pit of blackened debris near an old Buddhist pagoda that had been long since abandoned.

When the slick had descended to twenty or twenty-five feet from the cluttered jungle floor, Lieutenant Fletcher, who had been on the helo's intercom, received word from the pilot and in turn told his squad to "Go!"

All of 1st Squad knew that something was wrong and quickly obeyed by jumping out of the side doors. It was a long plunge for men laden with an average of one hundred pounds each of gear and weapons. As soon as the guys hit the ground, everyone scurried off to the side to avoid the main rotor in the event of the slick's crashing.

As it turned out, the helo would have crashed if 1st Squad hadn't jumped when ordered. The pilot later explained that, as he was lowering the helo carefully to avoid most of the trees and the pagoda, its low RPM warning light had come on. After the squad had exited, the pilot still had difficulty in coaxing the power from the helo's engines to ascend from the tight LZ.

In 2nd Squad, we had watched the whole show from our slick while circling the LZ clockwise. As usual, I was seated on the edge of the starboard door with my combo weapon on my lap and my legs hanging out while watching the strange carryings-on below. After the first slick had finally lifted out of the LZ, we quickly moved into the same pit of miry clay and jumped to the ground from only ten feet. It was a molar-jarring thud, but at least it wasn't from twenty-five feet.

While Trung Uy and Dai Uy were conferring with each other, I ensured that the 2nd Squad guys were okay. I noticed that Doc Holmes was sitting over to the side by the radio and appeared to be in a lot of pain.

"What happened, Doc?" I asked quietly.

Doc grinned and answered, "I think I broke my leg."

All I could do was encourage him. "Well, hang in there, Doc. Don't give up the ship."

Dai Uy had decided to leave half of Trung Uy's men at the LZ with Doc, while the rest of us, ten in all, went on a reconnaissance of the area. Knepper and Tam were assigned as point and soon led us to a hootch that probably had been abandoned shortly after the cluster bomblets had detonated. We set fire to the hootch and continued on our recon eastward toward an old French-style building that the Seawolves had spotted near where one of the cluster bomblets had detonated. The thick jungle and numerous irrigation canals made it very difficult to penetrate and remain alert and ready to act aggressively against an enemy ambush. It was so hot and humid, we felt like we could barely breathe the stifling air. Sweat soaked our cammies and washed some of the cammi paint from our faces, which, naturally, drained into our eyes. It stung like lightning and almost continually blurred our vision. And last but not least, the CBU had thoroughly pissed off the wasps and other insects that buzzed around our bodies and on our sweaty faces throughout the operation.

That portion of the Binh Dai district reminded me of some miserable times I had spent in the T-10 jungle located in the northern portion of the Rung Sat Special Zone in 1967–68.

Once we had reached the French plantation building, we set our defensive perimeter and took a short break for a salt tablet, water, and a couple of C-ration candy disks apiece. Shortly afterward, Dai Uy and I left the psyop documents inside the once beautiful French building for our enemies to ponder over. We examined the nearby cluster-bomb damage and were surprised at what little destruction it had rendered. At least it didn't leave a deep crater filled with water like thousand-pound GP bombs did in the Run Sat. It wasn't nearly as destructive as we had been led to believe. I'd been told that the fuel/air bomb would basically vaporize all vegetation and flesh as thoroughly as God had destroyed Sodom and Gomorrah. We concluded that we couldn't rely on the cluster bomb to eliminate many—or any—VC/NVA troopers who were hidden in bunkers.

"What we need is one of the old double-fused M121 ten-thousand-pound GP bombs, called 'daisy cutters,' that the army utilized in 'seventy for creating large LZs and destroying enemy troop concentrations," I whispered to Dai Uy. He nodded in silent agreement.

While I was pondering visions of a dozen Hercules C-130 aircraft dropping M121 daisy cutters on our AO, northwest and approximately 150 meters from our position, a VC fired two warning shots. In a heartbeat the situation turned into a cat-and-mouse game, and I wasn't too sure who the mouse was.

Dai Uy motioned me over to him and said, "Smitty, I want you to take point and give Knepper a rest. Tam will stay behind you. Set an azimuth of three-six-zero degrees and patrol toward the signal shots. We don't want contact, we just want to recon for signs of any heavy enemy activities and emplace our surprise gifts."

I nodded and whispered, "I'm ready if you are."

Dai Uy grinned, slapped me on the side of my head and continued. "When we reach that point, I'll give you the signal to change our course to 090 degrees, and we'll return to the old pagoda and our insertion point. The Seawolves will try to keep Tu Uy aware of our location, and he will vector us by radio to his location if we get off course a bit."

We continued on our silent patrol for another hour and succeeded in avoiding the enemy during our short reconnaissance. Once we had returned to the old pagoda and linked up with the rest of the platoon and our SAS mates, I assigned defensive perimeter positions—wagon-wheel formation—for our squad.

Afterward, I went over to Lieutenant Fletcher and Mr. Kleehammer. "Dai Uy, I suggest that we recon by fire just prior to the slicks' arrival for extraction. If the VC are closing in on us, our fire should keep their heads down until after we've extracted."

"That's a good idea, Smitty, let's do it," Dai Uy said. "I'll give you the signal when to yell, 'Fire for two minutes.' "

After I had gone to each man and explained to them what we were going to do, I returned to Dai Uy and waited while Trung Uy coordinated with the Sea Lords, Seawolves, and Black Ponies for extraction and fire support.

Everyone was excited for we knew that the enemy were close at hand; we occasionally heard VC small arms firing at the gunships and OV-10s.

Finally, Dai Uy gave me the signal for us to start our two-minute reconnaissance by fire followed by my yelling, "Commence firing!"

Hell seemed to break loose as twenty-one of us opened up along a 360-degree circumference. Our 40mm HE rounds didn't travel far before they hit some form of vegetation and detonated with deafening results. Hundreds of 7.62mm and 5.56mm rounds were clipping through the jungle growth as a warning to our adversaries to keep their heads down.

After two minutes I yelled, "Cease fire."

The silence was deafening. Our hearing was so far gone that we didn't hear the slicks approach until they were almost upon us.

While the Seawolves and Black Ponies were making rocket and minigun runs nearby on suspected enemy positions, we soon heard the Sea Lord slicks' whump-whump-whump as they neared our position. The first slick appeared directly over our darkened pit of an LZ and descended low enough for Tu Uy and 2nd Squad to climb aboard.

After we had loaded, I sat on the outside edge of the starboard door of the slick with my boots planted firmly on a skid; I was ready for a long jump to the ground as I watched our helo's tail rotor chip off part of the tile roof from the old pagoda. I was amazed that our pilots were taking so many chances to extract us, carefully and calmly manipulating the helos; the consequences of the most minor mistake would spell doom for us all. I'll never be able to thank these guys and our BSU/MST mates enough for saving our asses so many times over the years.

After we had extracted, the second slick descended and extracted Dai Uy and 1st Squad. I watched the helo's main rotor chop off the top of a nearby coconut tree as the pilot carefully climbed vertically out of the LZ.

I turned my attention to the Black Ponies and Seawolves and watched Russian .51-caliber machine-gun tracers zip toward one of the Seawolves. Whoever the gunner was, he was good; some of his rounds were hitting the helo. "It's time to get out of Dodge, mate," I yelled at the Seawolf's pilot.

Everyone was relieved once we reached an altitude of approximately one thousand feet. We also began to cool off and dry out. While we were on our way back to Dong Tam, I had begun to feel the effects of the op—all of us were mentally and physically tired, ready for a few cool ones. Even the beautiful sunset failed to inspire me.

After we returned to Dong Tam, Doc was escorted to the Navy dispensary, where the medical staff put a cast on his broken leg. The rest of us sat down with our Seawolves and MST mates and our SAS cohorts—the Sea Lord and Black Pony crews had returned to their home base at Binh Thuy—for debriefing. The general consensus was that: we were lucky we hadn't patrolled into an ambush, and the CBU-55B Black Death bomb wasn't what it was chalked up to be. With that we went our ways to clean weapons, gear, and filthy bods. Another good op—no one was killed.

The next morning, August sixteenth, Lieutenant Morrow and I headed for Saigon. We stopped at Ben Luc, where Lieutenant Taylor's Quebec Platoon, Seal 1, was located, to inquire about utilizing Hien, their interpreter, to be November Platoon's agent handler for our intel nets. Unfortunately, the platoon wasn't there. By the time we had walked into N-2 at NavForV, everyone had gone to lunch.

Lieutenant Morrow shrugged and suggested we walk to the Cock and Bull restaurant for lunch. He was buying!

"That's the best offer I've had all day, sir," I replied.

With that, we walked around the corner to Phan Dinh Phong Street and had a meal of prawns, shark-fin soup, and a couple of Heineken beers.

After lunch, and working on charts and intelligence reports, Lieutenant (jg) Washburn and I returned to Dong Tam on the narrow two-lane highway and managed to avoid a collision with an ARVN truck driver who was trying to get around a much slower Vietnamese bus headed to the marketplace with farmers and their families. I had to quickly pull over to the edge of the road—the rice paddies frequently began within a yard or so of the pavement—to avoid him because he was coming directly toward me in my lane.

In 1969, when I was PRU adviser in My Tho, I was on that same stretch of the QL-4 highway driving a jeep between Saigon and Dinh Tuong province when an ARVN driver pulled a 2½-ton truck into my lane and started playing chicken. Strangely enough, our two vehicles were the only ones on the road at that time. The only equalizer

I had was my Smith & Wesson M-60, .38 Special revolver. With my left hand I quickly drew it from my shoulder holster and aimed it toward the driver while I guided the jeep with my right hand to the edge of the road just shy of plunging into the flooded rice paddies, which were a couple of feet below. I was about to begin shooting when the driver chickened out and pulled his truck back into his lane, narrowly avoiding a collision. It sometimes took drastic measures to alter the course of events.

It seemed, in my experience, that during the Vietnam War many indigenous folks had very little hope for the future, and for whatever reasons, had become very suicidal. In '69 two of my PRU in Sam Giang district, very good operators, were sitting in their small one-room house drinking *ba xi de*, rice whiskey, with their girlfriend. For some reason they decided to pull the pin on an M-26 frag grenade, and placed it in front of them—they were sitting on a floor mat—and watched it until it detonated in their faces. Later that day, Al Huey and I had to go there and take care of the details of the gratuities. War has many strange and tragic faces.

CHAPTER SIX

To make perfectly clear that action contrary to
orders was not considered as disobedience or lack
of discipline, German commanders began to re-
peat one of Moltke's favorite stories, of an incident observed while visiting the headquarters of
Prince Frederick Charles. A major, receiving a
tongue-lash from the prince for a tactical blunder,
offered the excuse that he had been obeying orders, and reminded the prince that a Prussian officer was taught that an order from a superior was
tantamount to an order from the King. Frederick
Charles promptly responded: "His Majesty made
you a major because he believed you would know
when *not* to obey his orders." This simple story
became guidance for all following generations of
German officers.

—Colonel Trevor N. Dupuy

On the morning of August seventeenth, Dai Uy, Lieutenant Z. (NILO), his Vietnamese navy counterpart, and I
drove to Vinh Kim village, Sam Giang district subsector,
to meet one of the S2 (intelligence) agents, but we were
told that the agent wouldn't be available until 1200 on the
nineteenth. We visited the adviser's hootch looking for
Captain Campbell, and were told he had gone to Saigon.
After I got additional Order of Battle information and the
coordinates and names of all outposts within Sam Giang

district for our OB overlays and artillary fans, we returned to Dong Tam.

After lunch I was sitting on our small porch reading—
the base electric generators were down at that time for
several days—when Dai Uy, Trung Uy, and an Army
warrant officer drove up in our jeep. As they walked to
our barracks stairway, I recognized the warrant officer to
be my first cousin, Eddie Dean Smith, from the little village of Brazos, Texas, which was approximately a mile
from the Brazos River and ten miles south-southeast of
Mineral Wells. I had spent many happy weekends in the
Brazos area during my youth visiting with my numerous
relatives, swimming in the river, hunting deer, wild hogs,
and squirrels, and in general running wild and woolly
over the countryside. Eddie Dean was six years younger
than me, but his older brother, Gary Allen Smith, and I
had spent most of our time together jumping off the old
railroad trestle's sandstone piling into a deep water hole.
Gary Allen had joined the Navy in '64 as a Naval Air
Cadet and was commissioned an ensign. In '65 Gary and
his lovely wife Geneva, who lived in Coronado, California, occasionally invited me over to their small apartment
for dinner while I was attending UDT training. It was a
fun time for all of us.

I decided to get in my first licks and yelled down,
"Well, look what the dogs drug in! Hey, dude, what's
happenin'? What in the world are you doing out here in
the midst of this heathenous wilderness scratching around
in this neck of the woods, Eddie Dean?"

Sanguine in nature and never one to be without a fast
quip, Eddie Dean looked up at me, gave a salute and
replied, "I've been reading my tea leaves, and heard you
guys were having some problems, Gary! I also heard
you had been shootin' at pigeons and killin' buzzards."

Dai Uy was getting a bit distressed at our family banter

and interrupted, "He's volunteered to be our FAC pilot and vector us into our future helo op targets once I've gotten authorization through his chain of command."

"I'd be careful, Dai Uy. Eddie Dean has been known to hold with the hare and run with the hounds."

Trung Uy spoke up and said, "Why, you guys not only speak what sounds like the same perverted dialect of English, you even look related."

Eddie Dean sniggered and replied, "Well, I hope so."

Eddie Dean's arrival was a very pleasant surprise. Now I would get to go on combined operations with my Army cousin.

Dai Uy had met Eddie Dean by chance at the nearby Dong Tam base runway. When Lieutenant Fletcher introduced himself as the OIC of SEAL Team 1's November Platoon, Eddie Dean mentioned that his retarded cousin Gary Roger Smith was a SEAL. Dai Uy told Eddie Dean that that same retard was in fact a member of his platoon, so Eddie Dean decided to visit us for a spell before his return to Vinh Long to change FAC planes.

After all of our handshaking and teasing, and after Eddie Dean had passed all pertinent information relative to his chain of command to Dai Uy for future coordination, Eddie Dean suggested that I accompany him to Vinh Long, hit the PX for replenishment of refreshments, and return to Dong Tam later that afternoon. Dai Uy seconded the suggestion, and off Eddie Dean and I went to Vinh Long via the northern areas of Cai Lay, Cai Be, and Giao Duc districts of Dinh Tuong province for reconnaissance. (Vinh Long provincial capital and province was south and across the My Tho River from Dinh Tuong province.) Later that afternoon, Eddie Dean dropped me off at the Dong Tam runway and returned to Vinh Long.

While Eddie Dean and I were out having fun, Senior Chief Bassett had been very busy trying to cumshaw a five-KW generator for our barracks. One was supposed to be delivered to our barracks by the nineteenth. The eighteenth was a slow day. We still didn't have any base electricity, and only hoped that Chief Bassett's supply buddies in Saigon would come through with that magic generator.

Later that day, Tam and I went to the Chieu Hoi Center and interviewed a Hoi Chanh by the name of Phu, who had been the executive officer of the VC 261A Main Force Infantry Battalion until February '71. Phu was thirty-two years of age and an average-looking Vietnamese man except for his left hand, which had been badly mangled from a helicopter rocket and minigun attack that took place in '69. I quizzed him as to the organization and locations of units of his battalion. Phu's answers were accurate and he seemed to be sincere. Most important, he was motivated to accompany us as a guide on operations within his old AO. I gave him two personal history statements, (PHS), with the thought that he might be very valuable as a principal agent (one who handles other agents). I briefed Phu on what I expected if I hired him. He assured me that he had ample operational information and would have his reports written within a few days.

Tam and I drove over to Sector S-2 and talked to another Hoi Chanh, named Dang. Dang's information was so incredibly enticing that I didn't believe him. When I quizzed him as to the identification and location of his former VC units and whom he was subordinate to, he didn't know.

Later, while Tam and I were returning to Dong Tam, I asked him his opinion of Dang.

Tam quickly replied, "He too full beaucoup shit!" I laughed and agreed with him.

I spent the next morning reading intelligence reports on

the VC MR-2, Dong Thap One Regiment and its 261A MF Infantry Battalion.

After lunch, Doc, Eberle, Same Tam, and I headed for the Sam Giang district subsector to debrief one of the Vietnamese S-2 agents about several targets near the Route 66 canal's first curve. We took our basic field gear and weapons with us because of recent increases in VC ambushes of vehicles throughout the province. Once we had reached the cutoff that went south for five klicks to Vinh Kim village, we turned off QL-4 and stopped. Same and his Stoner, and I with my M-16/XM-148, rode on the jeep's front fenders with our weapons at the ready. We traveled as fast as we dared and watched carefully during the five-kilometer trip until we reached the district subsector.

While the guys went to a local Vietnamese street vendor to get a coconut or papaya crush, I went to S-2 and checked in with Staff Sergeant Pham. He told me that the agent was on an operation. I thanked him and left. That was the second time within the last two days that the Sam Giang district S-2 (Vietnamese) had previously agreed to our debriefing one of their agents, then held the agent incommunicado before our arrival.

The guys and I visited with Major Bigelow (DSA) for a few minutes before our departure. Bigelow was a very personable and likable fellow.

Because we had little else to do, I decided to drive to the Chau Thanh subsector—approximately two kilometers northwest of My Tho—and get a list of the ARVN outpost names and coordinates for our OB situation map's overlays with artillery fans.

When we had returned to Dong Tam, Chief Bassett's 5KW generator was sitting beside our barracks. It was in nearly new condition. All hands helped with the electrical hookup to the barracks, and the job was completed at midnight. Everyone was jubilant once we had enough electricity for overhead lights and the bar's refrigerator and fans.

August twentieth was a day when all hands began to understand the rewards of being slow to speak, slow to anger, and quick to listen. Seaman Eberle continued to oversleep and was very slow to get up. Our omniscient senior chief decided that the only solution was to assign Eberle as the reveille petty officer and gave him a clock with a loud alarm set for 0630. Chambo bitched about the unkempt condition of our vehicles—so our omnipotent senior chief assigned Chambo as the platoon's first lieutenant department head. Hayden complained about the platoon's slothfulness in keeping our barracks, shower area, and Johnny clean—so our sovereign senior chief assigned Hayden as the Master at Arms. After the chief's new assignments, he collared the rest of the guys and kept them busy improving our living conditions for the better part of that day.

Out of respect for the senior chief's dominion, I kept my mouth shut and headed for the intel room, where I spent the next few hours updating our OB situation maps and overlays, and intel report agent dossiers.

Later, in the afternoon, Dai Uy returned from My Tho with information on the location of the VC 341X MF Engineering Battalion HQ. Cai Be district Police Special Branch Chief Muoi and his young and pretty ex-VC lass would accompany us on another helo op the following day. My cousin Eddie Dean was to be the "shotgun," or FAC pilot, to vector us to the VC headquarters. Because Doc Holmes still had a full-length cast on his leg, he was to accompany Eddie Dean in the O-1 Cessna and familiarize Eddie Dean with our tactical SOPs. Dai Uy gave us the warning order at 1430 hours. We spent the rest of the afternoon preparing our gear for the next day's op.

On August twenty-first Dai Uy gave his PLO at 1400 hours, and at 1630 gave us another updated briefing at the Seawolf helo pad. That was followed by discussion among shotgun, Seawolf, and Sea Lord pilots about the best avenues of approach to the target, shotgun (FAC) vectoring, and so on.

By 1745 we had picked up Chief Muoi and his "sweetie" and three PSB operatives at the Cai Be district subsector and were sitting in our Sea Lord slicks looking down at the rice paddies, swamps, and tree lines that we were clearing by only a few feet and at nearly one hundred knots. Shotguns Eddie Dean and Doc were already on station and were busy vectoring our Seawolf and Sea Lord helos on the prearranged avenues of approach.

At 1800, as the sun was getting low on the western horizon, we inserted near several hootches that were approximately three to four hundred meters from the tree line where the VC 341X Battalion headquarters was located. During and after our insertion, we received light AK-47 and RPD machine-gun fire from the ominous tree line. We knew that the VC had a well-developed bunker complex for their battalion's administrative offices and equipment within the narrow but dense forest, and we were prepared to destroy them in any manner we could.

Dai Uy and 1st Squad quickly assaulted their assigned hootch and found it empty. "Killer's" and Mr. K.'s and my 2nd Squad assaulted our hootch and managed to grease one of two VC who were sprinting behind it toward the nearby tree line. Neither I, with my XM-148's 40mm HE rounds, nor Chambo and Little Bear, with their M-60s, were able to get the surviving VC. Same's Stoner and our SAS mates with their SLRs also struck out due to the range and the VC's circuitous route and natural cover. Trung Uy quickly called in one of the Seawolves to get the VC with its minigun. We watched with awe as the

Seawolf gunship came in low as a charging lion, with his minigun blazing at six thousand rounds per minute. The poor fellow was literally lifted off his feet by the impact of the hundreds of 150-grain bullets smashing through his body and was thrown forward approximately eight to ten feet, just before he would have reached the safety of the tree line. Everyone cheered and waved at the Seawolf pilot, copilot, and door gunner as the pilot violently lifted the helo just in time to miss the treetops and banked hard to the left. We watched the door gunner as he leaned almost completely out of the side door—he was wearing a safety belt—with his pedestal-mounted M-60 blazing away at 550 rounds a minute toward the source of tracers that were coming from directly below him.

"Those guys are great!" I yelled to Quear. All of us, as always, were very impressed with the professionalism of our HAL-3/VAL-4 airdale buddies and thankful for their faithful support.

Unfortunately, we had again lost the element of surprise. Shortly after we had inserted, Chief Muoi told Dai Uy that the VC had been somehow forewarned of our coming and, naturally, were forearmed and entrenched for any assault against their well-concealed positions. The tactical situation had degenerated to the principle of mass—we were now out of our element. Nathan Bedford Forrest, a Confederate general, was supposed to have said, "The firstest with the mostest wins the battle."

However, the tactical situation did allow us to fire and maneuver. Dai Uy wasn't one to give up, and decided that we would feign flanking movements against the main source of the VC small arms fire by 1st Squad moving to the left and 2nd Squad moving to the right in single files—with the enemy at right angles—for a maximum rate of fire when needed. Our objective was to draw continual enemy fire by our fire and movement until they had exposed their exact positions long enough for the Seawolves to locate and destroy them one by one with their 2.75-inch rockets, 40mm HE rounds, 7.62mm minigun, and their M-60 machine gun.

Second Squad gradually moved, using the leapfrog method, toward right flank and the tree line, as did 1st Squad. Once each squad had taken cover behind a rice dike or other available cover, Dai Uy gave the word to commence firing for no more than thirty seconds and at a slow rate of fire. We then continued our leapfrogging to left and right flanks to other positions of cover and fired for another thirty seconds.

The VC swallowed our ruse hook, line, and sinker. The Seawolves' gunships had a heyday destroying the VC battalion headquarters. November Platoon and our SAS mates weren't credited with many KIAs that day, but our Seawolf partners were. They were fearless under fire and were magnificent in their line of duty.

As in all good things, time ran out on us. It was last light, and time for platoon rendezvous and extraction. The Seawolves had begun to drop an occasional para flare to illuminate the enemy positions and to aid our extraction. While the Seawolves continued their strafing and rocket runs, we set up our H formations, marked at each corner with blue-lensed strobe lights, and extracted shortly after o'dark-thirty.

Despite vexations from many quarters, there was no doubt in my mind that night that, as a team, we were invincible!

> Four brave men who do not know each other will not dare to attack a lion. Four less brave, but knowing each other well, sure of their reliability and consequently of their mutual aid, will attack resolutely.
>
> —Colonel Charles Ardnant du Picq,
> *Battle Studies*, 1880

The next day we received word that five SEAL Team 1 guys had been caught smuggling heroin into the States from Vietnam. Because I didn't condone the use of drugs and I had never seen or heard of any of my teammates using any form of drugs, I was stunned. I was very disappointed with those guys and was sad, because I really liked all of them. They were good operators, very likable, and always seemed to be highly motivated.

Later that evening Dai Uy had Chief Bassett muster the platoon and our SAS mates in our bar. We had a group discussion on the legal and moral problems of using drugs, the Navy and team policy of no drugs and reasons why, as teammates, we couldn't, wouldn't, and shouldn't approve of the use of drugs. We unanimously condemned the use of drugs—other than alcohol, of course—and vowed to police our own ranks, if necessary. When we finished talking, it was near midnight and time to hit the sack.

August twenty-third was another very disappointing day. Items were constantly disappearing from our living space. Finally, a couple of the guys searched our Kit Carson scouts' lockers while they were in My Tho and found our stolen operating gear, several of our S&W pistols and revolvers, money, fans, sheets, poncho liners, mosquito nets, civilian clothing, uniforms, and other things. The TV set that was in our lounge was also stolen, and our scouts were the only Vietnamese allowed in our barracks. Because we had caught them with our stolen gear in their lockers, and they had dishonored our trust in them, there was only one choice, and that was to get rid of them gradually and covertly. In the meantime we moved them down below where our MST mates had berthed previously. We were not very popular with our scouts after that.

Starting on August twenty-sixth Doc and I were to be the first to go on R&R. I spent five very relaxing days in Honolulu fishing, diving, sailing, eating great meals,

listening to Martin Denny and his band at the Royal
Hawaiian Hotel during the evenings, and visiting my favorite bar, Davy Jones Locker. Diamond Head and the
Waikiki beach were just as beautiful as they had been the
previous year when I was there on R&R. It was great to
get away from Vietnam and its pressures and look at our
beautiful round-eyed women again.

On the morning of September third I was eating a sandwich at Mama-san's across the street from NavForV in
Saigon while watching the pretty Vietnamese maidens
walk by with their *ao dais* (long, silk tunics) flowing in
the breeze. I always thought of the Vietnamese women as
being very pretty, feminine, soft-spoken, and dainty. After my quick breakfast, I went to the NavForV's drafting
department to visit with Petty Officer Lightfoot and
checked to see if he had completed the three VC Order of
Battle block diagram training-aid charts that I had asked
him to make for me. The charts were not only completed,
but Lightfoot had done an exceptionally professional job
of constructing them. Later, I managed to catch a ride to
Dong Tam, and arrived in time for lunch.

The first thing I was told was that our SAS mates had returned to Nui Det. Everyone missed them. Later that afternoon, about half of us started our first $1\frac{1}{2}$-to-two-hour tae
kwon do lesson at twenty dollars and twenty lessons per
month, to be paid in advance monthly. Our instructor was
Captain Kim, who had a second degree black belt. He was
a very good instructor and seemed to enjoy teaching us.

After supper, Senior Chief Bassett asked me to alter-
nate with him as the bartender for our busy bar during the
evenings. A couple of the guys had begun to drink too
much and were becoming more and more difficult to get
up in the mornings. Chief's solution was for he and I to
control the bar and to secure it no later than 2400 each
night except for special parties.

At 0830 on August fifth Chief Bassett, Compton, Same, Hayden, Chief Thompson (our staff photo interpreter), and I headed for Saigon in our diesel five-ton truck. Hayden, Same, and Compton were going on R&R, Chief Bassett was to cumshaw goodies for our living spaces, and Chief Thompson and I were to work on intel-related matters. I was driving the truck, Thompson sat in the middle, and Bassett on the right, while the rest of the guys were riding in the back. We were forced to stop time and again because of the heavy, disorganized traffic. The temperature was well over 100 degrees, the humidity was in the ninetieth percentile, sweat beads were running down the cracks of our butts, there was no breeze, and we were all getting very irritated at the Vietnamese and their chaotic traffic conditions.

"Hey, Smitty, the next time you stop, continue revving the engine," instructed Hayden, an ardent prankster.

Not knowing why, I asked, "Why should I do that?"

All three of the guys in the back started laughing. "Our truck's exhaust pipe is broken off under the right front fender, and it just happens to be pointed directly to our right. Each time you rev the engine, a cloud of black exhaust fumes shoots directly into any cab or motorcycle that's alongside," Hayden explained.

Bassett and I laughed at the thought. Each time we were forced to come to another stop, Bassett would guide me to move forward, left or right a few inches until we had a vehicle or motorcycle exactly alongside our right fender. Because the traffic was often packed, there was little chance for the targeted victim to escape. Once Bassett gave the word, I would race the engine and make life absolutely miserable for our neighbor and anyone else in the immediate vicinity. At first all the poor fellow next to us knew was that there was an incredible black cloud of hot fumes enveloping him from his left. In a matter of seconds the driver showed symptoms of a clouded vision, choking spasms, dilating of the pupils, and faintness.

Same yelled, "I think he's suffering from carbon monoxide poisoning."

"Yeah, maybe you ought to climb down and give him mouth-to-mouth resuscitation, Same," Compton quipped.

At our next intersection we managed to ambush a nicely dressed Vietnamese male motorcyclist. After a good shot of blackened soot on his clean white shirt, the fellow jumped like a heart-shot armadillo, revved his engine, popped the clutch and sideswiped several cabbies as he disappeared around the corner.

Chief Thompson, who had come over with Bassett and the boys, was a small, wiry fellow with a good crop of bushy eyebrows and a pair of large, cauliflower ears. For some unknown reason, the normally phlegmatic Chief Thompson spoke up and asked, "Did you hear about the ol' gal that had a wooden baby?"

No one answered until Same, being a little naive, finally said, "Why, no, I haven't, Chief."

"She got nailed by a carpenter," Thompson answered without a sign of emotion.

Bassett started laughing and commented, "Why, you conjuring old fart, now I know why you never say much. I always knew you photo interpreters were a strange lot."

"Yeah, you perverse, nasty old goat," I teased as I nudged Tommy with my right elbow.

A big grin came over Thompson's face, which I couldn't have beat off his puss with a ball-peen hammer. He was always easy to please, and he was now one of the guys.

By the time we reached NavForV, all of us were in a festive mood. The rest of the day was a piece of cake. Even Lieutenant Van Heertum couldn't make me mad.

The next morning, September sixth, Dai Uy and I

drove to My Tho. Lieutenant Fletcher continued his coordination with two Vietnamese Saigon PSB personnel, PSB chief Hue and Cai Lay PSB's district operations chief Muoi, and debriefed two PSDFs—South Vietnamese People's Self-Defense Force, which was composed mostly of old men and boys—concerning ten NVA Rear Services personnel who were reported to be located approximately six to seven klicks north of the Cai Lay district's subsector, near the My Phuoc village.

In the meantime, I went to the Embassy House to see Mr. Tai and Mr. Bai and to pick up a few translated Chieu Hoi reports and diversionary name traces. As I was about to leave, Mr. Bai invited me over to his house for a Ba Muoi Ba (French "33" beer). I accepted, knowing that he was going to try to elicit information about November Platoon's intelligence information nets, among other things. I knew that Chief Hue (PSB) probably had penetrated five of our six nets through our principal agents and/or interpreters—I just hadn't proved it yet.

After we walked to his home and sat down with a beer, Bai, who spoke nearly perfect English, opened by saying, "Smitty, because you have been my good friend since 'sixty-nine and 'seventy, I will be glad to help you in any way and on anything that I can."

I lifted my beer as a toast and replied, "I am thankful that you and your father-in-law, Chief Muoi," of the Province National Police, "have always been my faithful friends. I know that you and Chief Hue are aware of my problems with some of our agents. If you and he have any recommendations or advice, I would be very grateful. I have much to learn."

Bai smiled and was very pleased with my confirming our friendship and request for professional advice. Later, I asked him to draw a block diagram of the PSB's organization at sector and subsector levels and to explain to me how they might parallel the VC security sections at the same provincial and district levels. Bai was flattered and had soon drawn two rough block diagrams when I asked him another question. "I understand that neither the Company nor PSB directly runs the Chieu Hoi Center anymore. I've been told that President Thieu has created the Ministry of Chieu Hoi. Is that true?"

Bai took a sip from his beer and replied, "What you say is true. PSB has people there only to debrief or interrogate the Hoi Chanhs."

"An example would be political indoctrination chief?" I quizzed further.

"Yes," answered Bai somewhat nervously.

Bai had inadvertently confirmed to me that the intel info net that November Platoon had inherited from Victor Platoon had always been penetrated by PSB through our principal agent, code-named Oscar. Prior to Oscar's current employment as the chief of PIC—Provincial Interrogation Center, run by PSB—he was working at the Chieu Hoi Center as the PSB's political indoctrination chief. However, Doc Bryant was told, and was convinced, that Oscar was an ex-Hoi Chanh. In that way, Oscar would be eligible to receive wages as Victor Platoon's principal agent of their intel net. It was no wonder that Oscar had, at that time, refused his monthly pay of 10,000 piasters from us because I had continued to insist that he fill out past histories on all of his sources of information. His refusal only confirmed that he and his sources had been working for PSB and were simply collecting a little extra money for themselves, Chief Muoi, and Chief Hue.

Well, Oscar's net will have value in other ways, I thought to myself as I lifted my beer to Mr. Bai.

Later that morning, Dai Uy and I met again at the Embassy House and returned to Dong Tam. Dai Uy gave his warning order to myself, Knepper, Eberle, Waneous, and our Kit Carson scouts.

At 1520 the MST folks took me to My Tho by MSSC to pick up the four PSB operatives and two PSDF guides. After our return to Dong Tam, Dai Uy gave his PLO at 1730. The briefing went well until Dai Uy explained to the PSB operatives and the PSDF guides that we were going up the Rach Ba Rai canal by MST's LSSC and MSSC boats for twenty-one klicks.

The four PSB operatives and the two PSDFs became very agitated with the head man, exclaiming, *"Choi Oi!"* which translates as "Oh my God!" That expressed my feelings exactly. The VC and NVA had always controlled Rach Ba Rai canal (above Snoopy's Nose) and had inflicted hundreds of U.S. and Vietnamese casualties on that stretch of water. I didn't feel that a few NVA rear echelon grunts justified the risk.

Finally, the senior PSB operative stated emphatically, *"Khong duoc!* No good. Beaucoup VC. You go, we stay."

By 1830 all fourteen of us were aboard a U.S. Navy reefer truck and headed for the Cai Lay subsector. Chief Bassett borrowed a truck from one of his chief admin'er buddies next door and drove us to Cai Lay village, where he would remain overnight until we returned from our mission. Knepper and I sat to the rear of the reefer with our M-16/XM-148 combo weapons at the ready and the back doors cracked just enough for us to keep an eye on our posterior. Once we had reached Subsector, we switched to two U.S. Army weapons carriers and were driven to an outpost located just north of the QL-4 highway and a couple of klicks west of the infamous Rach Ba Rai canal, where we lay low until o'dark-thirty.

At 2230 hours we headed west for a couple hundred meters until we crossed a small canal, then patrolled north for six to seven klicks toward the target area. By 0300 we had lost all communications with Subsector; our PRC-77 had gone dead, and our spare battery and extra handset didn't solve the problem. Unfortunately, our squad radio didn't have enough range to reach Subsector, and we were in the midst of Indian country. If we got into deep trouble, we would have little chance of outside support.

By 0530 hours we reached the hootches where the ten NVA Rear Services troopers were supposed to be berthed. I had previously suggested to Dai Uy that we concentrate on setting up perimeter security and fields of fire near the hootches and let the Vietnamese enter the huts for the actual capture. My previous experience with the PRU, Biet Hai, and LDNNs taught me that the South Vietnamese forces seldom worried about their responsibilities of security, especially after the firefight was over.

After we SEALs were in position, the PSB operatives and the two PSDFs entered the two hootches carefully and quietly. Within three or four minutes, which seemed like an hour, we began to hear a low-toned, unintelligible voice that was followed by shrill feminine voices filled with terror. Shortly afterward I heard the senior PSB operative named Ho Van cursing.

It wasn't long before Ho Van went to Dai Uy and our new interpreter Son and explained that the NVA rear echelon troopers had moved on to another area the previous afternoon. There were only women, children, and one old man inside the hootches.

We decided to hang tight until first light to begin our patrol back to Subsector through the enemy-controlled area. The Rach Ba Rai's banks and the adjoining dense jungle was an area that was known for its punji stakes, booby traps, snakes, and Communists. We hadn't gotten very far when two Seawolves came flying over the area about 0700. Thank God for friends, I thought.

Because the areas nearest the canal consisted of dense

brush, nipa palm, and jungle growth, the Seawolves were unable to find us. Dai Uy fired two green-star cluster pop flares so the Seawolves would know our location and be aware that we had no radio communications and that emergency extraction was not needed. Unfortunately, the PSB operatives decided to go off without telling us where they were going. Apparently, Ho Van and his buddies felt they had lost face, and would meet us later at the canal.

Dai Uy and the rest of us continued toward the infamous canal through areas of very dense jungle growth with *Tu Dia* (Death Area) signs on the edges of all of the rice paddies. As expected, it was a very hot and humid trek to the canal. Tam, our head scout and an ex-VC sapper, was very capable of guiding us through such dangerous areas.

Once we reached the canal, we spotted Ho Van and his operatives nearby. As previously agreed, Ho Van signaled a water taxi—a large motorized sampan—by waving his M-16 rifle and ordering it to come over to the west bank to pick us up. I hadn't had the pleasure of riding a water taxi since I worked with the PRU in Kien Giang province in '69. I always carried a few piasters with me to pay for services, such as our taxi ride, that might be needed. It was an enjoyable ride. However, we didn't let our guard down. Everyone kept his eyes peeled for any sign of the enemy on either bank.

We reached QL-4 and Cai Lay village by 0900 hours and shortly afterward were able to bum a ride to the Cai Lay subsector. After Dai Uy had checked in at the MACV compound and notified Major Kaike of our compromised op and our safe return, we boarded our reefer truck and headed for Dong Tam.

I looked at Dai Uy Fletcher, who was sitting on the floor of the truck, staring at a large leech slowly moving up his pants leg looking for a meal. I commented with disgust, "I believe it's becoming increasingly harder for us to clear AOs without their becoming compromised before we even have a chance to get in the field. Apparently, the VC have informants or penetrants in almost all of the Vietnamese sector and subsector TOCs."

"I'm afraid you're right, Smitty," Fletcher replied as he gingerly pulled the three-inch leech from his cammi bottoms. He carefully placed the leech on the deck, caressed its slimy topside from head to stern and said, "However, we do get results when we operate with the Cai Lay PSB and Ba To's group." Dai Uy slowly pulled out his K-bar knife, with the tip pointing upward, while concentrating on the leech. He continued, "We'll simply work harder and operate smarter and smash our enemy decisively like this." Dai Uy brought the pommel of his knife down hard and mashed that leech flatter than a deuce of spades.

We were all feeling a bit grumpy because of our lack of success. It seemed we'd gone farther and fared worse than at any time during my previous four tours in 'Nam.

Waneous spoke up and said, "All right! We're turning south and heading for Dong Tam. We'll have a hot meal before we know it."

We had gotten only a few hundred meters when we came to a dead stop beside an RMK-BRJ (American construction conglomerate) truck loaded with asphalt. Once our truck had stopped, it became very hot in the reefer, and soon all of us were dreaming about chugalugging a refreshing, ice-cold beer—even a Ba Muoi Ba would do.

Eberle became visibly annoyed and started mumbling to himself. Waneous and I decided that we had best open the back doors slightly for a little fresh air to cool off the situation.

Waneous looked at me and I looked at him—we both knew what we had to do. Our frustration levels required action. It was get-even time. I handed him a CS grenade—Waneous was closer to the door than I was—and said, "Wait until we start to pull forward, then drop our messenger of thanksgiving down on the pavement."

Waneous looked at me, then to Dai Uy with an expression of absolute glee.

Eberle, with a sullen look on his face, saw and heard what was about to happen and commented emphatically, "Revenge is good for the soul."

After waiting patiently in our humid oven for more than ten minutes, our truck finally began pulling forward very slowly. Waneous leaned forward and clandestinely dropped the CS grenade to the pavement below as we pulled alongside the RMK-BRJ truck. The Vietnamese driver didn't hear the spoon fly away from the grenade or the hissing of the gas as it slowly formed into a huge cloud. On the other side of the road and going in the opposite direction was a Vietnamese Lambretta that was loaded down with eight passengers and their baggage. No one seemed to notice or pay any attention to the white cloud that was drifting across the highway toward them.

When the CS gas enveloped the outside worker, who was standing in front of the truck filled with asphalt, he didn't know what to do. He didn't understand what was happening; couldn't see or hear anything out of the ordinary, but he sure felt his eyes watering and his lungs choking from something. The poor fellow was obviously perplexed, and became frantic in his actions by rapidly walking downwind, where he found no relief from the unknown mist. His body movements became spasmodic as he started shuffling around in confusion, seeking relief. By that time all of us were peeking out the back of the reefer with tears streaming down our cheeks as we howled in laughter at the poor guy.

The truck driver was preoccupied with watching his fellow worker's antics in disbelief and amazement until he got a whiff of the gas. It was no wonder that RMK-BRJ employed him as a truck driver, for he knew trouble when he smelled it. He leaped from the truck cab, hit the pavement peeling rubber off the bottom of his sandals, sprinted past his battered, bruised, and bewildered buddy and headed for the wide open spaces of the adjacent rice paddy, which was located conveniently downwind.

By this time the occupants of the Lambretta had become concerned at the unusual antics of the truck driver and the worker, who had been walking into the truck as if blind. They must have thought that he had been recently chewing too much betel nut, until they also got a good snort of the sickening smoke. While he sprinted to the east, one of the occupants let out a curse implying that there had been incest within his immediate family. Two women screamed and cast their packages and parcels aside and joined the rest of the occupants as they abandoned the Lambretta and turkey-trotted through the muck toward the center of the rice paddy and the weeping truck driver. The addled worker finally worked his way to the edge of the field, where he fell into the marshy rice paddy in exhaustion. At least we weren't leaving the place in carnage, I thought as we continued on our way.

We were in a great mood until we returned to our barracks, where we were told that we had no water to clean our weapons, gear, and bodies. It appeared that the ARVN 7th Division had the last laugh after all—they controlled the source of water.

The next morning, September eighth, all hands assisted our Seabee mates in running an underground water line from the U.S. Navy compound under the perimeter fence to our shower area, located in the midst of our friendly Vietnamese pals and their barracks. Senior Chief Bassett had come through again. The Seabees even furnished the materials. By evening the water line was laid and November Platoon was finally able to take much needed showers.

At 0800 on September ninth, Dai Uy gave his warning order for the seven of us—himself, Tam, Knepper, Quear, Chambo, Eberle, and me. Our mission was to locate and destroy the VC Dong Thap One Regiment's technical subsection. This unit monitored U.S. and ARVN sector and subsector TOC broadcasts and transmitted—by captured PRC-25 and fifteen-watt radios—false information to the ARVN TOCs and field units. A VC specialist had broken the ARVN's code. Unfortunately, the men of the Technical Subsection had a nasty habit of moving their location at least once every ten days. And at night tripwire grenades were set around their enclave. This VC unit was located in Ham Long district, Kien Hoa province, just across the river from Dinh Tuong province. MSS and 525 sources stated that there was a possible local VC company within the area of the technical subsection, which was always guarded by a platoon of local VC. There was no doubt in my mind that Dai Uy had become very frustrated by our lack of success in the field. I found out what it was like to be under pressure from Staff the previous year while I was advising the Biet Hai and LDNNs. Unfortunately, little had changed in '71.

Later that morning, Doc and I went to My Tho and requested an update on 525's intel report on a POW camp that was supposedly located in the northern portion of Cai Lay district. After our return to Dong Tam, I prepared my gear for the next day's op until our tae kwon do practice with Captain Kim at 1630. After Dai Uy had given his PLO at 1900, we hit the sack to catch a few hours of shuteye before our 0230 reveille.

For some reason, I wasn't able to sleep that night. I kept thinking back to the days of the early sixties when I was working in the North Texas oil field wrenching sucker rods and pulling tubing out of the oil pumping units for McAllister Well Service, located in Wichita Falls, Texas. I never forgot those 110- to 115-degree days when the sweat pouring down my shirtless upper body, which was coated with paraffin and oil, felt like a continuous column of centipedes plodding downward to parts unknown. The pay was poor and there were no benefits.

Yessir, I thought, I love where I am and I love my profession with SEAL Team 1. I'm serving my country and I have a true cause, with a sense of urgency. I'd rather die serving my country and living life to its fullest than live to be an old man who had done nothing more than wrench sucker rods, only dreaming of something more. I finally went to sleep knowing that I *was* living my dream every day.

CHAPTER SEVEN

The plan was smooth on paper, only they forgot
about the ravines.
> —Russian military proverb

Reveille was shortly after 0200. Because the moon was
exceptionally bright, we decided not to go until later that
evening. Everyone hit the sack until 0730, at which time
we hurriedly dressed and sprinted to the Navy chow hall
just prior to its closing.

After breakfast, Dai Uy, Trung Uy, and I drove to My
Tho and continued our collection of information from
NILO John on a target in Tanh Phu district, Kien Hoa
province. From there we went to 525 and asked Larry if
he would develop a target analysis on the VC POW camp
in Cai Be district. Larry and his crew had always been
good at supporting us in any way they could.

At 1900 Dai Uy gave his PLO again, and at 2230 hours
our seven-man squad was speeding west by MSSC up the
My Tho River toward the Ham Long district in Kien Hoa
province. It was a great night for an op—it was almost
pitch-black.

After Lieutenant (jg) Washburn and his crew had inserted us approximately ten klicks upstream of the ferry
crossing between Dinh Tuong and Kien Hoa provinces,
we set security and listened for a while before beginning

our patrol. Tam and Knepper, who were the points, soon led the patrol south toward the Bai Lai stream that was about two and a half klicks inland.

We encountered what proved to be an immense system of irrigation canals that were the remnants of an old French plantation system. The canals were spaced approximately four yards apart. Each one was about five feet deep and six feet wide, with steep banks. The canals were lined with thick brush, trees, and jungle undergrowth, which also added to our enjoyable patrol.

After I had managed to pull myself out of one canal and was in the process of moving on my hands and knees to the next one, my left hand—my M-16/XM-148 was in my right hand—suddenly dropped down into space. I had only moved four to five feet instead of the expected four yards when I almost fell headfirst into another Communist canal. That night reminded me of another pitch-black night that I had spent in Panama while going through Jungle Warfare School in '67. I began wishing that we had some of the previous night's moonlight. Unfortunately, that was only the beginning of our trek. We must have crossed a couple hundred of those damn canals prior to 0600, when we finally moved to within fifty meters of the Ba Lai stream. All of us had had enough of irrigation canals for a while.

Dai Uy sent Knepper and Tam forward to recon the immediate area on our side of the stream while we set security and listened. After Knepper and Tam returned, they reported a small campfire directly across the stream. With that new information, just before false dawn Dai Uy had us move closer to the bank of the Bai Lai for surveillance, being careful to conceal ourselves in the brush.

As the light increased, a twenty-by-twenty-foot rock building gradually appeared approximately one hundred meters directly across the stream from our position. A small campfire was lazily blazing and crackling in front of the structure, and cords of wood were stacked next to it. We could hear subdued voices, but hadn't seen anyone. We didn't see any radio antennas anywhere either.

· Knepper, followed by Dai Uy and Tam, decided to cross the stream, knowing that the rest of us would take care of our side. They were moving into the brush on the opposite bank when a motorized sampan came from upstream, west to east, between our positions. I didn't want to open fire because Dai Uy, Knepper, and Tam were directly across the stream, but I aimed my combo weapon at the occupant of the sampan until I saw that it was a beautiful woman. If she had been a man, I would have taken him out with a single round from my M-16. I should have shot her, but for some reason I hesitated.

The woman hadn't seen Eberle, Chambo, Quear, or me, but she did see Dai Uy and Tam standing near the stream. For whatever reasons, Dai Uy and Tam didn't call or signal her over to their position. The pretty lady killed her engine and drifted downstream until she disappeared around a bend. It was to be expected that she would beach her sampan and sound the alarm. Sure enough, within two minutes we heard two VC warning shots approximately two hundred meters to our left flank. We were now compromised—there was no chance for tactical surprise. With that, Dai Uy decided that he, Knepper, and Tam had best recross the stream and get back to us.

Fletcher immediately had us head toward the My Tho River. We knew then that if there was a VC company nearby, it was likely we would have a running battle to the My Tho River. With that in mind, we headed northeast for our new objective and hopefully a rendezvous with Trung Uy Washburn and MST's MSSC.

Oh shit! I thought, we'll have to cross all of those damn Communist canals again. I looked at Chambo, wondering how he was coming along with his twenty-pound-plus M-60 machine gun and five hundred rounds. He saw me look back at him, frowned, shook his head and slipped into the next canal with his arm reaching up toward me. I winked at him, grinned and pulled him up and out of the muck. With two more paces I slid into the next canal. I knew that as tired as we were, if we got into a serious firefight, we would be in trouble. We couldn't move any faster than our slowest man.

After several hours spent climbing in and out of all those canals again, we finally made it to the My Tho River. After we set security, Dai Uy radioed MST and requested extraction. Trung Uy Washburn and his crew were screaming downstream in the middle of the My Tho River when we gave them a "Mark, 090" on our radio for a right flank turn toward our position. Within ten minutes we were safely aboard the MSSC and headed for home.

After our return to Dong Tam, we spent the remainder of the day cleaning up. I, for one, hit the sack early.

Yessir, those canals sure took the starch out of us, I thought after I had buried my head in my musty pillow. We were one tuckered bunch of squids that day.

September twelfth was a good day to catch up on some of my admin duties, like updating our enemy OB overlays and card files, agent report filing and dossiers, SEAL intelligence reports, constructing aerial mosaics of future targets, and other mundane tasks. Later that day we had PT and a three-mile run.

On the morning of September thirteenth all hands scattered to the four winds. Dai Uy, Trung Uy, Knepper, and Chambo dropped me off in My Tho at Sector TOC while they went on to Ben Tre in Kien Hoa province to coordinate another op. I tried to catch the sector slick to Vinh Long to do some coordinating work—not available, I was told. I tried to bum a ride with the Shotgun 15 FAC pilot to Vinh Long—too late, I was told. I visited Larry at 525 for a while and inquired about their target analysis for us on the VC POW camp in Cai Be—it's not completed yet, I was told. Apparently, it was one of those days—either I was out of sync with the world or the world was out of sync with me. I finally decided to get my butt back to Dong Tam before something did happen. I radioed our MST buddies at Dong Tam and asked them to come and get me—we'll be right there, I was told. Larry volunteered to give me a ride down to the river, where I was to rendezvous with the MSSC. I knew then that I had made the right decision. After lunch I spent the afternoon working on intel files, and we had tae kwon do practice with Captain Kim at 1630 hours.

At 2030 Dai Uy gave a combined warning order and PLO—everyone was always ready to go on emergency ops within five minutes. We were to go on a combined op with the Ben Tre Kit Carson scouts in Kien Hoa province. There would be a total of twenty-three of us—thirteen SEALs, Son, our interpreter, eight scouts, and one Hoi Chanh guide. Our target was a VC POW camp for ARVNs (no Americans) that was located a few klicks southeast of the Mo Cay subsector in very dense jungle (of course) near the Ham Long River. A VC company of the 560th VC Local Force Battalion and their Rear Services unit was reported to be in the immediate vicinity of the POW camp as security. MST's LSSC and MSSC would act as blocking elements on the river and be used for emergency extraction and fire support if needed. Doc Holmes was to ride with our MST mates because of his leg cast. The HAL-3/VAL-4 folks would also be on standby at Binh Thuy for emergency extraction and fire support. We were to carry extra two- and 2½-pound M-5A1 C-4 blocks for contingency purposes. All thirteen of us would be carrying a very heavy load.

By 0700 hours the next morning, September fourteenth, we had loaded our two jeeps and driven to My Tho, where we caught a ferry to Kien Hoa province and Road 6A to Ben Tre.

The ride was a lot of fun. We had two guys on each jeep ride forward for security: one guy on each fender. We got some strange looks from a few of our Navy and Army folks, apparently because both of our jeeps were slightly overloaded and we were driving very fast. Hayden teasingly said, "It can't be because the tires are too low, Chief. I aired them up to sixty psi yesterday."

Barron demonstrated our attitude best: "Hey, man, if we don't mind, it don't matter. Up yours, buddy." We were on our home turf and they knew it. Our attitude was: we know what our job is and we're good at it—now let us do it and get the hell out of our way. Actually, we knew what we were doing because some of us had paid for our mistakes with our own blood.

We arrived safely at the Kit Carson scout camp where we climbed aboard a five-ton truck with our KCS comrades and headed for Mo Cay district on Road 6A. After we crossed the Ham Long River by ferry, we continued south until 6A forked. We turned left and drove for a few meters to a convenient point, where we parked the truck and left with two guards (Objective A). From that point we patrolled half a klick or so until we arrived at an ARVN outpost (Objective B).

I was amazed that such a small PF outpost could survive in this area. There were several known VC/NVA main and local force units in the general area that could have easily overrun the small ARVN contingent. Later, however, we began to suspect that the friendly outpost wasn't so friendly after all and was probably being used to monitor U.S. and ARVN activities covertly as part of a VC early warning network.

From Point B we turned east into a thick growth of nipa palm, tall coconut palm trees, some type of bamboo thickets, wild banana plants, and other lush delta marshland vegetation on the jungle trail that we were traveling. It reminded me of the Rung Sat Special Zone's T-10 area—it had an eerie darkness to it. It was also full of VC/NVA, centipedes of up to twelve inches, huge sun spiders with leg spans of up to six inches, poisonous snakes, and the source of fungus or jungle rot that created red patches on our skin—one of my fungus patches remained on my back for several years after the Vietnam War. The jungle bramble threatened to choke those foolish enough to pass that way. However, the scouts never hesitated, and continued to move forward at a good pace. I sure hope they know what they're doing, I thought.

We continued the patrol, following the scouts for three to four klicks, when we encountered a large VC/NVA stronghold. Fortunately, it wasn't occupied at that time. The reinforced bunker complex was interlaced with L-shaped fighting trenches that had punji stakes in strategic locations. The bunkers were cleverly concealed with natural growth and were arranged so there was always interlocking defensive and supportive fire from all avenues of approach.

We were fortunate that we had the scouts with us. If the SEALs had gone in without them, and a VC 560th Local Force Battalion unit had been awaiting our approach, we would have been ambushed and shot to pieces. That would have been a classic case of tactical surprise, and a superb example of cover and concealment. It would have taken a large combined operation of infantry, air, and artillery to box in the enemy force and destroy them in place. Our Army and Marine buddies had been dealing with this type of warfare for years in the central highlands and the Parrot's Beak/Iron Triangle area. There were several cases in

'67 in which companies of Army or Marine troops had patrolled into well-concealed, brigade-sized VC/NVA forces that were in combination bunker and intricate tunnel complexes. The end result was that U.S. units were annihilated. The enemy strongholds had been located on high ridgelines or outcroppings with a commanding view of all avenues of approach from below. They were generally concealed and somewhat protected from the air by triple canopy forest. The NVA's bunkers were positioned with forethought and were extremely well-camouflaged. They usually had 61mm, 82mm, 107mm mortars, 57mm and 75mm recoilless rifles, 7.62×39mm RPD and 12.7mm machine guns, small arms and sniper fire, and shoulder-fired RPG-2s and RPG-7s with their HEAT rounds (High Explosive Anti-Tank) on nearby ridges or fingers and other points of advantage to ensure that all defensive fields of fire were interlocked with each other.

It was no wonder that those Army and Marine companies were wiped out—the weapons and ammo supply that they had were carried by hand or on their backs. When U.S. reinforcements were sent in by helicopter, they sometimes suffered terrible loss of life and equipment and were forced to turn back.

I had nothing but the greatest respect for our Army and Marine mates who spent weeks and sometimes months in the field chasing their elusive and very capable VC/NVA regular army adversaries through some of the most difficult terrain in the world. They were the true heroes of the Vietnam War because they sometimes had to stand fast and face their enemy until one side had destroyed the other.

After we had passed through the unoccupied enemy bunker complex, we quietly continued the search for our target—the POW camp (Objective C). We hadn't traveled much more than five or six hundred meters when we came to a hootch. After November Platoon set security, the scouts went into the hootch and searched it. They found a small clay cooking stove in the corner that had warm charcoal and ashes still in it. We wondered if we hadn't already been compromised, but only time would tell.

The Kit Carson scouts continued past the hootch and toward the elusive POW camp, keeping a close watch for any signs of the 560th VC LF Battalion or their Rear Services unit. They soon found one VC serrated grenade that was being used as an antipersonnel mine. It had an instantaneous type fuse and was anchored with twine to a small tree trunk next to the trail. Monofilament line was tied to the safety pin. The almost transparent fishing line was strung across the trail at ankle level and was secured to a sturdy bush. Now I know we're compromised, I thought.

I found out later from Son, our interpreter, that one of the scouts told him that the VC had left a marker of three sticks on the trail as a warning to other VC that there were booby traps ahead. All Kit Carson scouts were ex-VC, and they had no trouble finding two more of the same type booby traps within another one hundred meters.

We hadn't gotten fifty meters past the last booby trap when the scouts spotted a VC lookout that was set up ahead of us and reported that the VC Rear Services unit was just beyond the lookout. For unknown reasons, neither the scouts nor the VC fired upon each other. Maybe the VC were more confused than we were. It was obvious that we were compromised. There would be no chance of liberating any ARVN POWs that day. Dai Uy, Son, and the senior scouts debated the situation for at least ten seconds—the decision was to abandon our search for the POW camp, leave the immediate area, and return to the truck by another route as quickly and safely as possible.

Because all of November Platoon was heavily laden

with extra demolitions and ammo, it was a long, hot, and humid patrol back to the outpost. For the first hour of our return trek, we didn't even stop for a water break, and a couple of the guys were beginning to show signs of advanced dehydration. However, we did come upon a friendly old woman and a younger woman who were cooking hot rice cakes that were mixed with banana and shredded coconut and wrapped in banana leaves. Everyone was famished because we hadn't eaten since breakfast. After we set security, Dai Uy had Son tell the two women that we would gladly pay them for the rice cakes. Our only request was for them to make as many of the cakes as quickly as they could. As I recall, we all got to eat two delicious, steaming cakes apiece. The ladies were very happy when they were given 500 piasters for their kindness. That was probably more money than they earned in several months.

After our fortuitous meal, we returned to the scouts' truck a little before suppertime. All hands were in a hurry to get back to Dong Tam for a hot meal. Those rice cakes had only whetted our appetites.

The scouts drove the truck to the ferry that crossed the Ham Long River, where we rendezvoused with Doc and our MST mates and boarded their MSSC. We waved good-bye to the scouts, and entered the dangerous Giao Hoa canal, which would take us northeast to Ben Tre and eventually to the My Tho River. Lieutenant (jg) Washburn had the coxswain pour the coals to the MSSC until we were skipping along the surface at sixty miles per hour. It didn't take us long to reach Ben Tre.

At Ben Tre, eight of the guys off-loaded and drove our two jeeps back to Dong Tam via the ferry that crossed the My Tho River. The rest of us rode the MSSC through four corners (sometimes called crossroads), where the Giao Hoa canal crosses the Bai Lai River. This was a very dangerous route and was near the spot where my very good friend Chief Frank Bomar (X-ray Platoon) was killed in December of '70. Once we zipped through the crossroads, we continued down the Giao Hoa canal until it entered the My Tho River. Dong Tam was almost directly across the river from that point. We finally made it back at about 1900 and headed straight for the mess hall.

After I cleaned my weapon, gear, and body, I lay down, as did the other guys, until debriefing at 2230. Our debriefing was mostly a matter of formality—we all knew that we had given it our best. Even Eberle was too tired to complain about anything. At least we hadn't made any major mistakes, nor had we suffered any casualties.

The next three days were filled with our normal activities, including tae kwon do practice, a run to NavForV in Saigon for supplies, and continued preparation for our next mission. Mr. Kleehammer and Senior Chief Bassett departed for Camp Alfa at Tan Son Nhut on their first leg of the trip to their R&Rs in Hawaii. Our op in northern Cai Be district that had been scheduled for the afternoon of the seventeenth was delayed for twenty-four hours because there were no available HAL-3 helos.

On the morning of September eighteenth Dai Uy gave the warning order for our operation that afternoon. Afterward, Fletcher, Hayden, and I drove to the Embassy House in My Tho and picked up Mr. Bai, the OSA interpreter. From there we drove to Cai Be and met with our good friend Chief Muoi concerning a 525 report of a POW camp in the northern part of his district. According to Muoi's information, the 525 agent had fabricated a very general report on the POW camp. That was only one of the many dead ends that we encountered while trying to cross-check—through separate sources when permissible—such an important target as a POW camp.

After we returned to My Tho and dropped off Mr. Bai

at the Embassy House, we drove straight to the Navy mess hall at Dong Tam for lunch.

At 1430 Dai Uy gave us the patrol order. Our targets were the security chief of the Y-4 (VC Saigon/Gia Dinh Sub Region VI Political Office) training unit and ten to fifteen Rear Services cadre. Our adversaries were reported to be residing within a specific group of hootches. We intended to kill or capture the whole brood of vipers.

The northwestern area of Dinh Tuong province was at the southern edge of the Plain of Reeds and was sparsely settled. There were company-sized VC/NVA units of the VC Dong Thap 1st Regiment and a few units of the NVA 9th Infantry Division located in large bunker complexes that were generally hidden in tree lines. I had been consistently plotting COMINT Green Hornet fixes—Communications Intelligence of VC/NVA radio transmissions—on one of our situation map overlays as another method of cross-checking our sources of intelligence information. Our plottings, which we got daily from ARVN 7th G-2 adviser Major Scott, indicated that there was a VC radio station in the vicinity of our target.

The personnel assignments were as follows:

P/L: Lt. Fletcher with CAR-15	AP/L: Smith with M-16/XM-148
Chamberlain with M-60	Knepper with M-16/XM-148
Hayden with M-60	Quear with M-60
Same with Stoner	Waneous with Stoner
Compton with Stoner	Barron with M-60
Eberle with Stoner	Tam with M-16
Phu (Hoi Chanh) with AK-47	

After we test-fired our weapons and rehearsed our SOPs, we loaded our two Sea Lord slicks at 1815 and headed for the wagon wheel in Giao Duc district, where we rendezvoused with the Seawolf gunships. Our Sea

Lord slicks and our two Seawolves dropped down to approximately seventy-five feet and set a northeasterly, low silhouetted course for our target, located on the northern border between Cai Lay and Cai Be districts, just south of the Kinh Thuong Mai Di Song My Tho (Route 66).

Dai Uy decided that we should insert first and then have the Seawolves pound the surrounding area with miniguns, M-60s, and rockets if needed. Our insertion was outstanding. Both slicks went in abreast and flared thirty meters from the main target hootch. We all jumped from the skids at about ten feet and hit the deck running toward the edge of a small canal between us and the hootch. There we kneeled for a lower silhouette, keeping watch for VC running away from us and toward other hootches.

As rehearsed, I yelled, *"Lai dai, mau len!"* ("Come here, hurry up!") several times with no response. Dai Uy had us wait for about one minute before he told me to throw a CS grenade inside the hootch. The rest of the platoon covered me while I jumped the canal and threw the grenade through the door of the hootch. After I returned to our skirmish line, we waited.

Within two minutes three women and five children came out of their bunker and out the door of the hootch, crying and vomiting. One of the women kept crying, *"Choi Oi!"* ("Oh, my God!) in between fits of vomiting.

While Tam and Phu instructed the women and kids to cross the canal and move behind our skirmish line, Dai Uy motioned for me to go inside the hootch and throw another CS grenade into the bunker, then return. I donned my small riot control gas mask and did as ordered, with no results.

Fletcher told Tam and Phu to quickly interrogate the women and find out where the VC security chief of Y-4, his training unit, and Rear Services cadre had gone. In the meantime Dai Uy and several of the guys searched another nearby hootch and the surrounding area on our left flank before it got too dark. There were no VC there either.

The results of Tam and Phu's interrogation of the three women only told us what we already knew: "No good! VC go fast tree line before helo come."

After Tam warned the women and kids to remain in front of their hootch until after we had extracted, the four of us quickly patrolled to two hootches that were approximately one hundred meters to our right flank, and we found nothing there. We scoured the areas around the hootches—nothing.

As we were headed toward Lieutenant Fletcher's squad, I looked at Roger and commented, "Damn, it looks like we're gonna get skunked again."

Roger only shook his head without comment and spit a long stream of Copenhagen tobacco juice onto the back of Phu's right boot heel.

I looked at Roger and quipped, "Good shot, mate. My sentiments exactly."

After we linked back up with Dai Uy, it was 2000 and almost pitch-black. Fletcher had us move south of the hootches about seventy-five meters, where we formed two H formations for extraction. The Sea Lord pilots soon radioed Lieutenant Fletcher, saying that they couldn't spot our eight uncovered strobe lights and requested that we use a pop flare to illuminate our position. Not eager to spend the night with our Communist enemies, we fired a para flare directly overhead so that our HAL-3 buddies could see us and extract us.

The Sea Lord pilots later told us that they couldn't see our strobe lights until they were within seventy-five meters of our position. One of the problems with night insertion and extraction was that the pilots had trouble with their depth perception and had a tendency to crash into objects or the ground, catching the nearby troops in the helo's main rotor. Understanding that risk and knowing we didn't have a hot LZ, our Sea Lord pilots came in slow and easy and landed without incident.

Our return to Dong Tam was uneventful and unusually quiet. We were generally a happy lot. However, all of us were frustrated that night because of our inability to change the tactical situations. We knew that every time we cleared our AOs with TOC, our missions were generally compromised before our departure from Dong Tam. We used all of the tricks of the trade, including getting several U.S. Army district senior advisers to clear our multiple AOs at the last moment or for the longest period of time that the ARVN 7th Division and the Vietnamese district chiefs would allow. We knew that the VC had informants in the ARVN's sector and subsector TOCs. We also knew that the only way we could catch our enemies unaware would be to operate without telling anyone when and where we were going. The solution was very tempting. The only problem was that if we were to unilaterally take the initiative, some of our staffer/admin'er buddies would ensure that the consequences would be severe, and by the time they got done with us, we would have felt and looked worse than a gutted warthog. Even if the results were spectacular, we would be condemned if certain staff members couldn't claim the glory. None of us were willing to pay that price. Whatever happened to our military objective of finding and destroying our enemy? I asked myself as I looked out the starboard helo side door into total darkness.

After the Sea Lord slicks dropped us off at Dong Tam, we headed directly for the chow hall. While we were eating, Same felt something biting his calf muscle. He pulled his Levi's pants leg up and found a huge leech attached to his calf. The bloodsucking parasite was six inches long and bloated with an estimated eight to ten cc's of Same's blood. Everyone gulped down their dinner and hurried to our barracks, where we stripped off our clothes and carefully searched ourselves for leeches. That was one time that we cleaned our bodies before our weapons and gear.

Same and Waneous found several more leeches on their legs. The leeches' bites left triangular marks that were approximately three-sixteenths of an inch in diameter. Because of the anticoagulant that the leeches injected into the wound, the bleeding didn't stop for approximately an hour.

Waneous looked at Doc Holmes and said, "Hey, Doc, can you do anything to stop the bleeding?"

Doc was always known to be compassionate, and demonstrated his concern by replying, "There's nothing wrong with your leg, you wimp. It's all in your head. Take two salt tablets and drink a glass of water."

"And what in the hell are the salt tablets going to do?" Waneous asked in frustration.

"The salt will stop the bleeding from the inside," quipped our loving corpsman.

Same and Waneous also found a few leeches that were on the outside of their pant legs. Those blood-starved leeches were only three inches in length. I didn't have any leeches on me because I had tied my cammi leg-bottom laces securely around the tops of my jungle boots. However, none of us had rubbed mosquito repellent on our uniforms before the operation. We had paid a heavy price for that error in judgment. From that time forward, all of us were very careful to squirt repellent all over ourselves and especially on our boot tops and our cammi bottoms.

The next day was spent working on OB maps and overlays, filing systems and trips to Ben Luc, Vinh Long, Saigon, etcetera.

On the morning of September twentieth Dai Uy, Trung

Uy, Chief Thompson, Staff Sergeant Mai, and I went to Sector in My Tho where the province chief, Colonel Dao, presented us our awards and letters of appreciation. Later that afternoon, we practiced tae kwon do under Captain Kim.

The twenty-third of September was a busy day spent in preparation for another operation. At about 1330 hours Lieutenant Fletcher, Roger Hayden, Son, and I drove to My Tho. While Dai Uy was visiting with 525, I went to the Embassy House to see Al. I requested his permission to allow Bai to reproduce organization charts and coordinates of the VC Mang, the NVA 111th Regiment, the NVA 9th Division offices, and units within Dinh Tuong province for me. Al readily consented.

Before I left, he mentioned that he was planning a type of Beacon operation and asked me if I was using this type of equipment. I told him that I had the equipment but hadn't developed its capabilities due to my agent handler/interpreter problems. Al said that after the October third South Vietnamese national elections, he would contact me and go from there.

After my short visit, I went downstairs to see Mr. Bai at the translation office and asked him to draft the VC Mang, NVA 111th Regiment, and NVA 9th Division organization charts and the coordinates of their office and unit locations. Bai assured me that he would.

That afternoon, we practiced our tae kwon do from 1530 to 1805 hours with Captain Kim. Our workout had been particularly brutal because of the terrible heat inside the metal building. Afterward, everyone headed for our little bar for a few cold refreshments.

CHAPTER EIGHT

Warfare is like hunting. Wild animals are taken by scouting, by nets, by lying in wait, by stalking, by circling around, and by other such stratagems rather than by sheer force. In waging war we should proceed in the same way, whether the enemy be many or few. To try simply to overpower the enemy in the open, hand-to-hand and face-to-face, even though you might appear to win, is an enterprise which is very risky and can result in serious harm. Apart from extreme emergency, it is ridiculous to try to gain victory which is so costly and brings only empty glory.

—Emperor Maurice,
The Strategikon, ca. A.D. 600

September twenty-fourth started off as a beautiful day for an operation. We were all well-rested and ready for a scrap with the VC—or at least we thought we were.

Trung Uy gave his warning order at 0800 hours, immediately after everyone had gotten back from the Navy mess next door. I was to be 2nd Squad leader, while Trung Uy would act as the 1st Squad leader and the patrol leader. Lieutenant Fletcher would go along with Kleehammer as his adviser. The rest of the morning was spent preparing our gear and weapons for a potential knucklebuster. In other words, we were going to carry a maximum amount of ammunition and ordnance just in case.

Killer gave his PLO at 1230. We were going to try to capture Ba Tin, the commanding officer of the VC 341st Engineer Battalion (Dong Thap One Regiment). Ba Tin's office was located within a reinforced bunker complex. As usual, the VC complex was very well camouflaged and was located in the midst of a thick jungle area adjacent to local farmers' homes, rice paddies, and gardens on the Sam Giang and Cai Lay district border south of QL-4, just two and a half klicks west of Ba To's hamlet near Song Sam Giang. Our guide was to be a VC POW accompanied by Chief Muoi and his four PSB operatives. This ought to be interesting, I thought—this VC grunt hadn't even Chieu Hoied!

After the briefing, we went to the river and test-fired our weapons. Then we went on to the helo pad, where we rehearsed our SOPs until the Sea Lord slicks arrived.

At 1430 hours all fifteen of us—Tam and Son included—loaded our two slicks and headed for Cai Be to pick up Chief Muoi and his five men. Unfortunately, a severe thunderstorm struck while we were in Cai Be. All of us were shivering from the cold air and rain in the back area of the Huey slicks, and the pilots returned to Dong Tam, where we would wait until the rain slackened.

The rainy season had begun in earnest about the first of September and wouldn't be over until the following April. The storms generally struck every afternoon and sometimes continued for several days, making it a tough time to operate. The whole delta and its rice paddies were flooded; the delta streams were swift and out of their banks, which made them hard to cross. It could get fairly cold, especially at night, and sometimes it was hard to get fixed wing and helo air support once the clouds dropped too low. However, a wet, cold, and nasty environment was our forte and the reason we were sent to the delta.

I grinned as I looked down at QL-4, the national highway, as we flew east rather slowly because of the heavy rain. We were no more than fifty feet above the paved surface. I reflected back to 1961 when I was working at the Bridwell Hereford Ranch headquarters, which was located about six miles from a small German-Catholic village called Winthorst in north-central Texas. I enjoyed my stay there and lived in the bunkhouse with five other hardworking bachelors. Chores began at 0530 sharp for all hands. After Scotch and I had completed our initial chores—Scotch mixed specialized feed, while I fed it to the bulls—working with fifty two-year-old registered short-horn Hereford bulls, we went to the big barn, where I took my turn milking a big old long-legged Guernsey cow just prior to breakfast.

During those milking times there were several cats and a multitude of playful little kittens hanging around begging for a squirt or two of milk direct from the tit. The little urchins would close their eyes and open their mouths wide to receive their portion of the white elixir with which I occasionally covered their faces. They never seemed to mind the mess—they just sat back and took their time licking it off their paws.

One morning an old mama cat got a little careless. Ol' Bessie had wrapped her dung-laden tail around my face, causing me to spill from the milk bucket. While the cat was concentrating intently on licking up the puddle of milk, Bessie apparently decided she would get back at me by lifting her left rear hoof high enough to place it into the nearly full bucket. She never did have much of a sense of humor, especially after I told her what I thought of her and secured her tail to the hobbles on her back legs. At the early age of twenty, I was about to get my first lesson on feminine revenge. Bessie brought her hoof down dead center and hard on the top of that mama cat's round head. It was a sight to behold—in less than a second, mama cat's head went from four inches in circumference to something flatter than a silver dollar, with a diameter of a medium-sized frying pan. The cat's reflexes took over, and the carcass started flopping against Bessie's hind legs.

Bessie, sensing that something was wrong, got spooked, and before I could grab the milk bucket and get out of the way, she kicked the bucket over, spilling that day's milk allowance and knocking me and my one-legged stool ass-over-teakettle. The rest of the cats had all of the milk they wanted that morning. Unfortunately, we bunkhouse boys didn't get any fresh milk with our meals that day.

Such were the trials of a cowpoke sloggin' through cow crap, I thought as our Sea Lord slicks started setting down on the Dong Tam helo pad. As I looked out the slick's starboard door at the rapidly flooding quagmire surrounding us, I could see that not much had really changed in my life. The main difference was that the pay and benefits were better. If I got killed, Mom and Dad would get $10,000 and the government would bury me. A cowpoke never had it so good, I thought as I slapped at Same's head to let him know that I was glad he was my friend and teammate.

The rain finally stopped at 1615 hours, and fifteen minutes later our two heavily loaded slicks were skimming the rice paddies at about one hundred miles an hour with two Seawolves slightly above us, covering our flanks. Kleehammer had decided against prepping the bunker complex before our insertion, in hopes that we might retain the element of surprise. Basically, he was hoping for a miracle.

Once the helos flared at about six feet altitude, 2nd Squad and I peeled out of our helo and quickly took left flank, while Kleehammer, Fletcher, and 1st Squad took the right. We didn't even have time to find a good place to hide before we started receiving small arms fire. We were only twenty-five meters from the thicket of jungle that was at twelve o'clock, or directly in front of us. Mr. Ba Tin definitely had units of his VC 341st Engineer Battalion located in that thicket somewhere.

Both of our squads immediately returned fire and bravely set a classical frontal skirmish line as everyone took cover behind a rice dike—in other words, we dove into the mud and called for our Seawolf gunship buddies to rain 2.75-inch rocket warheads and minigun projectiles on Ba Tin's head. Nothing fancy, just effective; nothing heroic, just for survival.

On that day, all of us were reminded of what the Marine and Army grunts had to put up with, sometimes on a daily basis, against conventional VC/NVA forces.

On left flank, Chambo hosed down the source of the enemy fire with his M-60, while I threw in a few 40mm HE rounds to open up holes in the bush. Same, Waneous, and Compton opened up with their Stoners, and Little Bear carefully laid out a couple of 7.62mm bandoleers for easy access before he gleefully began expending his case of ammo.

On right flank, Hayden's and Quear's slow-firing M-60s were thump-thump-thumping at a measly 550 rounds a minute, while Chief Bassett's and Eberle's Stoners were filling in with chatter at a paltry 850 rounds a minute. Knepper, not to be outdone, kept a steady rate of 40mm HE rounds, blowing holes through the thick brush toward the sources of the VC rifle fire.

While the muzzle blasts from our firearms gradually reached a crescendo, Mr. K. was on his PRC-77 radio busily coordinating with the Seawolves for their first rocket and minigun run. The gunships' first targets would be only thirty meters from our skirmish line, and Trung Uy knew that there would be no room for error. However, because we were situated out in an open rice paddy, the Seawolves had no problems locating us at all times.

Prior to the Seawolves' firing run, Trung Uy called for both squads to cease-fire and to stand by. That meant we were to get our heads and asses down behind the rice dike. Naturally, being young, stupid, and impatient, we peeked over the dike, looked to our right and watched the gunships as they started their run from right to left flank in front of us. I watched the first two rockets streak toward the nearby VC bunkers, which were visible only from the air. The sight was awesome.

When the first two 2.75-inch rocket warheads detonated only thirty to forty meters in front of our position, I had a flashback to '69, when a unit of the U.S. Army 9th Infantry Division's Huey gunships tried to blow me and seventeen PRUs to bits one dark night. The only difference was that the rockets of '69 were detonating closer than thirty to forty meters, and it took the housemaids a week to wash out all of the crap from my tiger-striped cammi bottoms and jungle boots. That was a dismal and soggy night in more ways than one.

When both of the Seawolf helos had completed their firing runs and were making a hard left bank over our left flank, we watched numerous green and red VC tracers streaking upward behind the helos. It was obvious that Ba Tin's boys weren't very intimidated.

Chambo looked at me and asked, "Now that we have brought our enemy to bay, what are we going to do with them?"

I grinned and replied, "Call in more helo strikes until they cry uncle, or drop a fifteen-thousand-pound daisy cutter on them."

Chambo looked at me for a second, nodded his head and gave me a thumbs-up.

Again Trung Uy called in air strikes, and again the VC opened up with their AK-47s at the helos. Somehow those VC haven't gotten the message, I thought.

I leaned over to my left and told Same, who was carrying 2nd Squad's PRC-77 radio, "Now that we've got them entrapped, it's time to request a few CBU-55B FAE bombs to clean the VC out of their bunkers."

"Yeah, like we did in Binh Dai district," Same replied sarcastically.

"We only have two options: go in and clear the bunkers, or call in our slicks and extract. Let's see what Mr. K., Lieutenant Fletcher, and Chief Muoi decide," I commented. I knew that if Trung Uy decided that we would go in after Ba Tin, all of us would obey and give it our best effort.

Trung Uy had a very difficult decision to make, because (1) our image was at stake, especially if Chief Muoi wanted us to go in and (2) we would probably take heavy casualties because our VC enemies were combat engineers and would be prepared for anyone stupid enough to assault their reinforced positions. In addition, certain staff members would have jumped for joy at November Platoon's casualties because our loss would be their gain. Their existence and the personal awards they had been writing for each other would be justified in their eyes through our blood.

All of us knew it would only take one command-detonated claymore mine to wipe out the better part of a squad. We could expect to find booby traps used as blocking elements and VC riflemen positioned at well-concealed firing ports carefully cleared through the dense vegetation to ensure interlocking fields of fire from all avenues of approach.

It was during those times that the patrol leader really earned his pay and felt the terrible burden of combat leadership. The job carried with it awesome responsibilities, and during times of great decision, it was a very lonely position. The consequences of the patrol leader's decision could haunt him for the rest of his life, not to mention the lives of his men and their families.

Sometimes, missions had to be accomplished regardless of the cost. When allowed to do so, Kleehammer would have to weigh his options carefully. Was the target worth the loss of some of the most highly trained men in the world in order to maintain our self-image or to save the lives of hundreds or thousands later? In this case, I didn't think so.

Same soon passed the word from Trung Uy that we would not be going in after Ba Tin and his boys and to stand by for extraction. Without being too obvious about it, I let out a sigh of relief. In my humble opinion, I believed that Trung Uy had made the right decision.

Surprisingly, the only person who was mad about Mr. K.'s decision was Chief Muoi. For some reason, he wanted Mr. Ba Tin real bad. Some of my PRU were that way in '69 because the VC/VCI had murdered members of their families. Acts of revenge carried their own special curses and had terrible consequences for those involved. Acts driven by such motives were dangerous, self-serving, and should never be tolerated, I thought to myself, as I reflected on a couple of PRU missions.

I immediately told the guys to stand by for extraction and remain in our skirmish line behind the rice dike. I knew there would be no arguments there. Because of the sporadic enemy fire from twelve o'clock, we couldn't set up our normal H formation in the middle of a rice paddy with no cover available.

In this situation, the Seawolves concentrated maximum firepower on the VC bunker complex, while our Sea Lord slicks landed twenty or thirty meters directly behind us with their noses facing the enemy. The sequence of loading the slicks would begin with each squad's first fire team laying down a maximum rate of fire while falling back toward its slick. The second fire team would load the Sea Lord slick's portside. Once second fire team was loaded, first fire team would quickly climb aboard to starboard. The squad leader/patrol leader and the radioman would be the last to load, and the door gunner or the copilot would usually give the pilot a thumbs-up when everyone was aboard.

When our Sea Lord buddies landed directly behind 1st and 2nd squads, everyone opened up for a maximum rate of fire while both second fire teams loaded, followed by first fire teams. Within a couple of minutes all hands were loaded and continued to return fire at the VC from the helo side doors until the slicks lifted us from the flooded rice paddy.

After we had returned to Dong Tam, Dai Uy contacted Major Bigelow (DSA) at the Sam Giang subsector on secure-voice radio. Dai Uy suggested that Bigelow convince the ARVN district chief to request that Sector organize an ARVN sweep through the VC bunker complex with November Platoon, HAL-3's Seawolves, and VAL-4's Black Ponies on the following day, which was a Saturday. A short time later Major Bigelow called back and notified Dai Uy that the ARVNs at Sector and Subsector strongly hinted that they preferred not to operate on weekends.

Dai Uy called all hands into our little bar for our debriefing. He began by saying, "I think Mr. Kleehammer made the right decision this afternoon. I'm sorry we've had such poor results lately. However, there's little we can do about it. Mr. K. and Senior Chief, I think it's now time to attend to our wounded spirits. As soon as everyone gets his weapons and gear cleaned up, I'm buying the first round. Senior Chief, you'll be in charge. Mr. K. and I will spend the night in My Tho. Any questions?"

The process of healing our spirits with our MST buddies turned out to be an evening odyssey. For starters, the MST OIC, Lieutenant (jg) Washburn, volunteered to grill a bunch of chicken for dinner. Senior Chief Bassett demonstrated his appreciation for Mr. Washburn's condescension by keeping him covertly supplied with at least two triple scotches at all times while the young officer was tending the grill. The more scotch whiskey that Trung Uy Washburn drank, the happier he got and the more chicken he burned. Everyone was having a great time teasing and harassing each other. Much laughter, yelling, and occasional screams of pain echoed off the surrounding Vietnamese barracks' bulkheads.

UDT training had taught us that, when in doubt, we

Sao Lam, my good friend and mentor, being awarded another Vietnamese Cross of Gallantry, 1969. John, my friend of '69, is sitting in the rear with shades on.

SEAL platoon training at Camp Kerry, Niland, California, 1970–71.

Mike Platoon, on December 7, 1971, the last SEAL team platoon to depart South Vietnam. Standing (L-R): HMC William Hill with Stoner, BT1 Leonard Van Orden with M-60, BM2 Frank J. Czajkowski with M-60, RMSA David R. Hoover with M-60, RMSN William M. Foley with M-60, and ETNSN David W. Johnson with M-60. Kneeling (L-R): QMC Thomas A. Norton with AK-47; RMSN Steven R. Jones with PRC-77 radio and M-16 rifle/M203 40mm grenade launcher; YN3 John W. Chalvs with Stoner; Tan, a Vietnamese scout, with CAR-15; RM3 Thomas J. Christofer with Stoner; SFP2 Paul C. Bourne with M-16/M-203. Front row (L-R): LT (jg) Walter F. Merrick with Stoner, Lt. Michael S. McCrary with CAR-15/M-203, Quan with M-16, Nhge (age seventeen) with M-16, and Kit Carson Scout Nguyen Van Dung (age fifteen) with AK-47.

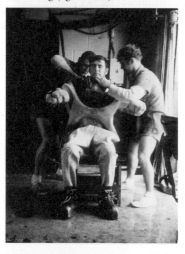

My turn to suit up. All evolutions were timed. Our instructor, Chief Jesse Lively, was one of the best.

SERE jungle survival course, Cubi Point, Philippines. I built a nice bohio out of a poncho, mosquito net, inflatable mattress, bamboo, vines, and parachute suspension line.

Entering the water with 190 pounds of the MK-5 deep sea diving rig on my shoulders at the Navy's diving school at Key West, Florida (fall/winter '72).

From left to right: Philippino Negrito instructor (SERE survival course), BM2 C. J. Dunn and RM2 W. W. Nehl (spring '77).

November platoon, Dong Tam, Nov. '71. Left to right: LT (jg) "Killer" Kleehammer, Doc Holmes, Rick Knepper, Gary Smith, LT "J.J." Fletcher, Leonard Same, Terence Wanous, Roger Hayden, David "Eb" Eberle, Gordon Compton, Gary "Chambo" Chamberlin, David "Little Bear" Barron, Layton "Your Lordship" Bassett. Ronald Quear is absent.

Left to right: NavForV journalist and photographer, KCS, Gary Smith, and Doc patrolling to Ba To's Hoa Hao hamlet. Notice mini–CS grenade on my back.

Doc Holmes crossing one of the many "monkey bridges" on the way to Ba To's hamlet.

LT (jg) Washburn being dragged through the benjo ditch butt first. Wanous is pulling on his left leg while Killer Kleehammer has his right arm. Chambo is coming over to grab Washburn's right leg. Before it was all over, Mr. Washburn wasn't wearing a stitch of clothes.

"Bad Medicine" Doc and the omnipotent Senior Chief Layton Bassett. It was time to head for the hills when those two got their heads together.

Left to right: Lou DiCroce, Gary Smith, and "Big" John Chalmers about to go on an Emerson SCUBA compass dive in the San Diego Bay in 1970.

My Korean UDT/SEAL/EOD counterparts near Chin Hae, South Korea, 1977.

The highlight of my naval career: shaking the hand of the last five-star general, Omar Bradley. He passed away several weeks later on April 8, 1981, while living onboard Ft. Bliss, Texas. "Deacon" Holmes stands to my right in the background.

After my advancement to master chief petty officer, it was time for reenlistment. Colonel Joseph Ostrowidzki, commandant of the Sergeants Major Academy, shipped me over for the fifth and last time.

Parachute requalifications for EOD Det. Whidbey Island. CWO-3 Clark George is about to exit off the CH-46's ramp after ABH1 Tony Tennyson and Master Chief Jim Collins.

Master Chief Boatswain Mate Jim Collins piping me over the side. The men in dress uniform were EOD officers and chiefs from various EOD dets and billets within the Puget Sound area, including the Whidbey Island NAS Ordnance officer. It was a very sobering ceremony—the finality of my retirement had begun to set in.

Gary Smith in his dress uniform, '69/'70. Note the trident above the ribbons. At that time, enlisted SEALs wore silver, the officers gold, but within a year or so, all UDT/SEAL enlisted and officers wore the gold trident. Initially, the trident was not well received by West Coast UDT/SEALs—for reasons of tradition we preferred the Navy/Marine Corps jump wings as our breast device and the UDT diving patch on the right upper arm of the uniform. To make matters worse, rumor had it that the army had designed the trident!

should torture the depraved until they began to love it. In other words, if your buddies love you, they'll demonstrate it by sucker-punching you when you're not looking, by kicking your stool out from under you, or, when you're in great pain from an injury or the flu, by telling you it's all in your head and giving you a salt tablet—if you want a glass of water, you have to get it yourself. That was the kind of perverted love that all SEALs preferred and understood.

I reflected back on a cold, dark night at the infamous Devil's Elbow on the Colorado River in October '65, when I was captured by a mob of loving instructors. As UDT trainees of Class 36, we had been frantically trying our best to evade our enemy instructors as we paddled from Davis to Parker dams in our seven-man IBS. We knew that if we ever got captured, we'd wish we were dead before they finished torturing us. That was the whole lesson—fight until you're dead, never surrender.

After our initial capture, Brother Moore and I were elected by our enemy instructors to suffer the consequences for the entire boat crew. It didn't take Moore and me long to realize that there was nothing we could do about it other than keep our mouths absolutely shut—except for name, rank, date of birth, and serial number—during our interrogation. And so we did, for a price.

The military principle of "fight until you're dead" was severely reinforced during our physical and mental torture. Gradually, our minds, emotions, and wills began to understand that our enemy was ruthless, and mercy wasn't a part of the modus operandi. For SEALs, capture meant only eventual death after unimaginable torture. I totally believed in my PRU buddies' slogan, "It is better to die with honor than to live in dishonor."

Once it had gotten dark, Same and I decided to ambush several columns of ARVNs that were soon to be marching in formation past our barracks. For some unknown reason, the ARVNs had a habit of marching by every evening about 2000.

Same looked at his Rolex watch and commented, "It's now 1950. If we're going to do it, we had better get in position, don't you think?"

I started chuckling and replied, "Yeah, and the slight breeze is just right. I'll go get a CS grenade off my web gear."

After I had retrieved the riot-gas grenade, Same and I hid in some high grass approximately ten meters south of the road. The conditions and terrain were perfect. There was a ditch that ran alongside the road that would be just right in which to throw the grenade. Also, the evening coolness provided an inversion that would prevent the gas from rising too quickly. As luck would have it, the breeze was coming from behind us and would carry the gas slowly north and directly across the road.

After we lay down in the weeds and waited for the ARVNs to arrive, Same looked at me, started laughing, and commented, "This is more fun than sitting on a real ambush. We'll teach these guys to sabotage our missions and steal our belongings. Revenge, how sweet it is."

I laughed and replied sarcastically, "Yeah, they'll never know who did it. We're at least thirty-five meters from our barracks. We can always blame it on the Vietnamese navy guys"—they lived behind our barracks—"if this gets out of hand. The main thing we must keep in mind is—don't get caught at all costs."

The ARVNs didn't arrive till 2015 hours. Their tardiness only justified our plan in our minds. When the ambushees were within approximately fifty meters of our concealed position, I pulled the pin and threw the CS grenade forward into the ditch, which was no more than fifteen feet from the center of the road. The inversion had held, and the gas drifted slowly over the road. Same and I were like little kids playing hide-and-seek. It was all we could do to refrain from bustin' out laughin' as the ARVNs rapidly approached our clandestine ambush.

Our Vietnamese buddies were caught completely unawares. It was a great plan and perfectly executed. The column innocently marched into the cloud and did well for at least two or three seconds until the front ranks disintegrated with loud cursing, coughing, and rapid shuffling of boots as they frantically scrambled and shoved each other around in circles. The momentum of the rear ranks kept pushing those in front farther into the CS gas and made matters worse. Many began rubbing their eyes, and some fell into the sewage ditches on both sides of the road. The almost invisible gaseous cloud was so large that no one knew where to run, or for that matter, where they were going. As far as they knew, they were surrounded. Within another few seconds the whole column was totally panic-stricken and retreated from whence they had come in total disarray.

Same and I laughed until tears were streaming down our cheeks. Once the ARVNs had backed off to a safe distance, both of us quietly belly-crawled all the way back to our barracks and went topside as if nothing had happened.

However, there just wasn't enough action to really complete the process of our much needed mental and spiritual healing. Something simply had to be done about the burned chicken.

When Washburn had most of the chicken overly grilled, Bassett, Knepper, Chambo, and Hayden went over and stood behind him. Not a word was said. Chambo, who had an opossum-eatin' grin on his face, began twirling a pair of nickel-plated Smith & Wesson handcuffs on his right index finger.

Trung Uy Washburn, knowing something was up, turned slightly to his left and noticed the flashy handcuffs spinning round and round. By nature he was a predator just like the rest of us—he just wasn't aware of it at that time. Before that day was over, he would have much better insight into his family's atavistic roots.

Trung Uy was an unusual JO (junior officer) in that he enjoyed our rough-and-tumble attention that we delighted in sharing with him, i.e., bathing in the benjo ditch, spiking his Scotch drinks with urine, and other forms of SEAL-type humor. It may have been that his mother truly loved him and even sang lullabies to little baby Washburn every night before she slapped the thunder out of him, or maybe she demonstrated her love by torturing him and promising to beat him a week before the actual act. Whatever the truth was, Washburn was our type of guy.

Mr. Washburn looked at the four knuckle draggers with concern, even though he knew that he was soon to be part of the fun in one way or another. Not knowing what else to do, he looked nervously down at the burning coals, turned over a couple of pieces of burned chicken legs, and asked, "Anyone want some chicken hot off the grill?"

With swift execution, Senior Chief and boys stripped him of all clothing. Once the task was completed, Bassett gave the final order. "Handcuff him to that electrical pole over there for all passersby to observe what a chicken burner looks like. Hayden, you can write, can't you?"

Hayden quickly replied, "Yeah, Chief, I think I can. I wrote my mama a half-page letter last month."

"Good. Go make a cardboard sign that says, 'This man is a chicken burner and heretic' and post it above Mr. Washburn where he can't reach it," ordered the big chief.

Hayden initially started for the barracks but stopped, turned around, and asked, "Chief, how do you spell 'heretic'?"

Bassett thought for a moment, then said, "H-a-i-r-a-t-i-c-k."

After Chief and his boys had taken care of Trung Uy Washburn, all of us headed for the bar in our barracks. In spite of Mr. Washburn's cursing and yelling, which was occasionally heard from below, everyone was having a jolly good time topside. Later, when the mosquitoes came out in clouds just before dark, Washburn's moaning and growning gradually increased until his piercing screams finally penetrated the walls of our crowded bar.

Finally, an hour later, Compton and Quear, being the only softhearted types in November platoon, went down and set Trung Uy loose. They returned his shirt and pants and brought him up to the bar for a hot toddy with his friends, comrades, and mates.

Trung Uy looked at me—I was barkeep that night—and said, "Smitty, give me a quadruple Scotch on the rocks and give everybody else a round on me."

Trung Uy Washburn had passed the test. He was one of the boys. Later, he proved it by sucker punching Eberle off his stool when he wasn't lookin', thus proving the old adage that character is shaped by one's own thoughts rather than by one's circumstances.

Yes sir, Mr. Washburn is one fine officer, I thought as I poured him his second quadruple Scotch.

CHAPTER NINE

No one starts a war—or rather, no one in his senses ought to do so—without first being clear in his mind what he intends to achieve by that war and how he intends to conduct it. The former is its political purpose; the latter its operational objective. This is the governing principle which will set its course, prescribe the scale of means and effort which is required, and make its influence felt throughout down to the smallest operational detail.
> —Field Marshall Carl von Clausewitz,
> *On War*

The next few days were filled with administrative and operational planning tasks of one sort or another. We had been assigned two new interpreters, Bay and Long, to replace the ones who had stolen from us—except Son, who was always faithful and loyal. On the morning of September twenty-sixth I had to take Bay and Long to Dong Tam's Navy LSB (Logistical Support Base) 21/30 admin office to meet the Vietnamese navy base commander and pick up their gate passes for getting on and off Dong Tam.

Afterward, Little Bear, Bay, Long, and I left Dong Tam for Saigon. It was an unusually pretty day considering it was rainy season. While we were driving through Cholon toward downtown Saigon, we noticed that the "White Mice"—the Vietnamese National Police—and Quan Cahn or Vietnamese Military Police had been reinforced at their checkpoints. Even the normally hectic Vietnamese traffic seemed somewhat subdued. During our meal at the small Meyer Cords café near NavForV, I overheard that the Vietnamese students were stirred up again and were on a rampage of burnin', lootin', and shootin'. Once we arrived at NavForV, I was ordered to drive our jeep inside the Navy's compound and leave it there until our departure for My Tho. Apparently, the reason for the increased security was that the Vietnamese students had burned another Navy jeep just outside the NavForV compound earlier that morning.

In '70, a U.S. Navy chief petty officer was killed by a Molotov cocktail while sitting in his jeep just outside of NavForV. It was thrown by a VC sapper who was riding by on his motorbike. The chief died a slow, terrible death. Frankly, I'd rather be shot.

There was also sporadic sniping from rooftops in the area. The situation was normal in that we didn't know who our enemy was. I doubt that anyone else did either, except the VC. It was 1500 hours by the time I had finished taking care of a few intel-related matters. On our return trip to Dong Tam, we decided to take the fairly new Korean highway that went to Cu Chi, the location of the U.S. Army's 25th Infantry Division, instead of driving through Cholon—the Chinese section—which was on the southwestern outskirts of Saigon. Considering the political situation, we thought it might be a safer route. It was an exceptionally pleasant and uneventful return trip to Dong Tam—we didn't even get run off the road by an ARVN truck.

The next day, most of the platoon went with the MST folks to Vung Tau by MSSC and LSSC. They were to rendezvous with Doc Holmes, Quear, and a few SAS troopers on the Australian R&R beach for an SAS party, and return with Doc and Quear to Dong Tam.

I enjoyed the rare peace and quiet, and took advantage of it by creating an aerial photo mosaic of a VC POW camp and updating intel files. However, all quiet times must come to an end.

At 1815 all of the guys returned safely from Vung Tau. As to be expected, everyone was severely sun- and wind-burned and very tired from riding the MSSC and LSSC over fairly rough seas.

Unfortunately, a freak accident happened to Dai Uy Fletcher while he was sitting on the bow of the MSSC on the way to Vung Tau. As usual, the boat was cruising at high speed when a large silver fish, two to three feet in length, leaped high out of the water forward of the bow. The MSSC was much faster than the cold-blooded vertebrate, so the fish hit Dai Uy's leg and bounced into his face. He suffered several deep cuts in his left thigh and had a bad cut on his cheek. Fortunately, it wasn't long before the others got him to an Aussie doctor, who sewed up his wounds in no time.

Two days later, on September twenty-eighth, Lt. (jg) Jon Wright and Petty Officer Holler drove up to our barracks in their five-ton truck, loaded to the gills with Oscar Platoon 2nd Squad's gear. They had made a long, dangerous drive from Solid Anchor all the way across the delta to Dong Tam. Lt. (jg) Nick Walsh, CE2 Gary Lawrence, ET3 Browning, RM2 Chuck Hollern, and RM3 Mark Lesher were moved to Ben Luc with Mike Platoon's Lt. Shannon McCrary, ENS Wally Merrick, Chief Norton, and others.

Solid Anchor (previously called Sea Float) was located near the southernmost tip of Vietnam and An Xuyen province on the Cua Lan River. I had sent some time there in '70 as a Biet Hai adviser. Oscar Platoon had been ordered to leave due to the Vietnamese navy's pressures on NavForV in Saigon. Obviously, all was not well with our

Vietnamese navy buddies down there, I thought. Our withdrawal from South Vietnam had a lot to do with the South Vietnamese government's and the Vietnamese people's attitudes toward us. In many ways, I couldn't blame them. The continuing withdrawal of all U.S. combat forces from 'Nam, which was completed by the summer of '72, made all of us feel like we were leaving our Vietnamese brothers when they needed us most. There was nothing more grievous than a friend who runs away when the going gets tough—especially when he or she is deceitful about it.

Nevertheless, it was a time of celebration for us; it was always good to rendezvous with our mates again. The remaining members of 2nd Squad would be arriving within the next few days. Trung Uy Wright, Chief Harris, Doc Jennings, RM2 Chuck Miller, GMG2 Bailey, PO2 Eddie Farmer, PO2 Mojica, and GMG1 Edwards (MST) would be staying with us for several weeks, we were told, until they received orders from SpecWar staff to depart for CONUS. Until then, Oscar Platoon was still on operational status, especially for Bright Light ops.

Later that evening, Dai Uy gave November Platoon an update on the general situation of SpecWar policies. Afterward, I gave my weekly enemy OB/intel briefing on enemy activity and potential targets for our platoons.

The next day, Senior Chief Bassett had us all frantically setting up double bunks in preparation for the arrival of Chief Harris, Miller, Bailey, and Farmer. Later that afternoon, Knepper and I worked on our operational gear in preparation for a three-day op in Ham Long district, Kien Hoa province, the following week. Tam and I were to be his point men. Knepper and I were looking forward to spending a little time in the bush sneakin' and a-peekin'.

Lieutenant Fletcher had previously decided to allow the senior enlisted men, and eventually the junior enlisted men, who wished to do so, to plan and execute their own operations. Dai Uy was very generous and farsighted like that; he always took good care of his men and encouraged all of us to do our very best. Because of my experience, I volunteered to be their point man and/or APL (assistant patrol leader).

I was soon to learn that attitudes like Lieutenant Fletcher's were a rare commodity in SpecWar, especially after the last of the SEAL platoons pulled out of the Vietnam War in December 1971. From 1972 onward many of our best operating officers/combat leaders resigned rather than spend their careers butting heads with admin'er officers—basically nonoperating SEAL officers/nonhackers with a chest full of phony medals. During the seventies, politics in the teams was at its worst.

That afternoon, eight more men from Oscar Platoon arrived from Solid Anchor. That night it was my turn as the bartender. It turned out to be a rowdy evening, all right.

Oscar Platoon's Doc "JJ" Jennings teasingly pestered me the better part of the evening and early morning by placing his face within six inches of mine. My natural reaction was to push him away to a safe distance. Having been sucker-punched at close quarters from my blind side while drinking a cool one at Shalamars—across the street from NavForV, in Saigon—in December '66, I had a tendency to keep a safe sucker-punch distance from those I wasn't sure of.

I knew that JJ was very intelligent and had a great personality. He was blessed with a chocolate complexion, was approximately five feet ten inches in height, medium-heavy in build, had a powerful set of shoulders, and most important, I knew he had a black belt in judo. I had first gotten to know him while he was serving with Lieutenant Todd's Hotel Platoon in 1970 while they were working out of My Tho. I was an LDNN adviser to a Vietnamese

SEAL platoon, and participated in Hotel Platoon's attempt at rescuing a U.S. POW in Kien Hoa province that summer.

Because I didn't understand JJ's persistent actions, I finally got irritated and said, "JJ, if you don't get your ass out of my face, I won't serve you any more scotch." I thought it strange at the time that JJ considered my comment absolutely hilarious, then he spilled his scotch-on-the-rocks down the back of my neck and hugged me for the third time. There were very few folks that I would allow to get close to me physically in those days. In fact, JJ knew what he was doing—he was playfully exposing my insecurity, as he would let me know soon enough.

In spite of a few complaints, the bar did finally secure at 0600 sharp. Reveille was at 1200 hours.

During the next couple of days, Compton, Doc, and I worked on intel-related tasks and extended the intel room by knocking out an inner wall. Chief Bassett and Same rewired the officers' quarters adjacent to our intel room. Lieutenant Fletcher departed for Taiwan on a five-day R&R, leaving "Killer" Trung Uy Kleehammer in charge. We were in good hands, though.

We continued to attend tae kwon do lessons with Captain Kim almost every afternoon. Most of us who took the lessons continued to bruise our bones and muscles—especially on our forearms and shins—during those two-to three-hour workouts. Some days we wrapped our hands and wrists with Ace bandages to protect our previous injuries and reduce the pain during the workout. After our workout, Hayden, Knepper, Chambo, Compton, Same, Waneous, Barron, and I would head immediately for our well-supplied bar to purchase a minimum of three ice-cold beers. We would apply one cold can of beer to our external wounds and chin-chin the other two beers for our internal ones. Our remedy sure as thunder beat Doc Holmes's remedy of two salt tablets or a malaria pill. By the time we went through the three-can sequence four or five times, the pain was miraculously gone. With our new-found strength, we worked each other over with our latest tae kwon do moves.

October third was the South Vietnamese election day. All U.S. personnel were restricted to their bases. U.S. intelligence reports stated that the following few days would be the most critical for the Vietnamese government. No one knew for sure what the results would be. Many truck-loads of Vietnamese left Dong Tam for My Tho that day, heading to their assigned voting booths. Same and I did not even consider any clandestine use of CS gas on our Vietnamese brothers as they drove by our barracks. There was always a better time and place for that.

For the remainder of the morning, November Platoon's tae kwon do group worked out under Captain Kim's care-ful tutelage while Killer, Lieutenant (jg) Wright, the se-nior chief, and the rest of the guys played volleyball. Naturally, by evening everyone was properly motivated to take care of his external and internal wounds. Because Senior Chief Bassett was barkeep for the evening, that left me free to pester JJ.

Later, after much posturing and humorous dialogue be-tween JJ and myself, I asked him a leading question: "JJ, what would you say if I told you that I'm farsighted?"

He looked at me for a second, grinned and opined, "You don't like me getting up close to you, do you, Smitty?" Without waiting for me to answer, he continued, "Have you ever heard of the eighteen-inch security bubble?"

"The only bubble I know about is your woolly head that's always before me," I teased as I playfully threw a few hooks and jabs at his ears and nose.

"You dummy, don't you understand that I've been try-ing to penetrate your eighteen-inch bubble ever since I got here?" JJ exclaimed prior to breaking out into his unique, hearty laughter.

I turned to Bassett, winked and said, "Chief, give JJ another double scotch-on-the-rocks. I'm buying."

I leaned over close to JJ's face and replied in a low tone, "Well, I think you have the right question, but the wrong answer. You see, when I was in the seventh grade, I had an English teacher who became infuriated every time she caught me gazing out the schoolroom windows, dreaming of running trap lines in Alaska's hinterlands. She was well aware of my love for the outdoors, and hated it. The problem was simple. I wanted to learn about trapping, and she wanted to teach me about syntax and sentence diagramming. The end result was that I temporarily forgot about trapping while she beat me severely about my head and shoulders with an eighteen-inch ruler."

I stopped talking long enough to down my Cuba libra, then continued, "Naturally for the short term, I regained a new interest in syntax and sentence diagramming. However, she loved to look hard into my eyes and get her ugly nose right up to mine for a while before she started whaling away at me. Her tactic absolutely unnerved me. Ever since then, I've been wary of folks who try to get up close, and especially in my face."

Doctor JJ got a sick look on his face. I couldn't tell if the cause was my story or his eight double and two double-double scotches.

Continuing, I went on to explain, "When someone gets real close to me, my subconscious takes over and he becomes that female English teacher. I expect her to begin pounding on me with that damn ruler. What I disliked the most was her intimidation, and my dread of that first swat—and I don't mean a sucker punch either—it would have been much kinder," I summarized as I wiped my eyes.

I looked sadly down at the floor, stepped on Bassett's stogie butt with the toe of my unpolished jungle boot, then looked up and straight into JJ's black eyes. I concluded my story by saying, "I don't want to live in the past, I just don't want to forget the lessons learned."

Doc had swallowed the whole works: hook, line, and sinker. "Oh surely, you don't think—" JJ cried incredulously.

I reached over and placed my arm around his brawny neck. "It's okay, JJ. You don't have to worry about me smacking you with a stick. Because you're my buddy, I would keep my distance and tell you, in a spirit of love, what I was going to do just before I used my fists and feet on you. That way, I wouldn't leave you wondering when I was going to discipline you. How do you like me so far?" I teased, then broke out into a gut-bustin' hee-haw.

JJ responded by grabbing my right hand from around his neck, quickly twisting it, kicking my feet out from under me and knocking me down on my knees before I could scream "carpetbagger."

"Never, never, ever tell a man when you're going to work him over. I'm now going to give you your first lesson, in a spirit of love, in a basic manipulative hold to enhance your shoddy tae kwon do. How do you like me so far?"

Not being in a position to argue, I tried another tack by pleading my case. "Damn, Doc, I already know how to bite off noses and ears, poke out eyes, crush throats, and shatter kneecaps, not to mention how to shoot 'em at long and short ranges and blow up the survivors! What more do I need to know?"

Doctor JJ smiled down at me and answered, "Finesse."

After that, JJ and I became even closer friends. Neither one of us ever mentioned the eighteen-inch-bubble thing again—there really wasn't any need to as far as I was concerned. I never did tell him that I made up the story either. And, oh yes, he did teach me some good judo moves and how to use a straight razor clandestinely. That was what I called finesse—slicing your Communist enemies wide open without them even knowing it until it was too late.

Over the years, I've often wished that I had more good, honest mates like JJ. My granddad Smith, who died in '43, was fond of saying, "You're a mighty lucky man if you gain a total of two or three true friends in a lifetime." I've been a little luckier than that, but my grandpa knew what he was talking about.

October fourth proved to be a day of organization and preparation for that unknown operation that was sure to come. Captain Campbell called by secure voice and notified us that Ba To's hamlet had been under heavy attack during the night by units of the VC/NVA 267B Sapper, 309F Heavy Weapons, and 261A Infantry Main Force battalions. The VC units managed to blow up Ba To's command bunker with several 75mm recoilless rifle HE rounds, damaged the hamlet's only half-kilowatt generator, and killed several of Ba To's PSDF men—People's Self-Defense Forces: government hamlet militia composed mostly of old men and boys. In general, they tried to wipe his little Hoa Hao hamlet off the map.

Captain Campbell also told us that Ba To had some good operational information for us and that he badly needed 40mm HE, 40mm para flares, and handheld pop flares. I told him that I would do my best to get the supplies that Ba To needed plus an M-60 machine gun. I immediately requested that Captain Campbell arrange for the sector Huey slick to take Doc, Mojica, and me to and from Ba To's hamlet on the morning of October sixth.

Later, I asked Petty Officer First Class Mojica—we called him Mo—to be my interpreter during the visit to Ba To's hamlet. I knew that Mo could speak the southern and northern Vietnamese dialects perfectly, and, most important, I knew that I wouldn't have to worry about the Sam Giang district chief confiscating the ordnance and/or M-60 machine gun from Ba To and his strategic hamlet. Mojica was only too glad to accompany me, and understood the urgency of the situation. Mo was a very valuable man to have around.

Mojica had become a legend among the SEAL and MST folks over the years. Mobile Support Team's home command was Boat Support Unit-1 of Naval Operations Support Group 1, located at the Naval Amphibious Base, Coronado, California, and Mo had served with MST in 1967 at Nha Be when I was with SEAL Team 1's Foxtrot Platoon. MST had delivered us from some tight situations in the T-10 area of the Rung Sat Special Zone.

By October 1971, Mojica had been in 'Nam for approximately seven years. He had married a very cute, petite Vietnamese lady—who was also of the Hoa Hao faith—and had a gaggle of kids. Mo had also spent a couple of tours with SOG—a special operations outfit cover named Studies and Observation Group—at the spook base in Da Nang from '64 to '66 as a crewman on the Norwegian-built "Nasty" class, eighty-foot PTF boats, which could speed along at a cool forty-five knots. As a crewman, he had some very interesting experiences north of the DMZ.

Later, we had tae kwon do practice from 1630 to 1830 hours. It was a long, hard, and hot workout. Because Captain Kim was a very good instructor, most of us were doing very well.

The next morning, I got up early and put together a cleaning kit for the M-60 machine gun for Ba To. Later, Doc, Compton, and I worked on our newest Dinh Tuong province enemy OB situation map with overlays.

After lunch, Same and I went down to our two ord-

nance conex boxes and completed staging all of the ordnance that Doc, Mo, and I would be taking to Ba To's
hamlet the following day. The list was as follows: two
cases of 40 mm HE (144 rounds), one case of M18A1
antipersonnel claymore mines (six each), 40 mm white
para flares (40 rounds), miscellaneous fragmentation grenades; smoke mini-grenades, CS mini-grenades, 3,000
rounds of 7.62mm linked ball ammo for the M-60, etc. It
was little enough, I thought.

At 1645 hours Same and I worked on our third tae
kwon do pattern until 1800 hours. At approximately 2000
hours, the Sam Giang district subsector, at Vinh Kim village, came under heavy attack. From our stairway, we
watched and listened to that night's action, which was
taking place approximately five to six kilometers northwest of Dong Tam. We couldn't help but wonder how
Major Bigelow, Captain Campbell, and the rest of the
Army boys were doing. There were a lot of mortar and
rocket explosions and small arms fire and tracers going
everywhere. There were at least two Huey gunships and
one Night Hawk—a Huey with a large spotlight—
circling the village. It was a great night for operating—it
was raining.

The sixth of October was to be a long and interesting
day. After breakfast, I spent a few minutes preparing my
field gear for Hayden's operation that night.

By 0830 Doc Holmes, Mojica, and I had loaded the assorted ordnance and M-60 machine gun aboard the sector
ship, a Huey slick, and landed near Ba To's war-torn
hamlet. Ba To and his followers were happy and excited
to see us. The feelings were mutual. Their smiles got
brighter when they saw all of the ordnance and the M-60
being off-loaded. It was good to hear that Ba To's immediate family hadn't suffered any casualties.

After things had settled down some, and while Doc

Holmes was compassionately caring for the hamlet folks' medical needs, I introduced Mojica to Ba To. There was an instant admiration and respect between them. Without further ado, I paid Ba To 16,000 piasters ($58.18) for his services during August and September. After he had peeked inside the sealed envelope, his grin got even bigger. Suddenly, hope showed in his eyes for his small Hoa Hao village.

Afterward, Ba To told Mo and me that he knew the exact location of the VCI's South Cai Lay district HQ. Ba To's defection-in-place action agent—no doubt a Hoa Hao—would rendezvous with us and guide us to the VCI HQ. His only requirement was that we pay him 20,000 piasters immediately after the operation. His bona fides would be based on the success of the operation and his willingness to Chieu Hoi to the Vietnamese authorities. The source also stated that he would have to bring out his wife and four children.

I was careful to have Mojica explain to Ba To that we were very interested and that I didn't think there would be any problems getting the 20,000 piasters or getting the informant and his family safely out of the area. I also told him that first I needed the approval of my superiors, and that I would notify him as soon as possible. Shortly afterward, when Doc finished issuing his plentiful supply of salt tablets and malaria pills, we returned to Dong Tam in time for lunch. However, there was little time for eating.

RM2 Roger Hayden presented his first combat warning order as a patrol leader at 1300 hours. Roger demonstrated good self-confidence, control, and follow-through. His basic briefing went as follows:

A. He presented a brief statement of the enemy and friendly situation in the vicinity of the target at grid coordinates XS078585.

B. The mission was the interdiction of a ten- to thirteen-man unit of the VC Dong Thap 1st Regiment Rear Services unit and their staging area.

C. General Instructions:

1. Personal gear: strobe light with different colored lenses, penlite, snaplink with Swiss seat, Sylva compass, K-bar knife with MK-13 day/night flare, morphine styrette, two quarts water, two LRRPs, water purification tablets, first-aid kit, para flares and smoke grenades, minifrag and mini-CS grenades, etc.

2. Personnel assignments and specific duties:

First Fire Team:

BM2 Knepper, point, M-16/XM-148 rifle/grenade launcher, prisoner handling gear

RM2 Hayden, P/L, M-60 machine gun (heavy), serum albumin

HM1 Holmes, radioman, XM-177E2, PRC-77 radio with extra battery and handset

SN Eberle, rear security, Stoner machine gun (heavy), serum albumin

Chief Muoi, two PSB operatives, and Son, M-16s

Second Fire Team:

RM1 Smith, point, M-16/XM-148 rifle/grenade launcher with Singlepoint, prisoner handling gear

EM2 Chamberlain, APL, M-60 machine gun (heavy), serum

RMSN Compton, radioman, Stoner machine gun (light), PRC-77 radio with extra battery and handset

EMFN Same, rear security, Stoner machine gun (heavy)

Three PSB operatives, M-16s

3. Visual Recon by PL and APL that morning.

4. Time Schedules:

a. Visual Reconnaissance: 0900–1000H

b. PLO: 1930–2030H

c. Equipment check: 2130H

d. Depart for Seawolves helo pad and rehearsals: 2145H

e. Depart Dong Tam: 2200H

f. Arrive target: 2230H

g. Depart target: 2315H

h. Arrive Cai Be: 2330H

i. Arrive Dong Tam: 2345H

j. Debrief at SEAL hootch: 0015H, all personnel involved

At 1930 hours, Hayden presented his patrol leader's order as follows:

I. Situation:

A. Enemy forces: covered earlier.

B. Weather: probable rain.

C. Terrain: targeted hootches surrounded by rice paddies. One small canal running between the hootches. The closest tree line is located 600 meters to left flank with another approximately 1,200 meters to our right.

D. Identification: Dong Thap 1st Rear Services cadre/guerrillas staging area.

E. Location: grid coordinates XS078585.

F. Enemy activity: source says the guerrillas have had a nasty habit of harassing the villagers and their PSDF (People's Self-Defense Force).

G. Enemy strength: ten to thirteen ugly Communist pigs with eight AK-47s, one M-16, one SKS, and one K-54.

H. Source of information: Chief Muoi, PSB, Cai Be Subsector. Enemy OB was cross-checked with our platoon's enemy OB situation map with overlays and files.

I. Friendly forces:

1. ARVN outpost: XS062584, XS062590,

XS062598, XS088598, and XS100580, and Chief Muoi with five PSB operatives plus Son, our interpreter.

2. U.S. Navy: two Seawolves and two Sea Lord slicks from HAL-3; and two Black Ponies with Smitty's old mate and mentor Lt. (jg) Sam from VAL-4.

II. Mission: Assault and destroy the Dong Thap 1's Rear Services cadre (10–13 armed men) and their staging area.

III. Execution:

A. Concept of operation:

1. Flight plan: The Black Ponies will rendezvous with us near the target. Our Seawolves and Sea Lords will follow Route 66 (Kinh Song My Tho) to QL-4 (national highway) until it turns south at the Cai Lay/Cai Be district line. From there we will take a straight azimuth of 315 degrees for 12$\frac{1}{2}$ klicks to the vicinity of our target. The Black Ponies will vector our helos to the vicinity of the target and drop para flares directly over our target just before our insertion. Time at the target shouldn't be more than forty-five minutes.

2. Insertion: The slicks will come in abreast on an azimuth of 230 degrees and insert both squads no more than fifty meters from the targeted hootches, which will be at twelve o'clock. First fire team will set a frontal skirmish line and take the right flank, while second fire team does the same on the left, keeping in mind that the small canal is between the two hootches. Once one of us exits the helo, then all must exit the helo.

Son, our interpreter, will *lai day!* the hootches. If the folks don't come out, Knepper and Smitty will move forward and throw CS grenades inside the hootches and return to their positions. At that point, we'll wait until something happens. When I give the word, we'll move forward and set up for hootch search and seizure. After the hootches are cleared, we'll search the surrounding areas for any hidden VC or documents.

    3. Extraction: We'll move approximately 200 meters on an azimuth of 090 degrees and set up our two standard H formations for helo extraction. All eight corners will be marked with blue-lens-covered strobe lights. And finally, all of us will extract or none of us will extract. If one guy can't make it, then none of us will.

    4. Actions at danger areas: SOPs.

    5. Actions upon enemy contact: return fire with a maximum rate of fire followed by fire and movement, fire and maneuver (leapfrog by fire team) to our extraction point.

    6. Rally point: extraction point.

    7. E&E: 135 degrees for 12½ klicks to high-way QL-4.

    B. Coordinating Instructions:

        Area of Operations: cleared through Subsector for seventy-two hours.

  IV. Administration and Logistics:

    A. Ammo and equip: Covered in warning order.

    B. Casualty plan: Set security around the wounded and/or dead and call for maximum fire support and extraction. No one will be left behind dead or living.

    C. Prisoner plan: SOPs.

        1. First fire team: Knepper and Eberle

        2. Second fire team: Smitty and Chambo

  V. Command and Signal:

    Radio comm plan:

Unit/Call sign	Pri Freq	Sec Freq
Cai Be Subsector/Amateur Papa	36.75	56.60
Black Ponies/Roper Lion 1	36.75	60.60
Seawolves/Roper Lion 2	36.75	60.60
Sea Lords/Paper Lion	36.75	60.60

At 2239 hours the Black Ponies dropped two one-million candlelight flares just prior to our insertion. At 2240 we inserted as planned before the two enemy hootches. For some reason, second fire team's PSB operatives failed to immediately tell the inhabitants of our hootch to "come out." I quickly yelled, *"Lai de! Toi day! Mau len!"* (Come here! Come forward! Hurry up!) Still no one came out. I hollered my message again and fired a few rounds through the thatched roof. Still there was no response.

I pulled a mini-CS grenade from my vest, looked at Chambo for his approval, because he was the assistant patrol leader, and went forward to the door of the hootch. I threw the grenade inside. After I had returned to our skirmish line, the wind shifted and blew the CS gas toward us. Chambo ordered everyone to move to right flank a few meters. Within a minute or so three women and five small children emerged from the hootch, crying and vomiting. Our PSB operatives immediately went into action and motioned for the women and children to come to our position.

In short order the Vietnamese PSB boys found out that the VCI Rear Services folks had departed the two hootches and headed northeast just prior to our insertion.

Roger Hayden decided that we should form a wide frontal skirmish line and move northeast toward two other structures that might be filled with Communists. During our eerie, shadowed march through chest-deep water, we received word that the Seawolves were making a firing run. I instantly became concerned and asked Compton, the radioman, to find out if the run would be with miniguns or five-inch/2.75-inch rockets, and at what distance and direction from our position. No word was passed back, and I was soon to find out why.

First fire team was also in water up to their chests when Doc Holmes let out a mixture of screams and groans.

Eberle, who was forward of Doc, turned around ready to shoot whatever was killing Doc when he saw our compassionate doctor throw Roger Hayden's broken M-60 down into the water. With that, Doc let out another series of screeches and moans while pulling at his genitals.

Crap! I thought. There can't be saltwater crocs this far inland! Maybe it's a python.

Eberle thought that Doc might need more than a couple of salt tablets, and asked him what was wrong.

Doc looked at Eb with eyes filled with horror and replied in an almost uncontrollable voice, "I've got two huge leeches hanging on my crank! Oooohhhhhh, shit. I hate these blood-sucking pud suckers! Eeeeiiiioooohhhhhh."

There was little we could do for poor Doc at that time. I waded over to him, retrieved Roger's M-60 from the bottom of the pond, and handed it back to Roger. All of us were fighting to control our laughter.

While Doc continued screeching, we moved forward to the second set of hootches, our secondary target. Hayden had the Seawolves begin their firing runs just behind our targeted hootches from three to nine o'clock, in hopes of killing any escapees, and to act as a blocking element. The two hootches were at twelve o'clock from our position. The gunship's 7.62mm GAU-2 electric miniguns, .50-caliber machine guns, and 2.75-inch rockets started impacting from thirty meters to two hundred meters from our skirmish line. When the Seawolves had finished their runs, one of the PSB operatives fired a 40mm HE round into a hootch. Naturally, Knepper and I got into the foray and launched a few 40mm HEs into the hootch also. After we had let off a little steam, the PSB boys searched the hootch, with negative results. To make matters worse, the Sea Lord slicks notified Hayden that they were running low on fuel and that we would have to extract or patrol out of the area for 12½ klicks. After considering our options, Roger took only a picosecond to request our extraction.

Hayden directed us to patrol northwest for fifty meters and set up our two H formations. The Sea Lords arrived with their spotlights searching for our H formations, but, because of the para flares, our blue-lens-covered strobe lights were very difficult for the helo crew to see. Since Doc was indisposed, Compton took up the slack and vectored the slicks to our position on his PRC-77 radio.

After our uneventful extractions, we flew to Cai Be district's subsector and dropped off Chief Muoi and his five men. From there we had to fly to Vinh Long province to refuel at the U.S. Army base before returning to Dong Tam.

Once we had returned to our barracks, Doc immediately stripped and inspected the damage done to his dork.

"Doc, did you learn anything?" I asked Holmes as I handed him a four-shot hundred-proof Old Granddad bourbon whiskey straight with no ice.

Doc looked up at me and said emphatically, "Yeah! I'll never wear any more button-type Levi's in the field again. I hate Levi's!" Doc grabbed the large dose of whiskey and downed it in one gulp.

CHAPTER TEN

... war has its own particular characteristics and in this sense it cannot be equated with politics in general.... When politics develops to a certain stage beyond which it cannot proceed by the usual means, war breaks out to sweep the obstacles from the way.... When the obstacle is removed and our political aim attained, the war will stop. But if the obstacle is not completely swept away, they will have to continue till the aim is fully accomplished.... It can therefore be said that politics is war without bloodshed, while war is politics with bloodshed.

—Mao Tse-tung,
"On Protracted War," 1938

The next few days were spent preparing for Knepper's op in Kien Hoa province and Doc's and my op in Cai Lay district, Dinh Tuong province. As always, Cai Lay district's Major Kaike (DSA) and Captain Campbell (DIOCC adviser) were very supportive and encouraging.

Tae kwon do practice continued on schedule. One afternoon, Same got carried away and managed to hit me directly on the left side of my upper lip, causing my teeth to break through to the outside. We continued as if nothing had happened. Later, while I was sparring with Captain Kim, I jammed my thumb and index finger on my right hand. I had to wrap both of my hands before the next day's practice and hope Same didn't pop me in the mouth again.

On October tenth Knepper gave his warning order and patrol leader's order. He did a fine job. Later that night, Knepper, Hayden, Chambo, Same, and Tam were inserted in Ham Long district, Kien Hoa province by Lieutenant (jg) Washburn and his faithful MST crew. I didn't go because of a sudden Asian flu bug that affected all of November Platoon at one time or another during that tour. That particular type of flu caused all platoon personnel to squirt out of both ends for a period of two to three days. It was a miserable illness, but paradoxically, the victim's condition was amusing for everyone else. The ground below our stairways was splattered with vomit and, during emergencies, refuse from the south end of the body. No doubt our Vietnamese comrades below didn't appreciate the stench or the mess.

When it was Roger Hayden's turn to get sick, he begged "Bad Medicine" Doc tearfully, "Doc, you've got to do something for me! I'm dying! I hurt something awful. Give me a shot of anything to help me . . . please."

Bad Medicine looked unmercifully into Roger's bloodshot, pleading eyes and replied, "There's nothing wrong with you, you wimp! Take two salt tablets and drink a glass of water."

Poor Roger did his best to sit up in his top rack, and with a face filled with frustration and rage, he yelled, "You $#&!*#& SOB! If I could get out of this rack, I'd kick your &#?!%*$@# ass and %$&#! in the hole!"

It was one of the most hilarious situations I and a half dozen bystanders had ever seen. Of course, all of us encouraged Roger by whining like little puppy dogs. As we were always told in UDT training, "The only easy day was yesterday!" However, within thirty-six hours Roger had almost totally recovered from the flu. Maybe Bad

Medicine's salt tablets did do some good after all, I thought.

The next morning Doc, Mojica, and I took a 60mm mortar, eight cases of 60mm illumination rounds, two cases of 40mm HE rounds, and one case of M-18A1 claymore antipersonnel mines to Ba To and his hamlet. As always, it was good to see Ba To. His people had managed to repair their command bunker and had gotten the generator working again.

Early that afternoon, Knepper and the guys returned about 1430 from their operation in Kien Hoa. They abducted three people: one old man of about fifty, his wife of thirty-three, and a younger woman. The old man was a member of a local VC assassination unit, according to the Phuong Huong committee's blacklist.

Shortly after Knepper and crew returned, Lieutenant Todd, the Det Golf OIC, arrived from Binh Thuy. His task was to present to us Commodore Spruett's (CTF 116) policies of our new "rules of engagement." Basically, we could no longer go on any offensive operations. We were not to open fire on any enemy units except to defend ourselves after being fired upon first. Lieutenant Todd was a messenger bearing bad news, but we were smart enough not to blame him for the new restrictions.

Initially, all of us were very angry and upset because of the new and very restrictive rules of engagement. Apparently, NavForV and SpecWar staff were terrified that SEAL team personnel might commit some type of horrible atrocity before we withdrew from South Vietnam. Considering the worsening attitudes and frustrations of November and Oscar platoons, Staff's fears were not totally unfounded.

After Lieutenant Todd had departed for Binh Thuy, Dai Uy called an all hands (MST included) meeting in our bar. Lieutenant Fletcher explained that everything seemed to deteriorate when he sent a memo to Commodore Spruett via Det Golf, stating that approximately twenty percent of our operations were being compromised due to the requirement of clearing our AOs through the government channels at Sector and Subsector. Commodore Spruett forwarded Dai Uy's memo to Admiral Salzer (NavForV) via SpecWar in Saigon. The admiral commented that if we thought our operations were compromised, then don't operate. Furthermore, we were informed that we would not be allowed to utilize helos for combat insertions. Such operations were considered direct assaults and not clandestine SEAL-type operations. It appeared to me that the rules of engagement were intentionally ambiguous. Dai Uy Fletcher concluded by saying, "That means we will pretty well shut down except for Bright Light ops."

We all agreed with our platoon commander. The remainder of our time in-country would be spent practicing tae kwon do, traveling to Cam Ranh Bay, attending Communications Security School at Nha Be, and so on.

The next day, October twelfth, Doc, Mojica, and I took another load of ordnance and fifteen hundred rounds of 7.62mm linked ammo to Ba To's hamlet. We didn't tell Ba To that we had been basically shut down operationally. As luck would have it, Ba To informed us that his action agent had decided to wait a few more weeks before coming out. I then explained to him that no helos would be available for some time due to extensive structural testing, which precluded us from going on any more missions in the near future. Everything worked out fine except that the sector ship wasn't due to return until 1600. Doc, Mojica, and I walked the two or three miles to Subsector and called for the guys to come and get us.

Later, during tae kwon do practice, I tore the skin off the bottoms of my feet. Immediately after practice, we knew it was time for another healing session with the inevitable three cans of ice-cold beer—one for the wound and two for the gullet. As it turned out, it was a night for everyone's hedonistic spiritual and physical healings.

On our trip to Saigon the following morning, Doc caught the right side of our jeep's windshield on a Vietnamese five-ton truck while trying to pass it on the narrow QL-4 highway. For a second I was certain that I would eat part of our windshield and defunct rearview mirror. After Doc pulled over, I got into the driver's seat and drove us safely to Nha Be. There, we checked on our platoon pay records, ate lunch on the Navy's APL-30, dropped Eberle and Little Bear off at SpecWar, and went to the PX at Tan Son Nhut.

Later, when we were between Cholon and Ben Luc on our way to Dong Tam, our jeep stopped running. Fortunately, we caught a ride with a Navy Seabee, who took us to SEAL Team 1's Mike Platoon at Ben Luc, in Long An province. With a little fancy talk, we convinced Chief Norton to tow our jeep to their hootch and give us a ride to Dong Tam. By the time we had returned to Dong Tam, without our stolen jeep, it was almost dark. As it turned out, we never did get our jeep back from Mike Platoon— they sold it to the Vietnamese.

About noon on October nineteenth Lieutenant Todd called and told Dai Uy that he had good firsthand Bright Light (U.S. POW) information, and that a Sea Lord slick would arrive at our location within the hour to fly us to Binh Thuy. By 1600 hours Lieutenant Todd, Dai Uy, Trung Uy Kleehammer, and I had flown to Bac Lieu city and were briefed by the local naval intelligence liaison officer.

The Navy lieutenant gave us an overview of the situation. He told us that several South Vietnamese ARVNs had escaped the previous day from a VC POW camp that was well-hidden within the forbidding Dam Doi Secret Zone. The ARVN escapees had seen one U.S. Army staff sergeant who was being held at that camp. Other sources confirmed that the staff sergeant was indeed a POW; however, no one was able to recruit informants who had access to the targeted coastal areas—those areas were almost totally controlled by the VC/NVA. There were several immediate disadvantages to our mission: (1) the government sector and probably subsector knew about the ARVN escapees, which meant that the VC were forewarned and forearmed; (2) the information was already over twenty-four hours old at that time; (3) the VC had always moved U.S. POWs to another location within hours of previous escapes; and (4) if the U.S. Army and Vietnamese ARVNs became involved, the whole operation would certainly be compromised before any of us left Sector. Essentially the SEALS probably wouldn't have the benefit of tactical surprise if we decided to try to rescue the staff sergeant. As it turned out, there were even more formidable problems.

Our NILO lieutenant then took us to the sector S-2 adviser, a U.S. Army major, for the sobering enemy order of battle surrounding the POW camp. There were approximately six hundred VC/NVA Main and Local forces within the Secret Zone. There were massive reinforced bunker complexes that ringed the POW camp. Even though the combined VC/NVA forces were undergoing training and reprovisioning, they would have been a formidable force to deal with on their home grounds. The Bac Lieu sector's ARVNs and an ARVN 21st Infantry Division regiment had already refused to go into the Secret Zone. To make matters worse, the POW camp was surrounded by mangrove swamps and covered by thick jungle canopy. It looked like a stacked deck to me; however, the decision was not ours to make. Our U.S. and Vietnamese superiors elected not to allow November Platoon to attempt to rescue the American POW.

Dai Uy, Killer, and I were a quiet group during our return flight back to Dong Tam that evening. Apparently, we were all wondering what that staff sergeant would have done in our place.

Two days later, HAL-3, VAL-4, and SEAL Team 1 were presented the Vietnam government's Unit Commendation ribbon and pennant with palm wreath and gold star, respectively. I had the honor of being the guidon for SEAL Team 1.

After our return to Dong Tam, November Platoon's tae kwon do crew practiced our patterns and free-sparred for a couple of hours. The following day we would be tested on our tae kwon do techniques, physical conditioning, and proficiency by Captain Kim and Lee. If we passed the tests, we would be awarded blue belts.

The morning of October twenty-second began by field-daying (i.e., thoroughly cleaning) the barracks and surrounding areas. Several of the guys and I later worked on intelligence files and plotted Green Hornet (enemy radio transmission) positions on our situation maps with overlays until 1600 hours, when we secured for tae kwon do warm-up.

Captain Kim and Lee arrived at 1700 hours, gave a short introduction, and started our testing inside the extremely hot and humid metal Butler building. Each two-man pair was required to go through each pattern on command, followed by one-step sparring. After all four pairs were finished, Captain Kim had each pair free-spar for thirty seconds, rest thirty seconds, then free-spar for one more minute. After a short rest he had us start over again and free-spar for another thirty seconds. When we had completed all that was required, Captain Kim collected fifteen dollars from each of us for our blue belts and rating cards, which he would issue a few days later.

Until then, none of us would know what degree blue belt we had earned.

During the morning of October twenty-third, Lieutenant (jg) Wright was notified by SpecWar in Saigon that a five-ton truck would arrive at our location within the hour to load all of Oscar Platoon's 2nd Squad and their gear for transit to Tan Son Nhut, where they would rendezvous with Lieutenant (jg) Walsh's 1st Squad. On the following day, Oscar Platoon would depart for CONUS via Air Force C-130 to the Philippines, followed by the Navy's VR-21 to NAS, North Island, Coronado, California. By 1300 hours Lieutenant (jg) Wright, BUC Jim Harris, and boys had departed for Saigon. I, for one, hated to see JJ and the guys depart—we enjoyed their company. Our barracks seemed strangely quiet and empty.

Same, Compton, and I spent the next few days working on intel matters, situation maps and overlays, while Senior Chief Bassett kept the remainder of the hell-raising rabble busy building November Platoon and MST a screened-in lounge between our barracks for evening flicks. The new lounge was also conveniently located next to our large bunker, for the occasions when our VC/NVA Communist adversaries rudely interrupted our movies with their 82mm HE mortar rounds.

On the evening of October twenty-seventh Captain Kim presented Same, Hayden, Waneous, and me with the fifth-degree blue belts. Our next belt to earn would be the fourth-degree brown. Knepper, Compton, and Barron received the sixth-degree blue belts. After Captain Kim presented us with our blue belts, he had us free-sparing, one-step sparing, and doing rapid executions of our patterns to sweat out any false sense of tae kwon do expertise. By the time he was done with us, we only had enough strength to drag our sweat-drenched, smelly bodies to our bar. It was fortunate for us that Captain Kim had departed—after several repetitions of our two-and-one medicine, everyone was ready to take on the VC Dong Thap One regiment barehanded. Such were the pitfalls of SpecWar youth during those last Vietnam War days.

Little Bear "Guano" was acting especially gloatful and insolent. He slithered over to Senior Chief Bassett, placed his smelly armpit around Bassett's shoulders and commented, "Senior Chief, you should start working out with us tae kwon do warriors for a change—it might give you a little backbone."

The omniscient Bassett instinctively knew what Seaman Little Bear was leading to. Instead of becoming defensive, the senior chief went along with Bear's game and replied with an easygoing question. "Why is that, Guano?"

"Well, you're so swaybacked that every time you do push-ups, you get grass burns on your belly," answered Little Bear in a spirit of effrontery, swagger, and superiority. My tae kwon do brothers and I were aghast at Guano's first-degree felony attempt at character assassination, and quickly collared him with the intention of disciplining our own and protecting him from the certain wrath of our senior chief.

After we had received our blue belts, Captain Kim sternly warned us to maintain discipline within our ranks and to demonstrate a humble attitude toward those who didn't believe in or understand the Korean doctrine and methodology of tae kwon do. Captain Kim summarized his admonition by saying, "I will personally hold all of you accountable to the code."

"Guano" had self-righteously violated the code within a couple of hours of Captain Kim's warning. Bear's flippant disrespect toward our platoon chief not only dishonored our chief, but his irreverence also cast a shadow on Captain Kim and ourselves. His disobedience of our strict code required the immediate application of "the letter of the law." A little blood wouldn't do any harm, either. The tae kwon do clan quickly appointed me the trial judge to charge "Guano" with his crime. This procedure was one of the techniques peculiar to November Platoon.

I gave Little Bear a stern look in the spirit of Judge Roy Bean of the Pecos and accordingly judged, "What you say is true, Guano. For by your words you shall be judged, and by your words you shall be condemned. First, you must always *outwardly* demonstrate respect and submissiveness for our rotund senior chief in spite of the obscene 'spray-tube' that bulges over his belt buckle." Known as Dunlap's disease: my belly dun' lapped over my belt buckle. "Second, what is *inside* your deceitful heart must be kept secret at all costs. You not only revealed that your motive was to murder Senior Chief's character, but, more important, you exposed the tae kwon do clan for what we are—a brood of vipers. To summarize, control of the latter—*inside*—is the means by which the former—*outside*—is achieved."

Because combat missions weren't always available, our platoon desperately needed a substitute, and soon. If we took out our frustrations about the war and the U.S. political situation on our U.S. Navy neighbors and gave them a sound drubbing, they would eventually throw us into the brig with the Marine "turnkeys," assuming they could catch us. If we took out our frustrations on our South Vietnamese brothers on a Friday, they would probably wait until Monday and sentence us to steal a couple of U.S. vehicles and an air conditioner or two for them and their homes. However, we had more respect for our South Vietnamese comrades than we did for our liberal politicians, media, and long-haired college hippies.

The only option was to take out our frustrations on each other. November Platoon's justification was: (1) we had to honor our own code—"the more you sweat in peace, the less you bleed in war"; (2) certain SpecWar admin'ers couldn't care less what we did to each other as long as we didn't embarrass them; and (3) a good knock-down, drag-out was simply a lot of fun and good for cleansing the heart. Because we were somewhere between war and peace, we thought, almost anything goes. As always, it was understood that no one was to be killed or seriously maimed.

With that in mind, I continued with assurance from below and with fearlessness from within and went on to say, "Your penalties are as follows: first, you must demonstrate your repentance with confession—that means you must *outwardly* be sorry for what you've done, and that you will become more deceitful and smooth-tongued in the way you exalt yourself in the chief's presence. You must get down on your knees and prostrate yourself before your tae kwon do brothers and apologize for having exposed our self-righteousness, pride, greed, feelings of superiority, and arrogance. Second, for your act of contrition, I sentence you to move your rack above Senior Chief's, so that he will have the convenience of instructing you in good eating habits and dieting methods. Any questions?"

Not surprisingly, Senior Chief didn't care for the thought of getting pissed on every night, among others things.

Little Bear Guano felt that his tae kwon do brothers had betrayed him. "You're nothing more than an apostate!" Guano yelled accurately.

Because I was a little on the small side—only 175 pounds when in 'Nam—and not overly stupid, I made a run for the door. However, it was too late—Guano tackled me at the threshold. In spite of my best efforts, he started dragging me outside of the barracks by my jungle boots. In no time at all I was involuntarily surveying the underwater depths of November Platoon's favorite recreational area—the benjo ditch.

The nearest we came to combat action in the next couple of days was when we received a call from Lieutenant Todd at Binh Thuy. We were ordered to get ready to go in on one of VAL-4's OV-10 Black Ponies that had crashed on the coast of Vinh Binh province.

Everyone was ecstatic. We were at the Seawolf helo pad and ready to go within fifteen minutes. A true cause with a sense of urgency at last! I thought as I tried to tempt Guano into sucker punching Same's left ear while he was tying his boot lace.

Shortly afterward we were notified that a HAL-3 Sea Lord slick had picked up the two downed pilots. A little while later we were told to secure for the evening, but we were to be ready to go in and destroy the Black Pony the following morning.

At 2100 hours we received another call, canceling the next morning's mission. We were very disappointed. Everyone was looking forward to destroying something and getting into a firefight. Our frustration levels were getting bad again.

A few days later, on October thirtieth, Lieutenant (jg) Washburn and his MST men arrogantly challenged Dai Uy, Trung Uy, and the rest of November Platoon to a tournament of volleyball games. The loser was to furnish and serve food and drinks for that evening meal as tribute to the winner. In our view, the stakes were high—our image, our food, and our booze.

The battle began at 1300 hours sharp. Strangely, MST managed to soundly thrash us for the majority of the first dozen games. November Platoon was getting desperate and frustrated. All of us knew that something had to happen soon. November Platoon hated losers—especially when *we* were the losers. Someone once said, "You show me a good loser, and I'll show you a *loser*."

With that in mind, Dai Uy called for muster just outside of hearing range of the gloating Mr. Washburn and his rabble as they continued trumpeting their premature victory. Recognizing that the MST guys were becoming too much like ourselves, Dai Uy offered a plan. "All right men, there's only one way that we might be able to win the tournament. We've got to distract them."

"Yeah! Tell us, Dai Uy! Tell us!" Chambo begged excitedly.

"I've got it! Let's get Senior Chief to take off his blue and gold so that his spray tube hangs over the front of his swim trunks," Little Bear Guano suggested.

Lieutenant Fletcher started grinning, reached down and pulled his UDT swim trunks off and thundered, "We'll razzle and dazzle them like this! Let's go get 'em!"

"Onward to victory!" whooped Lieutenant (jg) Klee-hammer as he cast his swim trunks at the feet of the unimpressed "Bad Medicine."

Within three seconds November Platoon was stripped stark naked. Everyone started shouting gutter-tongued threats, cheering and yelling insults as we danced madly to our positions before the volleyball net.

Incredibly, Washburn and mob didn't seem to pay much attention to our nudity, threats, or insults, but within a couple of hours the volleyball scores put us neck and neck with the MST team. Even Bad Medicine Doc was stumping for us from the sidelines. However, the Vietnamese navy commander of the 21/33 compound robbed us of our victory by sending one of his subordinates to tell Lieutenant Fletcher to report to his CO ASAP.

Dai Uy shook his head sadly and said, "All right, men, put your swim trunks back on." Naturally, everyone bitched and complained about our Vietnamese brothers not having a sense of humor.

Before Fletcher could get into a suitable uniform, one of our U.S. Navy admin'ers, Lieutenant Pliss, came over and, while laughing, told Dai Uy, "Now that you're dressed, everything is okay. The commander didn't want his men and their visiting families exposed to your depraved traits."

Later that evening, one of the U.S. Navy corpsmen came over and asked Bad Medicine Holmes if we were running a nudist colony. After Doc assured him that we weren't supporting any form of a nudist colony and that we were only being creative in trying to win the volleyball tournament, he was told the following story by the visiting corpsman: "I was taking my newly arrived doctor for a familiarization walk around our and the Vietnam navy's compounds. While we were on our way to the PX, I began telling the doctor all about the mad SEALs that live with the Vietnamese. As we reached the 21/33 compound and I was pointing out exactly where you guys lived, we came upon your unique volleyball game. It was hilarious! You guys were running, jumping, yelling, and screaming as if mad. 'Yep, that's the SEALs all right!' I told the doctor. We laughed all the way back to the dispensary."

Later, Senior Chief went to our freezer, dug out a case of steaks, and prepared a great meal for all of the volleyball tournament participants. Naturally, the refreshments were on the house. We were one, big, happy family. And best of all, no one was a loser.

During the next week, I spent a couple of days preparing for Tam's polygraph test. Because I had assigned him as our agent handler for most of our intelligence information nets, I wanted to confirm my suspicions that Tam was in fact working for PSB. Dai Uy agreed and told me to do as I saw fit. I contacted First Lieutenant Larry at 525, where he briefed me as to basic preparations and made an appointment for me with a Mr. Brantley at 170/5 Mai Khai Street, behind the old Annapolis BEQ on Plantation Road in Saigon.

My next step was to meet with Brantley for specific guidance and direction. I arrived at the building, with the usual terrorist grenade screen and carefully stacked sandbags before its entrance, reported to two U.S. Army security personnel and requested to see Mr. Brantley.

Within a couple of minutes Brantley arrived at the lobby and introduced himself by saying, "I've been expecting you." I presented him with my memorandum, formatted questions, dossiers, and organization charts of November Platoon's/Tam's agent nets. He referred me to an examiner named Archie S. I had heard about Archie from various intel community sources. He was a legend in his own time, and had a reputation of being one of the all-time best in his field.

After the initial amenities, Archie and I sat down and began discussing November Platoon's agent nets and specifically Tam, our agent handler. Archie had a masters degree in psychology, was very intelligent, and had a magnetic personality. He instructed me to carefully debrief Tam relative to each question about specific agent/informant intel reports and patterns. Archie cautioned me to carefully and tactfully strive for a sense of complete trust between us—which I had been doing. I had much administrative work ahead of me, and began to feel like an admin'er.

Two days later, on November tenth, I discovered by surreptitious methods that Tam was developing, at our expense, a very desirable agent net through Phu for PSB within the Tan Hoi village of Cai Lay district. I knew that in '69 the PRU/Company and 525 had spent years and beaucoup money attempting to establish unilateral agent nets in that specific area. That was one of the reasons why November Platoon always notified 525 and OSA in advance of the exact location of our next operation. That gave them time to make arrangements for the safety of their agents or to convince us to cancel the op.

Interestingly, during the early summer of 1969, Randy Sheridan, myself, and approximately thirty PRUs spent one night patrolling into the Tan Hoi village where Sao Lam set a klick-long string of five-man groups as blocking elements between the VC/VCIs nighttime homes and their daytime offices/bunker complexes. Their civil and military complexes were generally located within a nearby tree line, carefully camouflaged and reinforced by man-made and naturally thick jungle, nipa palm, brush, and other types of secondary growth.

At first light the VC/VCI began their early walk on a beautiful and peaceful morning to their office in the local tree line. Randy and I and several PRUs were hiding inside a hootch where we had the inhabitants tied, gagged, and guarded in one of its corners. Once we began hearing AK-47 fire from several of the other PRU blocking elements that were a kilometer to the north, the peaceful morning changed rapidly. Within a couple of minutes a male VCI came by our hootch, in a hurry to get to the tree line and safety. One of the PRU hailed the fellow to "come here." The look of terror on the VCI's face would have fit in any horror movie. For a second I felt sorry for him, but he took off running. At a range of only ten yards, one of us shot a fifty-five grain 5.56mm bullet at 3,200 feet per second through his head, probably by accident. The intent was to shoot over his head and capture him, because he was worth more to us alive than dead. The VCI was instantly knocked down in the middle of the path. The projectile entered his left temple and exited just above his right temple. Other than the two small holes, there was no other visible damage.

Amazingly, the unfortunate VCI frantically tried to get back on his feet. However, his equilibrium was a bit off and he could never quite get there. I was amazed because my past experiences had always shown that when a person was hit in the head with a 7.62mm or 5.56mm projectile, the skull disintegrated, leaving a tattered mess of skin, matter, and blood. Sometimes, the brain would be lying on the ground in one unit. If I hadn't witnessed the incident, I wouldn't have believed it. Within another minute one of the PRU shot a bullet through the fellow's heart, thus ending his futile attempt to escape and his hopeless condition. The results of that particular mission were seven VC/VCI killed and seven VCI captured.

CHAPTER ELEVEN

My first wish would be that my military family, and the whole Army, should consider themselves as a band of brothers, willing and ready to die for each other.

—General George Washington,
letter to Henry Knox

During the night of November fourteenth, units of the local VC/NVA 309F Main Force Heavy Weapons Battalion blessed us with over eighty rounds of 82mm HE mortar rounds from four separate locations to confuse the ARVN 7th locating equipment and to delay their 105mm counterartillery fire. The enemy also probed our perimeter unsuccessfully. Fortunately, the mortaring didn't interfere with our nightly flick.

The next day, Waneous and I drove to Saigon, where we returned crypto gear and radio equipment. Later, after we arrived at SpecWar, Lieutenant Morrow told me that SpecWar had officially received word to withdraw all SEAL platoons from Vietnam. I for one was ready to get out of South Vietnam; I'd had enough of the new rules of engagement. The air in the SpecWar staff offices seemed electrified. Everyone was excited and ready to return to Coronado, California, or Little Creek, Virginia, depending upon who was from SpecWar Group 1 or SpecWar Group 2. Lieutenant Todd rode with Waneous and me as far as Ben Luc, where we left him with Mike Platoon. He was to be the last OIC of NavSpecWar's Vietnam Detachment Golf. After we reached Dong Tam and spread the good news, everyone sat around in our bar until late, talking about how great it would be to return to the beautiful Silver Strand.

November seventeenth was one of those days that I dread. Mojica and I loaded the sector Huey slick with cases of ordnance for Ba To's hamlet. During our usual five cups of hot tea with Ba To and his family, Mojica and I explained to the Hoa Hao leader that we were returning to the States to be with our families for a while. I presented him with an envelope containing a few thousand piasters and thanked him for being our faithful friend and comrade. Thankfully, we had very little time for awkward conversation before the sector ships returned from the Vinh Binh subsector. Lord, how I hate good-byes, I thought to myself. Mojica and I shook hands with Ba To and several of his faithful men and quickly loaded the helo. The old man seemed stunned, and stopped smiling when he realized the finality of our departure. As our helo slowly lifted off, I sat down on the edge of the port door while my jungle boots tapped the helo skids nervously. I continued waving at Ba To and his brave Hoa Hao followers even though I wasn't smiling anymore either. Finally, the helo's nose dipped over a flooded rice paddy and gained altitude as we slowly banked to port and over the tiny hamlet below. As that little village disappeared underneath the helo, I knew in my heart that Ba To and his small hamlet would not survive the war much longer.

The next morning, Doc and I loaded the back end of our pickup full of ordnance and drove to the Vinh Kim subsector. Because I was unable to utilize the sector slick for the following few days, I coordinated with Major Bigelow and Captain Campbell and was given permission to leave our last load of ordnance for Ba To's hamlet with them. The ammo, grenades, pop flares, 40mm HE rounds, M-72 LAAWs, 7.62mm belted ball, 5.56mm ball, M-18 claymore mines, and so forth, would be kept in their MACV magazines until Ba To and his men could transfer the ordnance by shanks mare to their hamlet. I also gave Dai Uy Campbell all of our Sam Giang district 1:4,000 split vertical aerial photographic mosaics, maps, and office supplies to aid the professional support of their ARVN counterparts.

About noon, Commanders Schaible and Del Guidice arrived at our barracks from Saigon. Schaible was relieving Del Guidice as the CO of NavSpecWar Group Vietnam. "Captain" Schaible had been my SEAL Team 1 commanding officer from 1968 to 1970. "Captain" Del Guidice had been the CO of the same team from 1962 to 1964.

One of the reasons for their visit was to familiarize Schaible with all of the SEAL platoon locations, potential LDNN and adviser locations and support, platoon morale, etcetera. Captain Schaible was very impressed with November Platoon's intelligence or N-2/S-2 room, and the luxury of our living quarters, lounge/bar, and screened-in outdoor movie theater. Dai Uy managed to get Captain Schaible's permission for our platoon to attend the Vietnamese Airborne School and jump from one of the old C-119 flying boxcars before we departed South Vietnam. Naturally, our motive was to earn Vietnamese jump wings.

I spent most of November nineteenth preparing Tam's debriefing in preparation for his polygraph test. Later that afternoon, November Platoon went to the Seawolves' area and played volleyball until dinnertime. During our drive across Dong Tam, our jeep had another of its many flats. Our platoon first lieutenant, Roger Hayden, was soon tasked by Senior Chief to "take care of the problem."

After dinner, Lieutenant Fletcher, Lieutenant (jg)

Kleehammer, and I were invited to a sector intel community party at Mr. Bai's home in My Tho. Because it was evening and the two routes from Dong Tam to My Tho were subject to road ambushes, Dai Uy twisted Lieutenant (jg) Washburn's arm and convinced him to have his MSSC crew take the three of us to the Cuu Long restaurant, on the edge of the My Tho River near the old U.S. Army 9th "Juicy Fruit Row" beer joints, and wait for us until after the party. Once we were there, we caught a pedicab that took us to Mr. Bai's home.

The party was a slow starter until OSA Al and Jake finally arrived at 1910 hours, followed by Lieutenant Zig (NILO). Eventually several of the 525 crowd arrived, as did Chief Muoi (National Police), Chief Hue (PSB), Province Chief Colonel Dao, the Chieu Hoi adviser, and others. After everyone began to relax and enjoy the hors d'oeuvres and the bar's selections, Lieutenant Zig came over to me and inquired about taking over our intelligence information nets with our dossiers and other files. I assured him that I would assist him in any way I could and that I would leave all dossiers and other material at N-2 with Lieutenant M.

Shortly afterward, OSA Al came over and asked how I authenticated the information I recovered from Phu's two agents. I chuckled and admitted that that was my weakest point. I explained that I was forced to compare their information with other intel reports from 525, S-2, enemy OB, Green Hornet plottings, mosaics, elicitation from Mr. Bai, Sao Lam, the assistant PRU chief, and others. I also told him that Tam and Phu—agent handler and principal agent—were probably working for PSB, but that I wouldn't be able to confirm that until after Tam's polygraph test in Saigon. We then discussed the problems of establishing and managing so-called unilateral intelligence collection nets in South Vietnam and other foreign countries. It was an interesting conversation. I thought of Big John T., who was in 'Nam in '69 and '70. A lot of water had gone under the bridge since '69, when I was a PRU adviser. By 2215 hours Dai Uy, Trung Uy, and I departed so that we would have time to prepare for our early departure from Dong Tam the next morning for the day's parachute jump.

Reveille was at 0530 hours on November twentieth. In spite of the rainy season, it was an unusually clear and beautiful day. However, some of the guys didn't appear to be focusing on the beautifully brilliant sunrise. I knew how they felt. About half of the platoon hadn't had the opportunity to jump since their graduation from Airborne School at Fort Benning, Georgia.

After Senior Chief had Little Bear Guano take his mattress outside for its daily airing and drying, we loaded our five-ton truck with our steel pots (helmets), pistols, or revolvers and headed for the Vietnamese Airborne School located on the Tan Son Nhut air base just north-northwest of Saigon. Tan Son Nhut was the location of the South Vietnamese air forces, U.S. Air Force, Army, Navy, Marine Corps, Air America airdales, and international traffic from all over the world.

Because Dai Uy Fletcher had attended the Vietnamese Airborne School in '69 and knew his way around, we stopped at the Airborne School's headquarters. Within a few minutes Dai Uy returned with a Vietnamese staff sergeant who guided us to a concrete pad adjacent to a warehouse where Vietnamese Airborne students were busy suiting up in the original T-10 parachutes—that is, no canopy modification or steering toggles. In a short while we were issued our main and reserve parachutes and assigned a rectangular space near the aircraft loading area for suiting up. Fortunately, we had plenty of time to get organized. I wasn't surprised that some of the guys couldn't remember exactly how to put on their jump gear—I probably wouldn't have either if I hadn't had the opportunity to jump over the last couple of years. Chief Bassett and I speedily assisted those who needed help and had just completed our second check of each man when the old World War II C-119 boxcar pulled up for loading.

By 0850 hours a Vietnamese jump master came over and motioned us to load the aircraft by its off-loading ramp. By hand signals, we were assigned the starboard side's seats. I was the fourth jumper in our fourteen-man stick. Once the noisy old craft managed to lift itself from the runway, it wasn't long before the jump master signaled for us to "Stand up!" and a short time later to "Hook up!" to a steel cable that was located overhead. Finally the J.M. motioned for all of us to shuffle up tightly to the side door with our left hands on top of our reserve parachutes and the static line loops in our right hands.

While the red light on the top right of the starboard door was shining brightly, the Vietnamese Airborne J.M. controlled Dai Uy, who was the first man in the stick, by placing his left hand on Fletcher's right shoulder. Once the red light went off and the green light flashed on, the J.M. yelled, *"Di Di,"* or "Go," and slapped Dai Uy's shoulder hard. I noticed that Dai Uy, Trung Uy, and Senior Chief, who were in front of me, were watching the Vietnamese jump master intently for his last hand signal. Even though this was my forty-ninth jump, I admit that I still had butterflies in my stomach.

Suddenly, the green light came on and the jump master yelled, *"Di Di! Di Di!"* Within ten seconds all fourteen of us had exited the old C-119 rattletrap that was flying approximately 125 knots and at twelve hundred feet elevation. After I had counted "one thousand, two thousand, three thousand, four thousand," I looked up at my canopy and noticed there were no holes and that my parachute had completely inflated. I scanned the DZ and noticed that I was drifting rapidly toward a group of fifty-five-gallon barrels that were surrounded with rows of concertina wire. By looking between my jungle boots, I noticed that the ground wind was moving us along at about fifteen knots—that was normally the maximum wind speed for administrative jumps. Just before I landed, I saw Eberle make a perfect parachute landing fall—feet and then head. Because he was slow to get up and run around his canopy to collapse it, he was dragged for another one hundred yards into the concertina wire. I didn't have time to do much laughing—I soon realized that I would have to make a good PLF to keep from getting hurt on impact, and I also would have to really hustle around to the apex of my parachute to collapse it quickly before I was dragged into the wire. I hit the ground so hard that my helmet flew off and my head rang for a week. I also bruised my right knee and elbow, but I was okay. That was one of the hardest DZs into which I had ever jumped. Poor Chief Bassett landed in the middle of the concertina wire and came to a screeching halt. It took a half dozen of us to get his canopy and suspension lines freed from the wicked wire. Fortunately, no one was seriously hurt, but there were a lot of bruises, cuts, and two sore heads. Still, that was one day when everyone was happy and didn't worry about the war or the political situation at home. The parachute jump was great for our morale.

The following day, I covertly prepared Tam for the next day's polygraph test by telling him, as a cover story, that we were going to Saigon to CIMEC to visit a VC Hoi Chanh who had been a member of the VC Military Region 2 (Central Nam Bo) headquarters combat training section. I explained to Tam that I believed the Hoi Chanh would have information valuable to Phu for individual targets in the northern area of Cai Lay and Cai Be districts. Tam appeared to be very pleased and was properly motivated to go.

Later that day, Doc and I received the results of our chief's exam—Doc passed and I failed. That meant I would have to attend the six-month Radioman B school at the Naval Training Command, San Diego, before I would be capable of passing the technically difficult radioman technician's exam. I wasn't happy with the thought—I still hated anything that had wires in it.

Dai Uy, Tam, and I departed Dong Tam at 0630 hours for Saigon. I spent the next two days preparing Tam's polygraph test and waiting for the results and his debriefing by the examiner. The three major areas that I had the examiner cover were: (1) Tam's relationship to the Dinh Tuong province's Police Special Branch; (2) Tam's knowledge, if any, of a special undercover agent; and (3) Tam's involvement, if any, in the thefts that took place within November Platoon's barracks.

By the end of the second day, the examiner's conclusions were: (1) Tam admitted that he was carrying out errands for PSB but wasn't getting paid for his troubles; (2) Tam knew nothing about the special undercover agent; and (3) Tam was involved in the barracks thefts of November Platoon's belongings. I said nothing to Tam of the polygraph test results. Later, I gave him 500 piasters to catch a Vietnamese bus back to My Tho.

That afternoon, Dai Uy, Trung Uy, and I were kept busy preparing documentation (1149s) for all of our personal belongings and SEAL team gear for Customs inspection and return to the Strand by military conex boxes. Senior Chief Bassett, Roger Hayden, and Gordon Compton drove our pickup out to Warehouse 6 and traded it for a Scout. Dai Uy spent the afternoon in preparation for his departure to Taiwan, Republic of China. I wouldn't see him again until 1975.

At 1100 hours on November twenty-fifth, Lieutenant Todd called from Binh Thuy and told Trung Uy Kleehammer, "Get your men and gear ready! A Sea Lord slick is on its way to your location. You're going in on a downed helo." Because we were on nonoperational status as of the twentieth, our gear was packed and all of our ordnance had been given to Ba To. However, many of us still had our basic web gear.

All hands quickly loaded the five-ton truck and drove over to our U.S. Navy buddies next door. We borrowed M-60 machine guns, M-79s, M-16s, ammo, grenades, and smoke grenades. Within a matter of minutes we were ready and waiting at the Seawolves' helo pad, where we loaded the Sea Lord slick and flew directly to Binh Thuy. There we rendezvoused with Mike Platoon from Ben Luc. They loaded two Sea Lord slicks, which flew them eighteen klicks southeast of Can Tho to the Navy AirCo-Fac CH-46 crash site. Mike Platoon's mission was to set up a security perimeter around the craft until a Navy crew arrived to remove the main and tail rotor blades. After the CH-46's blades were removed, an Army CH-54 "flying crane" helo flew from Tan Son Nhut to the crash site, retrieved the CH-46 body, and returned it to Binh Thuy.

While we were on standby at Binh Thuy, Lieutenant Todd explained to us what had happened. Because of the low-hanging clouds, the CH-46's pilot was flying the craft between two and three hundred feet altitude. At one point the helo passed over a sampan carrying two armed VC. Both of the VC fired their AK-47s at the helo as it passed overhead, hitting the pilot in the leg and wounding several others. The pilot almost bled to death before he could set the helo down on the ground, after which emergency first aid was applied to stop the bleeding. Fortunately, the crash site was relatively secure, or free from VC. However, the situation was sure to change within a short period of time. No doubt the two VC were grandly promoted and given certificates of heroism.

After Mike Platoon returned to Binh Thuy at 1500 hours, all of us went to the chow hall and ate a great Thanksgiving dinner. As Boatswain Mate Joe Thrift was fond of saying, "Everyone was absolutely famished and drew sparks with their knives and forks while eating."

Everyone was beginning to get uptight and tired of waiting for our departure from Vietnam. Bassett paid the hootch maids through the end of the month, dismissed them, and thanked them for their loyal service. I went to My Tho and visited with my old friend Sao Lam, who had maintained his position as the assistant PRU chief of Dinh Tuong province. He invited me to drink, eat dinner, and spend the night at his home, as we had traditionally done many times in the past. In spirit, Sao Lam was and always would be one of my life's best friends.

Relief finally came at 0800 hours on the morning of November twenty-eighth when Lieutenant Todd inspected our barracks and surrounding area and told Trung Uy and Senior Chief that we could depart for Annapolis from Tan Son Nhut AFB the following morning. By noon of the next day we had secured our weapons, filing cabinet, and other items at AirCoFac, and spent the remainder of the afternoon at NavForV. Lieutenant Morrow kept me busy working on C&CI fund vouchers and making Xerox copies of four dossiers to pass to Lieutenant Zig. I was very fortunate to have had the opportunity to work with and (indirectly) for Lieutenant Morrow. He always encouraged me, thoughtfully guided me, and was never condescending. I was sorry that I would never have the opportunity to work with him again.

That evening, we visited the Navy EOD villa in Saigon. Captain Schaible was there also. The two of us discussed the importance of good intelligence information for a while, then he made his pitch. "Smitty, I congratulate you on the job you have done as November Platoon's intelligence petty officer. Lieutenant Morrow, Lieutenant Fletcher, and others have also told me of your dedication and expertise. I also know about your letters of commendation from Lieutenant Morrow and John B. of OSA. It's because of that that I want you to extend your tour here for another six months. You would be working directly for me with the intelligence community gathering specific information for pilot rescue and LDNN targets. Are you interested?"

I was flattered; however, I knew my limitations. "I'm sorry, Captain, I can't do it right now because I'm mentally and physically exhausted. I'm afraid that, under the circumstances, I'd be of little use to you. However, thanks for giving me the opportunity to serve under you again." After my confession and explanation, Captain Schaible didn't mention the matter again.

I was hardly in the mood to attempt explaining my emotions at that time. I knew that I would probably never return to South Vietnam or see my Vietnamese military and civilian friends again. Somehow, I felt our politicians back home were running with a white flag. Sadly, our liberal Congress, cultural elite, intelligentsia, and academe had set the agenda as designed by the North Vietnamese, and we, the military men, were reaping the bitter harvest—we had been sold out. In summary, I felt we were slipping our mooring lines prematurely.

We didn't depart Tan Son Nhut until the afternoon of December 2, 1971. Mike Platoon, located at Ben Luc, wouldn't be able to catch a flight out of country until the seventh. They were to be the last SEAL platoon to depart South Vietnam. They had been in-country from September to December of 1971. The platoon members were Lt. Michael S. McCrary, Lt. (jg) Walter F. Merrick, QMC Thomas A. Norton, HM2 Carey (returned to the Strand after one mission), HMC William P. "Doc" Hill, BT1 Lenord J. Van Orden, SFP2 Paul C. Bourne, BM2 Frank

J. Czajkowski, SF3 Randy Kaiser, RM3 Thomas J. Christofer, YN3 John W. Chalus, RMSN Stephen R. Jones, RMSA David R. Hover, RMSN William M. Foley, and ETNSN David W. Johnson.

The first leg of our trip was by a Navy C-118 to Da Nang for a short stop, then on to NAS Cubi Point, Subic Bay, Philippines. Once we checked into the UDT barracks, Senior Chief Bassett and Chief Thompson took Knepper and me to the Chiefs' club for a San Miguel brew before the club closed at 0100 hours.

The next day was spent visiting our UDT teammates Lieutenant Nelson, Lieutenant Winters, Chief Sick, and others. That afternoon, everyone rendezvoused at the U and I Club in Olongapo and really let our hair down. Bassett and I each bet a five-spot that Little Bear Guano couldn't eat two baloots—fertilized, half-developed duck embryos in the shells, which had been aged by burying them in a salty solution for a period of months—and keep them down for thirty minutes. Guano arrogantly accepted our challenge. I paid a Filipino three pesos and specifically asked him to get two rotten baloots.

Within a matter of minutes the indigenous fellow delivered the two darkly covered, large duck eggs to me. After I instructed Bear in the Filipino method of eating the baloots, I gave both of them to him. With all eyes watching, Guano carefully opened one egg and properly emptied the juice into his mouth without gagging. Next, he popped the whole black egg in his mouth and chewed and chewed and chewed. I was certain that we had him, but Little Bear somehow swallowed the mess without puking.

Once Guano was done, he said, "I need a little while before I eat the second one."

I reminded him that we had agreed to his eating both baloots quickly and that his thirty minutes didn't begin until he had fulfilled our agreement. Guano began looking a little green around the gills and nodded as he took the last egg from my hand. Unfortunately, when he cracked the remaining egg open, I saw it didn't contain a developed duck embryo. Not realizing that fact, Guano reinforced the principle of "mind over matter" when he popped the egg into his mouth and started gagging. Then he blew the egg out on our table. Immediately, all of the surrounding UDT/SEALs and Filipinos started yelling accusations and laughing at Guano's predicament.

Bear somehow retained his composure and declared emphatically, "No sweat, I'll eat it." He bit the egg in twain, swallowed it, did the same again, and successfully managed to keep the contents down for the agreed thirty minutes. After we begrudgingly paid up, we added another sobriquet to his handle—Little Bear "Guano" Baloot Breath. Later that night at the barracks, Baloot Breath confessed that he had a terrible time getting the baby duck guts, feathers, and bones of the first baloot down. While he was telling us this, he started gagging. Looks like "mind over matter" wins again, I thought.

Thankfully, the next morning we departed the Philippines and flew to Kadina AFB, Okinawa, where it was thirty-two degrees! There, we delightedly ran into SEAL Team 1's Kilo Platoon, their platoon chief, Doyle, and Lieutenant Commander Hendrickson, who was commanding officer of SEAL Team 1 from 1970 to 1972. They were returning from Korea after a couple of months of winter and submarine operations with our Korean UDT/SEAL/EOD counterparts.

A few hours later we departed Okinawa and flew to Naval Air Station Atsugi, Japan, for the night. The following evening, December fifth, we departed Japan for Midway, and arrived by 0740 hours the next morning. Several hours later we were on our way to Barbers Point, Hawaii, and arrived there at 1605 hours. Both platoons and Captain Hendrickson immediately headed for the Enlisted Men's club.

The club was practically empty and unusually quiet at 1730 hours. However, within a short time and after the first few chin-chins and pitchers of beer, all twenty-eight hoodlums told endless tales of incredible missions deep within the bowels of the VC and NVA's home turf that were only survived by superhuman strength, intelligence, and uncommon determination and expertise.

By 1800 hours, BMC Leon Rauch and his wife Sue, having received word that we were in town, arrived at the club. Leon and I had operated together as PRU advisers in Kien Giang province in '69. Now, Leon was serving as a Navy recruiter in Honolulu. The boatswain mate chief petty officer, being a great storyteller, soon overwhelmed all others with his top-secret, cross-the-border experiences of derring-do in Laos.

The following day, December sixth, we were told that our VR-21 flight had been delayed until 1400 hours. That was more than Lieutenant (jg) Kleehammer, Senior Chief Bassett, Knepper, Hayden, "Bad Medicine" Doc Holmes, and Compton could stand. They rented a taxi to the Honolulu International Airport and paid for a commercial flight to San Diego. That left me with "Deacon" Same, Waneous, Eberle, and Baloot Breath as the November Platoon's remnant.

At 1400 hours we were notified that our VR-21 flight had again been delayed until 2200 hours. By that time the five of us were almost ready to catch a commercial flight ourselves. Finally, after seven days of travel, the remainder of November Platoon, Kilo Platoon, and Captain Hendrickson arrived at North Island NAS, Coronado, California, at 1100 hours on December seventh. I was very thankful to be back to the good ol' U.S. of A. for a while.

CHAPTER TWELVE

The greatest difficulty I find is in causing orders
and regulations to be obeyed. This arises not from
a spirit of disobedience, but from ignorance.
                            —General Robert E. Lee

By the first of March 1972, I was enrolled in the
twenty-one week Radioman B School at the Naval Training Center, San Diego. The training was long and difficult
for me. All of my classmates were E-5 to E-6 and had
spent their careers working with shipboard radio and the
newer satellite equipment. Fortunately, I did manage to
graduate. I was tenth in a class of eleven with a final mark
of 84.28, proving that I still held to my hatred of anything
with wires. However, I did pass the chief petty officer's
radioman test that following July, justifying my having
attended the school, and best of all, I ran into my very
good radioman friend John Bagos. He had been assigned
to the comm shack in Nha Be, Vietnam, in 1967–68. My
life was never the same since.

In August, SEAL Team 1 had received permission
from the U.S. Park Service to allow six members of
November Platoon to descend the Colorado River by
IBS—a seven-man rubber boat twelve feet in length and
weighing approximately 290 pounds—from Lee's Ferry,
just below the Utah state line, through the Grand Canyon

to Lake Mead for a total of approximately 225 miles. A UDT-12 group and a SEAL 1 platoon had previously managed to survive the arduous trip down the treacherous river earlier that summer. One of the Park Service's requirements was that we had to put on football helmets and Kapok life jackets before entering each rapids. Interestingly, one of the earlier SEAL fellows, whose IBS had capsized at the Rock House rapids, was sucked underwater by a huge whirlpool for reportedly over three minutes. His Kapok life jacket eventually brought him back to the surface and probably saved his life.

After a long drive aboard SEAL team's five-ton truck from San Diego to Lee's Ferry in northern Arizona, both boat crews started inflating the IBSs with the large hand pumps. Lieutenant (jg) Kleehammer, Eberle, and one other person were in IBS number one, while I, along with a corpsman and another fellow—unfortunately, I have forgotten some of their names—took boat number two. Trung Uy Kleehammer's IBS blew a main tube because Eberle pumped it to the maximum three psi and did not allow for its expansion due to the rapidly increasing ambient heat. What was surprising was that Eb hated work, especially when the ambient temperature was running about 110 degrees. Fortunately, each IBS had an emergency repair kit that contained two rubber-lined metal disks held together loosely with a wire bolt, nut, and lock washer.

After Eb had finished with the temporary repair job, we finally shoved off into the beautifully clear and deceptively calm river. Trung Uy Kleehammer coxswained one crew, with Eberle in the number-two starboard position as strokeman and the other fellow to port, while the other crew had myself as strokeman, Doc to port, and the third fellow as the coxswain.

Unfortunately for crew number one, the temporary

patch was a weak one and leaked. That meant that the damaged main tube could not be inflated much above $1\frac{1}{2}$ psi—Eberle would have to periodically reinflate the IBS with the small hand pump throughout the day. The IBS was certain to be very unstable when entering rough waters because of its tendency to fold up from bow to stern due to low air pressure. During the next six days, Kleehammer's boat crew would spend a lot of time swimming in the 45-degree waters.

On the morning of the second day and just before we approached the infamous Rock House rapids with our small rafts, we pulled over and visited with the civilian coxswains—River Rats—who were absolute professionals at piloting their boats and pontoons safely through the canyon's violent rapids for their thrill-seeking clients. After they had examined our IBSs, one of them casually commented, "It was just last week that a lady fell from her pontoon"—three military-type U-shaped rubber pontoons were secured together and powered with an outboard engine, and were rarely upset when descending the rapids—"and was killed when she was smashed against the Rock House boulder." The River Rats advised us to maneuver to the left of the boulder, which was as large as a house and positioned in the center of the rapids, and warned us to remain in the center of the narrow stream. Otherwise, the current would overpower us and take our boat into the canyon wall where the river violently doubled or washed back upon itself, similar to a twenty-foot plunging (pipeline) ocean beach wave. Because the river's water level was temporarily moderately high, the rapids were not rated at their worst. Trung Uy Kleehammer and Eberle assured the River Rats that we would have no trouble getting through because of our vast experience in dealing with southern California's seasonally large surf. The River Rats smiled and wished us all the best as they and their customers sat down on a high spot, got out their sandwiches and soda pop, and prepared their 8mm movie and SLR cameras to document the Navy's best at descending the ominous rapids.

Trung Uy and his Cocky Crew decided to take the starboard channel while "Dumb Shit" Smith and unwitting crew went to port. One of my favorite sayings in those days was, "It's good to be humbled." Little did we know. Boat crew one with its noodle bow managed to get as far as the first pothole, where the IBS doubled, throwing its occupants into the air and floating downstream, where it remained in a back eddy. Boat crew two didn't realize the power of the current until it was too late. Despite our best efforts, we discovered that we were powerless to avoid the huge backwash off the canyon wall and, consequently, were flipped upside down in the midst of huge waves, potholes, and deep surface foam. I remained underwater for at least ten minutes, it seemed, before my life jacket brought me back to the surface and, unfortunately, underneath the IBS. The water was so violent, I had a difficult time getting out from under the IBS because of my life jacket's buoyancy and entanglement with the bowline. Once I extricated myself from the hectic mess and reached the surface, I found that I couldn't breathe, because the water was so cold that my lungs refused to function, and two feet of foam lay on the surface of the violent water, keeping me from the air. For a while I thought I was a goner. As I was gradually washed downstream, the foam disappeared and I began to regain my breathing. Eventually I noticed several heads with helmets appearing above the waves. After a long, cold swim for our rafts and paddles, we managed to get back under way with a much healthier respect for the deceptively powerful Colorado River and the Grand Canyon's walls. The consensus of boat crew two was, "We've got to get our act together!"

After a bit of brainstorming, the three of us decided to secure the bowline tautly to one of the stern D-rings. This would raise the bow somewhat, and the line would give Doc and me a handy lifeline to grab with one hand, while we gripped our paddles with the other and the main tube with our legs. Doc and I moved forward to the number-one position for better control of the boat and an improved view of upcoming potholes, whirlpools, and boulders. Also the coxswain would have the bowline to hang onto when all else failed.

Interestingly, one of the consequences of our bad judgment at the Rock House rapids was that the canyon wall had cut a foot-long gash in the bottom of our IBS floor, which flooded the boat with water. During the next couple of days, after we had survived several more rapids, we (Humble Crew Two) learned that the six inches of water that always remained inside our boat added much needed ballast to keep the IBS stable during our passage through rough waters and potholes. We never turned over again during that trip. Conversely, we lost most of our maneuverability when trying to dodge obstacles. In the end, Humble Crew Two decided to sacrifice maneuverability for stability. We urged Cocky Crew One to cut a slit in the bottom of their noodle-IBS and we received sneers of "pussies, nonhackers, gutless wonders" and worse from Seaman Eberle. Consequently, they dumped a total of six times during the first six days of the trip. Sometimes the best way to convince people is to let them have their own way.

By the third day, the River Rats and their clients never failed to gather at the next rapids to wait for the two small, black dots to appear from upstream. For them it was amusement time; for us, Humble Crew Two, it was serious time. After pumping the River Rats for their advice and studying the best approach to the rapids, Cocky Crew One soon amused the cheering crowd with their speciality—acrobatic dumping: crewmen flying one way and the floppy IBS sailing through the air to another. Humble Crew Two paddled their asses off trying to rescue their retarded teammates from the frigid waters. Someone had to do the dirty work.

We generally departed camp shortly after daylight. Within a couple of hours we passed the River Rats' camping place, which was located in a large concave place or sandy knoll adjacent to the river. Most of the Rats and their customers stood around their fire, leisurely drinking hot coffee and eating bacon and eggs. This was their usual routine. At about 1000 hours they would pass us in their motorized pontoons and continue downstream until approximately 1400 hours, when they set up camp again. They occasionally stopped during their four-hour journey to watch Cocky Crew One demonstrate their specialty at each major rapids. Each day, we paddled for approximately sixteen hours. The reasons were simple: if we were to remain on schedule for our rendezvous with the SEAL team's truck, and if we didn't want to run out of food—LRRPs and C-rations—we would have to keep our paddles in the water.

By the fourth day we were beginning to get very sunburned from the reflection of the sun's rays off the water. We continually rubbed oil over our bodies to prevent second-degree burns. Later that afternoon we were moving along nicely without a jutting rock or rapids in sight— all we had to do was occasionally steer the boat to keep its nose pointed downstream. Suddenly, without warning, the nose of our IBS took a six-foot dive into a hole on the downside of a boulder beneath the surface. All I had time to do was tuck my paddle under my right armpit, place my face on the main tube, grab the taut bowline with my left hand, and grip the main tube with my legs. Our IBS totally disappeared underwater into the backwash and eventually returned to the surface like a surfacing submarine. Somehow Doc and the coxswain had managed to hold onto the bowline and maintain their positions inside the boat until the IBS surfaced. On the other hand, I was completely out of the boat and barely hanging on to the bowline with my left hand. Doc quickly reached out, grabbed my left arm, and pulled me aboard. Fortunately, I hadn't lost my paddle, otherwise Eberle would have ribbed me to death. Our boat's water ballast definitely kept the IBS stable throughout the whole experience. That was one treacherous river. Mr. K. later commented, "One minute you guys were taking it easy, and the next minute you had totally disappeared from view."

On the sixth day we slowly approached the worst rapids of the canyon—Lava Falls rapids. We soon spotted the River Rats and their cheering clients on the left bank, atop a rock outcropping just upstream of the rapids. As always, we pulled over and discussed the best approaches to the rapids with the River Rat coxswains, studied the two routes, and made our decisions. The left approach offered many large and small boulders scattered throughout the rapids, and assorted potholes that would require some fancy boat maneuvers and a lot of luck. The right approach offered fewer boulder obstacles and potholes but had a canyon wall somewhat similar to the one at the Rock House rapids—if the coxswain misjudged the current, the IBS would be pulled into the backwash off the canyon wall. Humble Crew had had enough of canyon-wall backwashes and took the left approach. Having had enough of potholes, Cocky Crew lived up to their name and took the right.

Strangely, one of the River Rats naively begged Trung Uy Kleehammer to take him with them. Mr. K. readily agreed and shoved off with the passenger. Once their IBS was committed to the current, on the right-side approach, there was no holding back. If the crew could keep the IBS moving faster than the current, then they could potentially control the direction of the boat. If the paddlers slowed their pace to the point that the current became faster than the boat, then the crew forfeited a high percentage of the boat's maneuverability. Their survival and success would depend on the discipline of the paddlers, the leadership of the strokeman, and the management of the coxswain.

Cocky Crew initially seemed to be doing well and had just dodged a large rock when they hit one of the hidden potholes. Because of their IBS's butt-bucking habit, Mr. K. flew high into the air and landed in the river just aft of the boat's stern. Eberle shoved his paddle toward Trung Uy for him to grab, and was pulling him back into the boat when they hit another pothole. The crew and boat disappeared. The IBS eventually surfaced upside down, and shortly afterward the whole ball of wax was pushed into the large backwash off the right canyon wall. Within a minute or so we began to spot helmeted heads bobbing on the surface here and there while the IBS rapidly headed downstream upside down, like a snake crawling on uneven ground.

By that time Humble Crew was making their approach on the left. Once we had maneuvered to our chosen entry point, the current committed us. There would be no turning back. As luck would have it, we managed to survive several potholes, bounced off numerous boulders without bursting the spray tube or the main tubes, slid over large subsurface juggernauts, and made it to calmer waters. Our next concern was to proceed immediately downstream looking for Cocky Crew One and their unfortunate passenger. All of boat crew one, except Trung Uy, had swum to the bottoms-up IBS and were busy trying to turn it over. After we signaled to them that we were going downstream to locate Mr. Kleehammer, we heard yelling and spotted Trung Uy's hand waving as he floated into deeper and calmer waters. Deeper water and steeper canyon walls sometimes meant numerous back eddies—and so it was. We paddled our butts off for forty-five minutes before we were able to reach Lieutenant (jg) Kleehammer. The poor fellow was suffering from hypothermia and was unable to talk for several minutes. We quickly reached a large sand-bar and beached until the remnant of Cocky Crew and the River Rats and clients arrived.

Later, the River Rat that accompanied boat crew one commented, "I have never truly experienced the absolute power of the river until this day! It was an incredible ride!"

The last three days were uneventful, and on the afternoon of the ninth day, we pulled out on the east bank, where we rendezvoused with one of our teammates and his five-ton truck near the western edge of the Hualapai Indian Reservation near Lake Mead.

During that trip, several of the River Rats offered us substantial amounts of money for our IBSs. Somehow, I couldn't imagine even drunken clients being crazy enough to proceed down the canyon any farther than just below the Rock House rapids. It's been fun, I thought, but I never want to do it again.

By October of 1972 I was attending the EOD/Scuba Diver Course at the Naval Station, Key West, Florida. During the three-month school, RM3 Bruce Keyston—another Navy EOD student—and I, along with three other students, took the standard scuba course followed by the Second Class Deep Sea Diving course. The deep sea diver's course taught us the basics in the use of the old Jack Brown Shallow Water and MK-V Deep Sea surface-tended diving systems and, for the EOD students, the MK-VI mixed gas scuba system (nonmagnetic type) for deep diving while working on magnetically influenced underwater ordnance. CPO Jessie Lively, an old, humorous deep sea diver, was our class instructor.

During the scuba phase, our instructors occasionally took us a mile or so off Key West, cast out two lines, and slowly towed two of us behind the LCPL MK-11. Our mission was to watch for rock outcroppings with likely lobster havens, free-dive down to the bottom, and bag as many lobsters as possible with our Hawaiian slings. The more lobsters, the more pleased were our instructors. The more pleased our instructors, the less miserable were the students. It was always a day of fun, and the students were graciously rewarded with box lunches in return for several bags of lobsters for our instructors.

On one particular October night our scuba class was tasked to go on a 1,500-yard night swim by pairs. It was a beautiful starlit night with calm seas and warm water—an EOD/UDT/SEAL diver couldn't ask for much more than that. Each swimmer wore his UDT swim trunks, web belt, diving knife, with MK-13 day/night flare, UDT life jacket, fins, and face mask. About halfway through the swim I had my first and last encounter with a Portuguese man-of-war jellyfish. Fortunately, I was the only swimmer to get hit. The jellyfish's body is approximately six inches in diameter, with tentacles reaching a length of fifty feet. I never saw the varmint, but I knew he was around when I felt intensely burning stings around my neck and shoulders, arms and chest. By the time I finished my swim, my upper body felt as if thousands of needles were being stuck into me continually. I went to the corpsman, told him of my misfortune, and asked if he had anything to deliver me from my miserable condition.

"The only thing I have that may relieve your symptoms is epinephrine. Have you ever been given a shot of it before?" the doc asked me.

I assured him that I indeed had been twice injected when I was blessed with a severe reaction from eating mangoes (sumac family) while attending the Jungle Warfare School in Panama, and prior to that in Da Nang, Vietnam, from eating Philippine mangoes. Without further ado, the doc had me lie down on a table and injected me with the adrenal hormone for the third time. As in Panama and Da Nang, my heart raced madly for approximately five minutes, until the effects of the shot gradually tapered off. Within an hour the stinging and burning were declining, and by the next morning I was ready to hit the deck running.

On January nineteenth our five-man class graduated, and Bruce Keyston and I continued on to the U.S. Army Chemical School at Fort McClellan, Alabama, for the next two weeks. During the course, ol' Murphy managed to get to me again when I came into contact with contaminated gas-mask straps—mustard gas. The end result was a huge bubble that formed on the back of my head and neck that took several days to disappear. I was beginning to feel like the hunchback of Notre Dame.

When I went to sick bay, one of the Chemical School doctors seemed amused and commented, "I haven't seen one of these in a long time." Another walked up and said, "That's the first one of those I've ever seen." By the time the two doctors had poked fun at me, mused at the bubble, and placed a large bandage over the obnoxious mess, I was beginning to get a persecution complex. Ever so slowly I began to understand why BM3 Cleem—one of my UDT Training Class 36 classmates—exclaimed, "Why me, Lord? Why me, all the time?" when our UDT training instructors rained various forms of hell upon our heads.

In late February, Bruce, PHC Wyeth Heiliger, and I began our twenty-six weeks of basic Explosive Ordnance Disposal School at Indian Head, Maryland. Commander Moody was the CO of the school during the first couple of months, until my old SEAL Team 1 CO, Commander Dave Schaible, relieved him.

During the first several weeks, the three of us spent

much of our time crawling around on the bottom of the Potomac River with the MK-V deep sea diving rig and the Jack Brown shallow-water system, searching and working on underwater projects. All of our MK-VI scuba diving was done in the school's twenty-four-foot-deep swimming pool. After our diving phase, we spent several weeks studying underwater ordnance—mostly mines and torpedoes—including underwater reconnaissance and practical application of their RSPs (Render Safe Procedures). It was one of the most difficult phases of the school, and also one of the most interesting.

The EOD School's curriculum and standards seldom left students with free time during the week. We generally spent evenings at the school studying, even occasionally Saturdays, and nearly always Sundays. During the mechanical and electric fuse phase, I reported to the school by 0600 hours and studied until muster at 0730. I was amazed at how much information the school tried to cram into our heads. Sadly, my instructor's attempts at shoving a quart's worth of information into my pint-sized brain were not entirely successful.

In spite of the nervous twitch I developed while attending the school, there were good times to be had, assuming one was creative. Every afternoon after chow, my good friend Sergeant Les McGhee (Marine EOD student) and I purged ourselves of our anger and frustration during our rigorous PT and run. Because I didn't have my truck with me while attending the EOD courses, I spent most of my weekends searching for old bottles along the banks of the Potomac River and dreamed of more exotic activities after my return to SEAL Team 1. I spent one Saturday in Washington, D.C., visiting museums and drinking a couple of Heinekens at Bassins on Pennsylvania Avenue. The sidewalk tables and chairs reminded me of the Continental Hotel, which was across the street from the old

opera house, on Tu Do Street in Saigon. Another weekend I went with PO1 Ken Peck (SEAL Team 2) to Little
Creek, Virginia, to visit with the East Coast UDT/SEALs.
I especially enjoyed visiting with PO1 Drady again. We
had operated together on Dung Island in January 1968,
when he was with Demo Dick Marcinko's platoon and I
was with Lieutenant Van Heertum's dysfunctional platoon (see *Death in the Jungle*).

On April ninth I was finally promoted to chief petty officer with two other squids after enduring many trials and
tribulations throughout the day and surviving the chief's
initiation at the small CPO club that afternoon.

Earlier that morning I was given a booklet and was told
to memorize its contents NLT (no later than) that afternoon.
It was titled "The Beliefs and Characteristics of a Chief
Petty Officer." I was also given a "Charge Book" to carry
with me during my classes that was attached to twenty
pounds of diving weights to ensure that I wouldn't lose it.

The contents of the "Beliefs and Characteristics of a
Chief Petty Officer" were as follows:

1. A gentleman by seed, breed, and generation.
2. Intelligent enough to be willing to learn, cagey
enough never to rush forward eagerly.
3. Copper lined, double riveted, and gilt edged.
4. Adventurers and philosophers capable of the gentlest
thought and the bloodiest deed.
5. Slippery as an eel and twice as fast.
6. Nimbleness of mind and audacity of purpose.
7. Share what you have and give with a full heart.
8. Drink sparingly of all forms of tanglefoot.
9. Never walk in front of cannons or behind horses.
Stay as far away from your men as possible. That way
you'll never get shot at, shit on, or a ration of shit.

10. Keep your rifle high, powder dry, and don't rattle your balls.

11. Never believe in superstition or luck.

12. Remain staunch, honest, respectable, pay your taxes, believe in motherhood, and vote a straight ticket, knowing all politicians (especially Democrats) are dedicated to the welfare of our country.

13. Always pass to the right of a stanchion rather than to its left.

14. When dealing with subordinates, congratulations are offered, excuses considered, and alibis rebuffed.

15. And finally, every tub must stand on its own bottom.

The contents of the "Charge Book" read as follows:

This is your charge book. It is important to your well-being and future financial position. Before you reach the exalted position of Chief Petty Officer, you must go through many trials and tribulations. Your successful completion will be a major endorsement of your ability to survive under adverse conditions. For the duration of this traditional day, the following rules must be carefully observed:

1. Number each page.

2. Do not lose any pages! For every page that is stolen or lost, you will be charged two dollars.

3. You must surrender this book to any and all CPOs. It is for CPO use *ONLY*. How you handle officers is your problem.

4. Do not lose this book! Punishment will be immediate, severe, and costly.

5. This book *WILL* remain on your person at all times: i.e., head, shower, sack, PT, swimming, diving, parachuting, etc.

6. This book *WILL* remain neat and clean at all times.

7. Immediately after issue, locate and report to the Command Master Chief, Chief Master-at-Arms, and all other Chiefs, and serve them refreshments, polish their boots, shine their brass, or any other task demanded by them.

8. Memorize the Chief's Creed and the Navy Hymn. You will be required to recite or sing upon demand.

Toward the end of that afternoon at the CPO Club, Commander Dave Schaible was given the honor of being the judge. After I and two others were forced to endure the final devilment of Captain Schaible's judgments, we were awarded our CPO hats.

On July 19, 1973, I graduated from EOD School and after saying farewell to Captain Dave Schaible and many of my friends, I made hot tracks for the Silver Strand on the following day. Because I was returning to SEAL Team 1—a combat unit that was subject to capture—I wasn't allowed to attend the highly secret eight-week nuclear weapons course. Frankly, I wasn't disappointed.

Interestingly, the cost for me to attend the EOD nine-month course was eight hundred dollars. While I was assigned to SEAL Team 1 and UDT-12, I drew demolition and jump hazardous-duty pay of $110 a month. However, I had to take a reduction in pay because Navy regulations forbid trainees to draw diving pay—which meant that I forfeited $110 per month—at Key West, and was only allowed to draw diving or demolition pay (hazardous-duty pay) at Indian Head. All Navy EOD trainees were eligible to draw diving pay at sixty-five dollars a month versus fifty-five dollars for demolition pay (Army, Air Force, and Marine Corps).

Once I had reported back aboard SEAL Team 1, my jump and demolition hazardous-duty pay was reinstated and I was assigned to Alfa Platoon. My platoon commander was CWO3 James "Jim" Lake, who had previously served as an EOD technician. Temporarily, I was to wear two hats: platoon chief and the assistant platoon commander.

Gunner Lake was not only an excellent platoon commander overall, but he also understood and believed in the chain of command. Gunner was a rarity among SpecWar officers after the Vietnam War in that he applied the leadership principles of organize, prioritize, motivate, delegate, and supervise through his platoon chief. CWO3 Lake never interfered with, subverted, or coveted the platoon chief's authority with the men. Sadly, during the early peacetime years of the 1970s, SEAL platoon officers of Gunner Lake's caliber were always sought, but seldom found. A few years later I had one of my platoon commanders tell me in a fit of rage and in front of the platoon, "You don't have to think, Chief—all you have to do is do what I tell you!" So much for the chain of command and the proven leadership principles of organize, prioritize, motivate, delegate, and supervise.

For the first few weeks, Alfa Platoon was kept busy training Beach Master Unit 1 personnel in basic defensive tactics and weapons training at Camp Kerrey, located at the foot of the Chocolate Mountains, on the Navy Bombing Range near the Coachella Canal's Siphon 10.

Afterward, we traveled to the Naval Air Station near Fallon, Nevada, for five separate trips of a week in duration working with Lieutenant Commander Ritz and Senior Chief Renea LaMarsch in developing techniques relative to combined Airborne/SEAL SAR (Search and Rescue) concepts. The mock operations took place at an altitude of seven thousand feet twenty miles or so from the NAS, near the site of the first underground hydrogen bomb detonation. The basic scheme required Alfa Platoon to rescue a downed pilot before the token North Vietnamese military forces could capture him. The SAR training exercise goals were to: (1) develop communications procedures between the SEAL platoon, the downed pilot, and the aircraft On Scene Commander (OSC); (2) develop a unique, simple code system of reference points, time, azimuths, and distances based on previous experiences in Southeast Asia to guide us (SEALs) to the pilot; and (3) familiarize us with calling in night, fixed-wing strafing and bombing support through the OSC.

Senior Chief LaMarsch was responsible for organizing and leading his token Communist henchmen (SERE cadre) and for preventing our successful rescue of the downed pilot. As I was to find out, my half-frog, half-Injun (LaMarsch) adversary not only played by Communist rules, but added a few of his own.

Our first pilot rescue mission took place that October on a pitch-black night at an altitude of approximately seven thousand feet. The weather was cloudy, cold, and windy, with occasional snow flurries obstructing the visual reconnaissance of our adversaries with starlight scopes. We were finally able to work out the exact location of our pilots' hideout using our simple code system for azimuths, distances, and time frames with the OSC's aircraft. Occasionally, we had to coordinate with the pilot through the OSC because of communications problems. After our initial radio communication and authentication with the downed pilot, we moved one kilometer toward his location for the rescue. Much to our chagrin, "Black Jack" LaMarsch was sitting arrogantly aboard a small tank that was no more than a hundred meters from the downed pilot. It was easy to deduce that this was a setup—our "Communists" had surrounded the downed pilot and were waiting patiently for us. I bet they even have hot coffee, I thought.

After Gunner Lake and I discussed the obvious setup, we decided we would play our own dirty game. First Squad would make a direct attack on the tank to draw

Black Jack's goons away from the pilot while my squad (2nd) sprinted toward the pilot's position for the rescue during the firefight. What the token Commies didn't know was that we had a hundred or so artillery and grenade simulators plus a few CS grenades. (Imagine that!)

After I had signaled Gunner with two breaks of squelch on the radio—meaning that 2nd Squad was in place and observing him through our starlight scope—1st Squad made a standard frontal assault using only 5.56mm and 7.62mm blanks and smoke grenades until they were close enough to see the whites of their enemies' eyes. From that point forward Lake and crew cast numerous simulators into the midst of the enemy's warm potholes, spilling their hot coffee.

Initially, the skirmish was uninteresting until the artillery and grenade simulators began to detonate on and around the tank with brilliant flashes and loud kabooms. Moreover, when the CS gas floated amidst the Commies, the tank was immediately put into reverse and started a rapid retreat behind small bodies running in disarray up the hill to escape the explosions and CS gas. Gunner Lake and his warriors continued to pursue them up the mountainside until the tank threw a track and its chicken crew abandoned ship. In the meantime, 2nd Squad successfully rescued the pilot without firing a shot.

Later, at the Chiefs' club, Black Jack LaMarsch and cadre and Alfa Platoon each celebrated the training operation in their own way. As they rubbed their bloodshot eyes, LaMarsch and crew lamented the loss of their tank but rejoiced in their miraculous escape from the simulators and CS gas. On the other hand, we celebrated the successful rescue of our pilot. It's always good to be the winner, I thought as I slapped the sturdily built Black Jack on the shoulder and said, "It's good to be humbled, huh, Senior Chief?" I could tell by the look in his eyes that the war wasn't over yet. And during the following four exercises, that proved to be the case. Senior Chief LaMarsch and men were always worthy opponents and were responsible not only for making the exercises interesting, but also for challenging us and forcing us to perform at our best.

The members of Alfa Platoon who participated in those interesting exercises were: RM2 Michael Shortell, EM2 Hugh Street, GMG3 Gene Wentz, HM3 Robert Metz, SN Michael Hulama, SA Charles Buchanan, AE1 Harry Kaneakua, EN2 Kirby D. Horrell, SN Russ Brownyer, SN David Maynard, and SA Robert Wagner.

In between the SAR exercises, Alfa Platoon was kept busy training with the San Diego Mountain Rescue Team and, on weekends, participating in searches for missing day hikers. The Navy and Special Warfare admin'ers called it "Civic Action." Alfa Platoon was also tasked to participate in SEAL/HALO (High Altitude Low Opening) airborne operations and training two groups of Cambodian navy personnel at Niland and Vallejo, San Pablo Bay, north of San Francisco. As always, we were required to maintain our diving qualifications with periodic day and night underwater ship attacks using the Emerson pure oxygen scuba system, 120-foot dives and recreational diving for lobster, abalone, fish, octopus, and moray eel, using regular scuba at Point Loma.

Occasionally on Fridays, SEAL Team 1 and UDT had a "Monster Mash" of one variety or another. All of the evolutions except for the para jumps were timed and very competitive. The worst was a 4½-mile run at Balboa Park—some of the steep hills made me think of Mount Everest—and the best were static line and freefall jumps at Rolls Farm, located at the foot of the Otay Mountains on the Mexican border. Some Fridays, for the more masochistic, we had a course that required running the obstacle course, then swimming to the rocks or to Coronado's center beach—1 ½ miles—and concluding by running back to the command. It was always great fun, and during my later years with the teams, I had Saturday to recover.

In early May, Alfa Platoon received orders to proceed to the Black Meadow campground below Lake Havasu on the Colorado River by truck. Gunner Lake took his beautiful wife and ski boat for platoon water-skiing training. During our off hours, Gunner pulled two skiers at forty knots or so until they waved that they had had enough. Then the next pair would don their skis and we would head north or south depending on our whim. It was a great week for all of us.

The last day of our stay at the campground, Gunner and his wife decided to take us all to the London Bridge, which was located approximately fifteen miles downstream where Highway 95 crossed the Colorado River. The yearnings in our hearts required that we ski downstream to the London Bridge, partake of a few refreshments, and ski back to our campground. After we had reached the London Bridge and were enjoying a few brews, Coutts suggested that we streak the bridge for a little excitement. Our approval was unanimous.

Once we finished our beers and were filled with bravado, we started across the London Bridge without a stitch of cloth on us. Some folks were obviously offended, and some looked straight ahead poker-faced. Others were laughing and pointing as Coutts ran back and forth from one side of the bridge to the other, beating his chest and yelling as if he were in the old Tarzan movies.

When we had completed our streak, we ran down to the riverbank, loaded Gunner's speedboat—his wife modestly kept her eyes covered—and sped upstream. There was little doubt that we were rude and unpolished, but we were steadfast in a fight and had good hearts. Fortunately for Gunner's and my careers, nothing was ever reported to the authorities of the incident.

CHAPTER THIRTEEN

Untutored courage is useless in the face of educated bullets.
                              —General George S. Patton, Jr.

In late May, Alfa Platoon was tasked to support COS-
RIVDIV 22's two-week summer active duty training as
enemy aggressors for their Naval Reserve PBR sailors. In
keeping with the riverine environment, our operational
area was the Honey Island Swamp near the mouth of the
Pearl River located on the boundary between Louisiana
and Mississippi. Unfortunately, CWO3 Jim Lake had
been reassigned to another duty station. Consequently, a
Lieutenant (jg) B. became Alfa Platoon's new commander. My teammates, S.Sgt. John Gebhardt (Australian
SAS assigned to SEAL Team 1 on a two-year exchange
program), HM3 Robert Metz, GMG3 Dodd Coutts, EN3
Russ Brownyer, and EM3 Frank Richard were a great
group of guys with whom to play the role of swamp warrior for two weeks.

The home for each of us within the swamp was either a
bohio made up of a mosquito net, poncho, and air mattress or a military-issue jungle hammock hung in the
trees. Because of snakes, most of us lived in the trees. Our
mission was to maneuver (by small boat and swimming)
around the swamp, ambushing the PBR sailors and sabo-

taging their radio communications. All of us greatly enjoyed our role as the bad guys. Our role as guerrillas came naturally to us. Our individual weapons were blank-adapted M-16 rifles and M-60 machine guns. Our offensive ordnance was grenade simulators and pencil flares. Before and during our ambushes, I monitored the PBR radio frequencies on our PRC-77 and gradually learned the sailors' call signs. When the sailors were frantically trying to return fire during our ambushes, I occasionally slipped in covert statements and counterorders on our PRC-77. We had a grand time luring, deceiving, and confusing the sailors until they became aware of our tricks on the radio.

On one particular morning, the swamp's cypress trees, with their exposed knees and hanging Spanish moss and other swamp growth—similar to a tropical rain forest—were shrouded in moving layers of mist that seemed to float into one area and dissipate in another. Because Sasquatch/Big Foot was reputed to live in the swamp along with cottonmouth water moccasin snakes and alligators, it was sometimes a bit spooky.

Taking advantage of the eerie cast, low tide, and low visibility, we decided to ambush two PBRs that we heard slowly approaching our position. I had Coutts and Wagner undress, start talking loudly, and intentionally expose themselves, supposedly as they took a bath in the muddy river. In other words, the two nudists were to present the illusion of revealing everything while they exposed nothing. In short order the rest of us took our camouflaged positions among swamp trees with our grenades, blank-firing weapons, and pencil flares at the ready. Once they sighted our decoys, the PBR sailors naturally presumed that they had caught two stupid guerrillas with their pants down and poured the coals to their PBRs with their weapons blazing. They hadn't steamed fifty meters before pencil flares streaked over their bows and grenade simulators started exploding on the surface around their craft. Because of our nasty tactic of luring the PBRs into the ambush site—located in a narrow, dead-end inlet—the boats had a devil of a time with their fire and maneuver, fire and escape. The PBR sailors soon fled from our area of the delta swamp and marshland. I certainly couldn't blame them—we had stacked the deck.

I was not surprised that we saw and heard a wide variety of wildlife during our stay in the Honey Island Swamp. The most prevalent were birds, mudcats, snakes, and mosquitoes. Our only encounter with a cottonmouth water moccasin viper was on a muddy tidal flat just after sunset. In the dim shadows, the viper was little more than three feet in length, but was four inches in diameter at midsection—it had probably eaten a bullfrog. He was less than ten feet from us when he started hissing and moving aggressively toward us. He exuded a wickedness that reminded me of the viper that a PRU and I had encountered on a narrow dirt road one ominous night in '69 not long before we were ambushed. A man doesn't forget times like that. The hair on the back of my neck was still standing at attention well after we were able to move away from the water moccasin.

Harmless water snakes were common, wild hog tracks were everywhere, but alligators were seldom seen because of their generally nocturnal habits. We did see one alligator of five feet in length swimming on the surface about midday. He may have been searching for mudcats, because during the heat of each day there were large schools of the little—four to six inches—catfish packed closely together, swimming on the surface with their whiskers and mouths just out of the water. Their strange habit was supposedly necessary because of the lack of oxygen in the stagnant swamp water, which was filled with mosquito larvae. Some of the catfish schools must have numbered in the hundreds. White cattle egrets, bitterns, and herons were common and seemed to prefer standing on the cypress trees to wait for the mudcats to swim below them. One of the main differences between these animals and mankind was that we didn't need the food to justify our predations.

Hoot owls' and whippoorwills' lonely cries and haunting calls, the drone of mosquitoes and the light of lightning bugs penetrated all levels of the swamp during the night hours. Alligator gars of up to five and six feet in length and weighing well over one hundred pounds cruised along the surface looking for one- and two-pound drum or carp. Gars could be called the freshwater barracuda because of their occasional predations upon human fingers and wrists with shiny objects on them. In 1951 a 279-pound, ninety-three inch alligator gar was caught in the Rio Grande River, Texas. Our short stay in the Honey Island Swamp gave us only a small glimpse of the primeval life that still abounds in some not-so-remote areas of this world.

Interestingly, some of the local authorities told us that folks commonly disappeared in the swamp and were never heard from again. We were warned to be on the alert for the unknown and unexplained. For emergency purposes, each of us carried one M-16 magazine of 5.56mm ball ammo. We did find several small man-made structures containing personal belongings. However, we never encountered face-to-face any of the mysterious "swamplanders" during our stay.

On our return trip to New Orleans by vehicle, we stopped at a country Cajun bar and grill for a cool one and a hamburger. The atmosphere was oppressive and unfriendly. None of the locals spoke to us, and they looked at us suspiciously—maybe it was our short haircuts. It is my opinion that the country folk in the movie *Southern Comfort* were not portrayed out of character. Although I did acquire a taste for their chicory coffee, it was a relief to get out of that part of the country and back to the cheerful Silver Strand for a few days.

In June, Lieutenant (jg) B. and I flew to Washington, D.C., for briefings by the U.S. Customs (Treasury Department) number-two man and staff. Alfa Platoon had been tasked to develop a meaningful training course that would enable the Customs Patrol Officers (CPOs) to increase their interdiction of drugs and contraband crossing our international borders.

Two days were spent attending congressional subcommittee meetings in the Sam Rayburn Building concerning a squabble between the Border Patrol (Immigration Naturalization Service, Justice Department) and Customs Patrol Officers (Treasury Department). Fundamentally, Border Patrol wanted to change their primary mission of interdiction of illegal aliens to interdiction of drug smuggling and contraband. The Border Patrol's motive for requesting a legislative reversal of their primary and secondary missions was to increase the seriously low morale/job satisfaction of their patrolmen. For reasons of political power, the number of Border Patrolmen on our southern border was intentionally kept low so that the illegal aliens entering our country would not be restrained. And, to make matters worse, many a pregnant illegal alien came to the U.S. to have her child, thus qualifying the child for immediate U.S. citizenship. Because the illegal alien mother had no funds to support her child, she was eligible to draw Medicaid, food stamps, housing assistance, and welfare payments (city, county, and state funded) because of federally mandated laws. Because Democrats had generally controlled both houses of Congress since World War II, they continually refused to legislate funds to increase the number of Border Patrolmen on the U.S.-Mexican border. The Democrats were generating demand for their own social programs, leaving the Border Patrolmen in a powerless position with very low morale. Many of the frustrated Border Patrolmen had already transferred to U.S. Customs or DEA (Drug Enforcement Agency). It was tough being a loser.

U.S. Customs was forced to get into the squabble because the Border Patrol wanted to take over the CPOs' function at all Points of Entry along the border. Frankly, I sympathized with both of them. In the end, Congress refused to approve the Border Patrol's request for change of priorities and business went on as usual on our borders.

After the congressional meetings, Customs determined that Lieutenant (jg) B. and I should tour the U.S.-Mexican border (accompanied by CPOs) from Brownsville, Texas, to Nogales, Arizona, by vehicles and small aircraft to gain insight into the drug and illegal alien problems.

The border tour was enlightening, to put it mildly. Aliens were crossing the border everywhere day and night because there was no one to stop them. Drugs were being brought across the border by backpackers, vehicles, and small aircraft. Every few miles along the U.S. border there were crude, secret dirt runways with fifty-five gallon drums of 115/145 octane aviation fuel camouflaged nearby, where small aircraft could quickly land, drop off drugs, refuel, and depart. Customs Patrol Officers (in 1974) were similar to the Border Patrol in that they didn't have enough manpower, vehicles, or aircraft to stem the flow of drugs across our border. Customs estimated that they were interdicting no more than ten percent, and probably much less, of all drugs entering the U.S. However, Customs had, at that time, recently transferred many of their Sky Marshals, who had previously ridden aboard commercial airliners to deter hijackers, to the CPO program. Gradually, I began to understand the CPOs' mission and their weapons and tactical training needs. In many ways, all they needed were infantry trained personnel.

In 1968 SEAL Team 1 supported the Border Patrol in the interdiction of illegal aliens along the border in San Diego County for a short time during Captain Dave Schaible's reign. It was great training for platoons prior to their departure for Vietnam, and the Border Patrol loved it. A Border Patrolman would guide the SEALs to a main crossing point at the border, then turn control over to the platoon officer. Everyone's weapons were adapted for firing blanks, and the only ordnance utilized were grenade simulators, smoke grenades, and pop flares. All prisoner handling procedures were in effect.

Once the ambush was set, everyone waited for the "coyote," or alien guide, to guide his group across the line. When the aliens entered the "capture zone," the OIC initiated the ambush by firing a pop flare over them and opening fire with his CAR-15 (XM-177E2) for a few seconds. Yelling "Cease fire!" the SEALs jumped up and chased the aliens on foot. No doubt, the aliens understood that we were taking their trespass seriously. During one particular night, a platoon had set its ambush on the side of a hill above a deep ravine that was used by illegal aliens to enter the U.S. After the initial weapons barrage and pop flares deployment, the coyote about-faced and started returning for the border with uncommon speed. To the chagrin of the guide, PO2 Mike Thornton (Medal of Honor recipient) caught him from behind by the fellow's shirt collar. Because the ravine was steep, Mike was unable to stop, but managed to guide the coyote directly into a tree, which abruptly ended the footrace. Interestingly, the guide had a loaded pistol on his body. Nevertheless, the Border Patrol was later forced to cease utilizing SEAL platoons to interdict illegal aliens.

The lieutenant (jg) and I returned to the Silver Strand after an interesting but tiring trip. With a sense of urgency, I spent that evening, Saturday, and Sunday writing a nineteen-day training course that was to begin that following Monday.

Except for the first day and the FTX (Final Training Exercise) phase of the course each morning began with an easy PT and a run-walk-run. The CPOs received training in first aid, instinctive, live firing with M-16s, M-203 40mm grenade launchers, the CPOs' personal sidearms, night vision equipment, map and compass orientation, hand and arm signals, camouflage and concealment, stealth and night movement, patrol organization, planning and leadership, small unit tactics, surveillance methods, direct action tactics, prisoner handling, communications security, improvised booby traps, and sensors. The last five days and nights were called the FTX phase and were used to grade the effectiveness (professional and tactical) of the CPOs and the course curriculum. Through the Mission Directives, the CPOs were to apply all of the course objectives during the FTX. It was a butt buster, but morale for the students and Alfa Platoon was always high in spite of the incredibly long hours and seven-day-a-week schedule.

On the last evening at Camp Kerrey, I told the CPO class that they could sleep in that following morning. What I didn't tell them was how late they could sleep in. At 0700 hours sharp, Russ Brownyer and I went around to the southeastern end of the H-shaped building and peeked through one of the windows. No one was stirring, not even a mouse. I tossed a grenade simulator under the floor space, plugged my ears with my fingers, and watched the unsuspecting occupants as they snoozed quietly in their deck-gray-colored, double-deck bunks.

When the grenade simulator detonated, I was amazed at the results. The room instantly filled with fine desert dust from deck to overhead. The rack that had been directly over the grenade blast leaned to the right and came to rest on the adjacent bunk, dumping its occupants onto the filthy, littered floor. The blast of the grenade simulator had pushed the three-eighth-inch plywood floor upward with such force that the bottom bunk's starboard legs were driven through the plywood. I was rendered helpless with mirth and was unable to recover for several minutes. However, the students weren't nearly as incapacitated as I and, as soon as they heard my laughter, they swarmed out of the barracks in a spirit of playful revenge and, in disrespect for my position, dragged me over the bank and into the Coachella Canal for a good underwater cleansing. They were a great class with a good sense of humor.

On September 2, 1974, Alfa Platoon arrived at the Elmendorf AFB just outside Anchorage. From there we were bused to Fort Richardson's Camp Carrol to participate in exercise "Ember Dawn" with the Army and Air Force. Our first week was spent in preparation for our operations.

Just prior to our first operation, during our two-day isolation, RM3 Dave Smith and I spent much of our time familiarizing ourselves with a code-burster radio that transmitted tape-recorded Morse code messages within a couple of seconds. The purpose of the rapid transmission was to avoid effective enemy DF (Direction Finding) equipment that could determine our exact location of transmission. We also used carefully measured field expedient antennas for receiving CW (Continuous Wave) messages at specifically assigned times. Because of our closeness to the magnetic north pole, our compasses and radio communications became temperamental, and at times nonexistent.

On the night of September twelfth, a portion of Alfa Platoon flew aboard an Air Force Combat Talon C-130 aircraft to the Alaskan peninsula. Our mission was to destroy an enemy fuel tank farm that was located on the north side of the Naknek River near the small fishing village of King Salmon. The first leg of our mission was a jump into the tundra approximately seven miles north of King Salmon. The second leg would be traveling for two nights and hiding in tundra thickets during the following two days. The third and final leg would be the destruction of our target on the third night.

It was a beautiful evening, with the sun's reflections coming from just below the horizon, leaving a faint golden glow upon the many lakes and streams passing below us. All seven of us—Lt. (jg) Robert Baird, myself, Doc Moore, Coutts, Brownyer, Dave Smith, and Wagner—were suited up with our combat equipment, weapons, communications gear, food, water, and main and reserve parachutes. Dave Smith and I were the first two jumpers to exit the starboard door because of our extra heavy loads of radio communications equipment—over one hundred pounds each.

While I was standing in the door waiting for the green light, the lakes and rivers below worried me. I knew that the aircraft's computer exit point—determined by eight-digit coordinates—needed to be accurate. If we inadvertently landed in a lake or swift stream, we probably wouldn't survive long because of the thirty-two-degree water and our heavy equipment. Our bodies would start freezing up within two or three minutes after water entry, rendering us helpless. In 1968, "Friendly" Frederickson and a crew of Marine Force recon mates overturned their boat in the Potomac River during a winter training exercise. Freddie was last seen trying to rescue one of his mates. Because of the extremely cold water and because Frederickson and his mate weren't wearing life jackets, they soon disappeared underwater. However, in our case I needn't have worried.

When the green light flashed on, I immediately exited the plane, and 125 knots of wind and prop blast turned me aft as I plunged toward the tundra with my heavy load. Once I felt my canopy opening, I released my equipment bag, made one partial oscillation, and landed on the softest DZ of my naval career—an incredibly soft, spongy tundra. Later, we were told that we had jumped from an altitude of 250 feet. Normally, all military training static-line jumps were restricted to a minimum altitude of 1,250 feet. However combat jumps were normally at 250 to 300 feet altitude to reduce air time and the jumper's vulnerability to enemy ground fire, and to defeat enemy coastal radar systems. Because we were a Special Warfare unit working with Combat Talon and the Army, the altitude restrictions were lifted. With that in mind, there was no reason for us to have had our reserve parachutes snapped to the front of our harnesses—if our main parachutes had failed to open, we wouldn't have had time to deploy them before we hit the ground anyway. Regardless, all of us landed safely and quickly mustered for head count. U.S. Army Special Forces personnel were on the DZ waiting for us. Within a matter of minutes we moved from the drop zone and started on our three-night-and-two day trek across the treacherous but interesting tundra.

Because we were in some of the best brown bear hunting grounds in Alaska, I had gotten permission to jump with my old 8×57mm M-98 military Mauser carbine rifle with 180-grain soft-point ammo for bear protection. It wasn't much, but it was better than an M-16 with its small fifty-five grain, full-metal-jacketed (nonexpanding) bullet. However, as much as I had wanted to, we never saw a solitary bear.

Our first night's travel across the starlit tundra turned

out to be surprising in a variety of ways. One of the first things we learned was that not all tiny pools of water were shallow. In some ways they reminded me of some innocuous puddles that Dai Uy Fletcher and I had encountered in Vietnam. Because of the northern permafrost—a permanently frozen layer that was five or six feet below the surface—the tundra potholes were no more than chest deep and incredibly cold.

Our dark patrols were wet and cold and my Chippewa boots filled with water, but each night we were entertained by the heavens' aurora borealis, which was brilliantly and mysteriously displayed. During our difficult and punishing march across the thousands of uneven tundra hummocks, I would momentarily watch the heavens as through a darkened window—it was seemingly covered with slow-moving curtains. My next glance revealed that the curtains had been strangely removed as if from an opera stage. The phenomenon continued for several hours until it suddenly ceased. I also learned that the tundra was far more difficult to travel across during the black of night than a freshly plowed field, not to mention the bog holes into which I continually fell. During the day, while we were hiding in brushy thickets, we found many wild blueberries to snack on and to supplement our LRRPs. Russ Brownyer found a large wolf skull in one of the thickets the day before our final night.

During our last night, we finally reached our target—the fuel tank farm. After a reconnoiter of the tanks and their immediate area, everyone set security while Brownyer and I prepared the explosive charges for placement. Once we were ready, the two of us quickly moved to each tank and set the dual-primed, magnetic incendiary dummy charges at the level of the fuel. Keeping our "time on target" to a minimum, we quickly returned to our squad and all seven of us rapidly departed for our extraction point. Our mission had been successfully completed.

Four days later, during the night of September sixteenth, Alfa Platoon parachute-jumped into Dillingham's small airport, seventy statute miles northwest of King Salmon at the mouth of Wood River. We were successful in our mission to carry a timed special munition—carried by EN1 Mike Thornton—to destroy the entire airport and the surrounding countryside.

Later, during our patrol across the tundra to our extraction point, the Northern Lights were incredible, a light similar to the Milky Way—but much brighter—that went from one end of the horizon to the other. The lights disappeared within a couple of hours.

By October 18, 1974, all fourteen members of Alfa Platoon were aboard the USS *DuBuque*, LPH-8, and steaming toward Subic Bay, Philippines, at a leisurely rate of twelve knots. Lieutenant B. and Lieutenant (jg) Baird were the OIC and AOIC, with me as the platoon chief. The remainder of the platoon consisted of PT1 Charles Chaldekas, HM1 Walter Moore, RM2 Donald Beem, PN2 Michael Anderson, RM2 Tipton Ammen, EM3 Frank Richard, RM3 David Smith, EN3 Russell Brownyer, PH3 William Hoppes, GMG3 Dodd Coutts, and AN Robert Wagner. Our daily activities centered on intensive PT and running. Platoon training classes covered refreshers on advanced demolitions, intelligence, first aid, tactics, weapons, air and diving operations, diving tables, and working in our rates with the shipboard personnel.

On November fourteenth at 0800 hours, the *DuBuque* pulled into Subic Bay and docked at one of the piers. Everyone was chomping at the bit to set foot on terra firma for a while. During our stay aboard the USS *DuBuque*, all of us had been reminded of how fortunate we were to be members of Special Warfare versus crewmen aboard a Gray Ghost. One of the consequences of increasing the level of women in the Navy was that they took many of the shore-duty billets that might have been available for the seagoing male sailors. The result was that more and more male sailors were forced to spend most of their careers at sea with little time left to be with their families. The new policies were accompanied by a high divorce rate and lower reenlistment of the more desirable ratings—similar to the Army's MOS.

Within a few days after our arrival, EN3 Russ Brownyer, HM1 Moore, and I were tasked to train a group of Cambodian naval personnel of the Lon Noe government in the use of demolitions and weapons. The Khmer personnel had just arrived from Phnom Penh, the capital of Cambodia. Fortunately, the Cambodian naval warrant officer (Officer in Charge) could speak fairly good English and excellent French. I could speak fair English and worse French. Between the two of us and with the teaching principle of "show and tell," we managed to communicate well enough to accomplish the training objectives. As usually happens during times of war, we grew close to the Khmer trainees, realizing that their days in this life were probably short.

During the first part of January, I managed to win first place in my age group in the All Services eight-mile marathon. Lieutenant (jg) Baird took second in his age group, outdistanced by a Navy pilot who ran an average of four minutes and forty seconds a mile over a difficult course during the heat of the day—over 100 degrees, with high humidity.

January 20, 1975, began a four-week training exercise in riverine warfare called Lumba-Lumba, with a large class of thirty Philippine coast guard commandos. Because of Special Warfare's overcommitment and shortage of manpower, I was given only Tipton Ammen to assist me in the daily training classes and nightly exercises and missions.

The Philippine coast guardsmen were an excellent class. Some of them had been on raids against the Muslim Communist insurrectionists on the southern island of Mindanao the previous year. Each morning began with me leading PT and the run. I remember that one of the Filipinos was a very good runner and always had an infectious grin. Most members of the class were excellent in the bush when it came to cover and concealment, fire and movement, fire and maneuver. Tipton and I instructed them in small-unit tactics, weapons training, basic demolitions, booby traps, rappeling, and other areas of special and conventional warfare. Because of the long hours, Ammen and I seldom got to bed before midnight. However, there was never a complaint from anyone. The Filipino personnel were always professional and highly motivated. As all military instructors know, when the students are motivated, the instructor's task is half done.

On February twenty-fourth the commandant of the Philippine coast guard, Ernesto R. Ogbinar, presented me with their seventh "Plaque of Distinction." I was very honored.

A few days after the Philippine coast guardsmen had graduated, Alfa Platoon was aboard the USS *White Plains*, AFS-4, headed for Chinhae, Korea. Our platoon was to participate in the annual Foal Eagle winter exercises with our Korean UDT/EOD counterparts. During those four weeks, we trained and operated together aboard a U.S. diesel-powered submarine, made a night combat equipment parachute jump near Masan on March twenty-fourth, and trained our counterparts in specific areas that they had requested. The training phase was capped off with an FTX to test their and the instructor's proficiency.

Prior to our static-line combat equipment jump on the night of the twenty-fourth, Doc Moore and I had the opportunity while we were in Chinhae to gain added expertise in tae kwon do. Several evenings each week I hired a Korean sixth-degree black belt instructor to teach me personally. My kicking improved rapidly and markedly. Occasionally, I sparred with other black belts at the gym, and held my own mostly because of my physical condition. I contact-sparred with a regular U.S. Navy fellow who weighed about 220 pounds. He was as tall as I and certainly larger in bone structure. He was a worthy opponent and in excellent condition. My Korean instructor called it a draw. Frankly, I was glad that I didn't get my butt kicked.

On March twenty-third I received word that the members of the Cambodian class that I had trained at Niland during the spring of '74 were all dead. Most of them had stayed at my home for several weekends before their return to Cambodia.

Otherwise, my stay in Korea was a very enjoyable one. I especially admired the Koreans' industrious and respectful nature. Early every morning, I watched the citizens sweep the streets and sidewalks in front of their homes or businesses. All of the Korean homes that I visited were absolutely spotless inside and out. The Korean military forces and especially the UDT/EOD types were exceptionally well-disciplined and highly motivated regardless of the tasks. On April first PT1 Charles Chaldekas and I were presented with Plaques of Appreciation for our long hours of instructor duties.

After we returned to Subic Bay, I did get in a few free-fall jumps from CH-53 and CH-46 helicopters. We especially liked the 53s because they could reach high altitudes in a very short time. Most of our free-fall jumps were from ten thousand feet.

During the months of March and April the Navy was very busy supporting the evacuation of all U.S. citizens, advisers, and Vietnamese allies from Saigon and other areas of South Vietnam. It was a sad time for all of us. Our country and our Congress had lost much "face" with our Oriental allies. The Navy and Air Force had originally planned to stage many of the Vietnamese refugees on Grande Island—located at the mouth of Subic Bay—and Clark Air Force Base, near Manila, for the short term. However, the Philippine government objected to the U.S. using Clark and Subic Bay as Vietnamese refugee processing centers. Consequently, the refugee processing centers were set up on Guam and Wake islands. Those were ugly and disgraceful days for my country.

On the first of April we received word that two U.S. Merchant Marine ships were commandeered by desperate South Vietnamese refugees and ARVN troops. Obviously, they had been fleeing from the North Vietnamese invading army. The two ships supposedly departed Da Nang, sailed down to Saigon and Vung Tau, but were denied entry at both points. They then sailed on to An Thoi, located on Phu Quoc Island near the Cambodian border. The situation was apparently bleak there also. The commandeers' final decision was to head for Subic Bay, Philippines. The Merchant Marines aboard the two ships reported that people on both vessels were packed like human sardines—there was only standing room. The last word I received, on April eighteenth, was that after two weeks at sea, the poor refugees and ARVN soldiers were forced to stand in their own excrement for lack of anywhere to go to the head (bathroom). There were supposedly numerous robbings and killings, and starvation was a continual problem. Before the Philippine government denied their entry, the two ships were sent to off-load and quarantine the refugees on Grande Island. I had been scheduled to be used as an adviser and interpreter until I was told that I must prepare to go to Taiwan. I never did find out if the two U.S. Merchant Marine ships made it to Guam or Midway.

On April twenty-sixth HM1 Doc Moore, EN3 Russ Brownyer, and I flew to the Republic of China (Taiwan) to train their Navy UDT/EOD personnel in the use of the Burnett Electronics Model-512 Underwater Acoustic Receiving System. The Model 512 pinger receiver was used in locating underwater training mines—or any other object that had a pinger installed within or attached to it—off the southern coast of Taiwan during the Chinese navy's "Kang Ping #3 Maneuver" MINEX (Mine Exercise). Because I was EOD qualified, I worked directly with the Nationalist Chinese EOD divers in locating and retrieving the underwater mines using our M-512 pinger receiver.

When we arrived at Taipei, Lt. Jerry Fletcher met us at the airport. What a surprise! Dai Uy had been assigned as a naval liaison officer of the U.S. Embassy. He had married a beautiful Chinese woman named Janice. The next day, Dai Uy drove us down to Kaohsiung, where we reported to the Chinese naval base located at Tsoying. Lieutenant Fletcher introduced us to the commanding officer of the Chinese Navy Underwater Demolition Team, Captain Feng Chien. Captain Chien was approximately five feet nine inches tall, stoutly built at 180 pounds, in his early thirties, very charismatic and handsome. Later, Captain Chien introduced us to the CO, Lieutenant Commander Lee (O-4) and XO (lieutenant or O-3) of his small EOD team. I immediately recognized both of them. When I had first arrived at Key West in October 1972, they were just finishing their diving training and were leaving for

Indian Head, Maryland, for their EOD training. The following January, after I had graduated from Deep Sea Diving School, I saw them again for a time at the EOD School at Indian Head.

That afternoon, I trained several of the Chinese EOD personnel in the use of the pinger receiver in their swimming pool. The following day, all of us boarded a Chinese navy ship and proceeded to an offshore area where U.S. MK-55 underwater training mines had been dropped by U.S. Navy aircraft. We dived day and night for several days to depths of 100 to 120 feet in search of the mines. As an EOD diver, it was my first experience at actually locating and retrieving mines. The seas were calm and the water temperature was 80 to 85 degrees, with underwater visibility of up to thirty feet. We couldn't have asked for better conditions.

By May fourth, the MINEX was over. We had retrieved all of the mines that still had active pingers. Several mines had been lost because the pinger batteries had failed for one reason or another.

That evening at 2230 hours we arrived in Taipei, and at 0110 hours, May fifth, we were on our way by aircraft to Clark AFB, Philippines. After our arrival at Clark, we took a bus for Subic, and arrived there at 0600 hours. We were quickly taken to the USS *Blue Ridge*, LCC-19, where the three of us scrambled aboard for our final fifteen-day journey back to the Silver Strand. On May thirteenth I received word from the *Blue Ridge* comm shack that they had a message listing all E-8 selectees. I was absolutely thrilled to learn that I had been selected as Senior Chief (E-8). That meant a one-hundred-dollar-a-month increase in pay.

Our journey was spent cleaning up several berthing spaces that had been filled with the news media, Vietnamese refugees, and U.S. Marines during the evacuation of the last U.S. and Vietnamese from Saigon. I certainly didn't blame the Marines for making a bit of a mess because of their hectic duties and schedules in setting perimeters in and around Saigon to keep the North Vietnamese Army at bay through April thirtieth, the day that the Government of South Vietnam collapsed. I also found myself to be the senior man of SEAL Team 1's Alfa and Echo platoons, plus a group of Boat Support Unit's personnel. All of the officers and chiefs had wisely chosen to fly commercial air to California at their own expense rather than ride the *Blue Ridge*. I can't say that I blamed them.

The most recent bimonthly "Update" from the *Blue Ridge* crew had the following to say to their loved ones at home about their final days off South Vietnam:

UPDATE SUPPLEMENT

BLUE RIDGE and her crew are going to be late coming home. We hope this supplement to our last UPDATE of this deployment will explain why.

As told elsewhere in this issue, we departed Okinawa on short notice at Presidential direction. We were ordered to Vietnam. There, the crew of BLUE RIDGE rose to unprecedented levels of courage and determination as its hundreds worked as one to aid people in desperate need.

It was the people we came to help. They are our reason for coming home late. They needed us, and we were equal to that need.

For BLUE RIDGE, it began the night of April 29, 1975, as a giant South Vietnamese "Chinook" helo settled uncertainly to the deck with a frightened human cargo. It was the pilot's first shipboard landing.

It continued the 30th. One minute, all was calm, and the next there were helos swarming about like bees around a hive. Some landed precisely, some haphazardly, and one careened into the side of the ship. Crewmen and evacuees dove to the deck as hundreds of pieces of metal flew through the air. An entire rotor blade soared high over the ship and landed behind her. More arrived at a somewhat slower pace during that day and night.

The number of craft seeking refuge aboard BLUE RIDGE overwhelmed her, and flight deck crewmen trained to lavish loving care on helos were soon pushing empty ones over the side to make room for new arrivals urgently seeking a landing spot.

There were well-known people coming aboard— U.S. Ambassador Graham Martin, Air Vice Marshal Nguyen Cao Ky, and many more.

Less well-known but capturing the hearts of the crew, a South Vietnamese pilot volunteered to ditch helos in the sea. He defied danger doing it five times.

Reporters, representing ABC, CBS, and NBC, and many news agencies came aboard to report on the vital world news.

But now the job is done. Your loved ones on BLUE RIDGE have done their part—done it well. On a somber note, but with pride, we are on our way home to you.

Finally, we arrived in San Diego on the morning of May twenty-first. Sunny southern California never looked so good.

CHAPTER FOURTEEN

It is not the critic who counts, not the man who points out how the strong man stumbled, or where the doer of deeds could have done them better, the credit belongs to the man who is actually in the arena, whose face is marred by dust and sweat and blood; who strives valiantly; who errs and comes short again and again; who knows the great enthusiasms, the great devotions, and spends himself in a worthy cause; who, at the best, knows in the end the triumph of high achievement; and who, at the worst, if he fails, at least fails while daring greatly, so that his place shall never be with those cold and timid souls who know neither victory nor defeat.

—President Theodore Roosevelt

After my return to the Silver Strand, I was assigned to the Ordnance Department. I was now on the other side of the fence—I had reluctantly become a REMF. However, I did maintain my jump and diving requalifications, set up CW classes, present weekly demolition classes, and go on special assignments. I never forgot my responsibility as an admin'er to support all platoon members (operators) to the best of my ability. My position as an admin'er was to serve and support all SEAL platoons as needed.

On November nineteenth PO2 Kasco was killed during a free-fall exercise. We had been jumping from a C-130 at thirteen thousand feet above Rolls Farm, adjacent to the Mexican border. Because the weather was a bit cold, some of the guys elected to wear gloves during their free fall. Apparently, Kasco's ripcord (Piggy Back system) had gotten loose and was flopping behind his right shoulder. Whatever the reasons, Kasco was unable to deploy either his main or reserve parachute and was killed.

The following February, 1976, a group of us went to Yuma Proving Grounds, Arizona, for a week of free-falling. On one particular day we decided to jump despite fifteen to twenty knots ground wind, because the DZ was deeply plowed. The only trick was to get up after our PLF and outrun the canopy as we sprinted downwind. When that failed, we were forced to release one of the two capewells, which collapsed the chute. It was great fun jumping from a Navy C-117 fixed-wing aircraft, and good to get away from the Strand for a spell.

In May six volunteers were requested to go on a two-week marathon from Oakland to Sacramento, California, and back, for a total of 550 miles. SEAL Team 1 had traditionally participated in the annual Seal-A-Thon in support of the California Easter Seal Society. The two primary goals of our participation were to stimulate donations to assist crippled children and adults through the Easter Seal Society and to coordinate with the Navy recruiters to aid their recruiting efforts. Because I was bored with my mundane duties as the ordnance chief, I volunteered. My ordnance officer, Lieutenant (jg) Fox, a Mustanger, was probably happy to get rid of me for a couple of weeks anyway. With that, Lt. (jg) Carl Knos, HMC Terry Bryant, AE1 Harry Kaneakua, PM2 Richard Rogers, HM3 "Brother" Booker, BM3 Harry Nush, and "Happy" Smitty headed for Oakland. Mr. Knos took care of protocol while the rest of us did the running.

Our first engagement in Oakland was attending a California Golden Seals hockey game. We were given the game puck to carry to Sacramento to Governor Brown—who didn't take time to accept the symbolic puck—and return it to the Golden Seals hockey team. The next morning began our seven-day-a-week relay through the communities, where we were interviewed by four television stations, three radio stations, and nine newspapers. Additionally, a number of mayors, city officials, Navy League and Fleet Reserve Association members, and high school bands and track teams were on hand for our arrival or departure ceremonies. The most we ran per day was seventeen miles. However, Harry Kaneakua did run a little over twenty miles one day just to prove to himself that he could.

At the end of the day we were given free rooms at the local Holiday Inn, and the Golden Seals hockey team paid for our meals. Naturally, being totally depraved and full of vinegar, we headed for the inn's lounge and partook of the refreshments that were justifiably—in our deceived hearts—utilized to replenish our body liquids and heal our tired feet. Before the evening was over, the band usually invited us up on the stage to sing, "Old MacDonald Had a Farm." Loving the limelight, we sang with vigor and acted out our satire with animation for the chicken, the turkey, the dog, the cat, the pig, the ram, and the bull. During our presentation, the crowd became hysterical and fell to the deck as if having fits similar to a bunch of Holy Rollers. Once the audience had recovered, they threw substantial amounts of money upon the stage in appreciation of our humorous presentation and, more important, for the Easter Seal Society drive. In our own unpolished way, we collected several hundred dollars for crippled children and adults.

My highlight of the trip was when we stumbled into retired Admiral E. R. Zumwalt while running through

Concord on March seventh. Admiral Zumwalt had given a speech and was running for office against Senator Byrd of West Virginia at that time. Unfortunately, he didn't receive enough votes to replace Senator Byrd. It was a great privilege for all of us, however, to finally have the opportunity to shake his hand and to get a group picture with him. During Admiral Zumwalt's stay as the Commander Naval Forces Vietnam, he had protected SEAL platoons from being misused and needlessly sacrificed by conventional U.S. forces. On May 29, 1974, Admiral Zumwalt, while the CNO (Chief of Naval Operations) said, "I would take one SEAL one hundredfold over any Marine or soldier." I hope we'll always be able to live up to Admiral Zumwalt's statement, I thought.

Another enjoyable portion of the trip for me was when we ran across the San Francisco Bridge. It was a thrill; the view was spectacular. We also had fun on the Seal-A-Thon when ordering breakfast. Once the busy waitress came over to our loud and boisterous table to take our breakfast orders, I would usually get in the first lick by saying, "Give me a settin' of eggs [half a dozen eggs], a side of hog meat [a pound of bacon], and a side order of whippoorwill peas [a large bowl of grits]." Not surprisingly, as the waitress moved around the table, the orders were besmirched with provincial rhetoric.

The best joke I heard during the tour went as follows:

"The Self-Righteous Cultic Temple had just received a new preacher. Because the previous pastor had gotten too open about his lust of the flesh, lust of the eyes, and the pride of life, he got caught in a homosexual and monetary scandal. The attendance had naturally been low and the tithing nonexistent. In desperation, the new pastor had decided to visit a few of the temple member's households every morning to introduce himself and to encourage the delinquents to support and attend temple services that

Sunday morning so that they would receive a special gift of unknown tongues from a spirit.

"When he had reached the first house, he knocked on the door several times before a gray-haired, ugly old lady came to the door with her hair in rollers, no makeup, dressed in a threadbare housecoat and floppies. As soon as she saw him, she threw her arms around herself and exclaimed, 'Oh! Conway Twitty!'

"The preacher serenely replied, 'No, ma'am. I'm your new pastor. I'm Pastor Jones from the temple. I encourage you and your family to attend our temple services Sunday and receive a gift of unknown tongues from a spirit.'

"The preacher soon went to another temple member's home and knocked on the door. He knew someone was home because he could hear his favorite soap opera 'Days of Our Lives' on the TV set. In a couple of minutes a short, fat, middle-aged, flat-faced brunette with unkempt hair, clad in her pajamas opened the door, rubbed her bloodshot eyes, took one look and cried, 'You're Conway Twitty!'

"As usual, the preacher was imperturbable and replied, 'No, ma'am. I'm your new pastor. I'm Pastor Jones from the temple. I just wanted to stop by and encourage you and your family to come to the temple services this Sunday morning for a gift of unknown tongues from a spirit.'

"The preacher continued doggedly on to the third visitation and was soon knocking on another door. No one answered, but he thought he could hear the shower running so he tried ringing the doorbell. Finally the door opened and there stood an absolutely gorgeous blonde holding her bath towel over the front of her bulging breasts with both hands. As soon as she saw the preacher, she threw her hands around the preacher's neck, dropping her towel and screaming, 'You're Conway Twitty!'

"The preacher calmly cleared his throat and said with a

low voice, 'Hello, darlin'. Good to see ya. It's been a long time.' "

During May and June I was back at EOD School, Indian Head, Maryland, going through refresher for several weeks. All EOD technicians were required to attend refreshers at least once every three years. During the refresher I met BMC Dutch Miller, one of the most humorous and quick-witted old-timers that I had ever come across. We became fast friends for the remainder of my Navy career.

During July all SEAL Team 1 platoons, including most of the admin'ers, spent one week utilizing one of the Air Force's Combat Talon C-130s for airborne operations. As was peculiar to the SpecWar system, we jumped with tactical combat equipment day and night throughout the week and into a variety of tactical situations. The exercise was similar to a marathon FTX. In those days I loved to take risks. I wasn't afraid to take calculated chances. And then I broke my leg.

On July sixteenth, during an unusually wet night, I was standing in the door of the C-130 waiting for the green light to flash on. There was nothing but absolute blackness before me. I knew it was still raining outside because some of the moisture was blown into my face, sending chills running up and down my spine. The drop zone party's lights were not visible from the air. The aircraft's computer, however, had been programmed with the DZ's eight-digit coordinates. Finally the light turned green and I exited the door into the black night. I wasn't sure what altitude we had jumped from because Combat Talon had a habit of dropping us at three hundred feet or lower on occasion. Suddenly the DZ crew (HMC Terry Bryant) turned SEAL Team 1's ambulance headlights on. It was good that he had—otherwise I would have certainly smashed into the ambulance. I grabbed the right toggle, made a hard right turn and easily avoided the vehicle. Unfortunately, I hit the ground very hard and a loud pop came from my lower right leg. To say the least, it hurt like hell. Doc must have heard my cursing and soon saw me holding my leg while rocking back and forth on my butt in pain. Doc Bryant came over to me and asked, "Are you okay?"

Looking up at Doc with disgust (at myself), I smarted off and replied, "Naaaaa, I always grunt, groan, and cuss like this, you shithead. Help me get my right boot off while we still can."

By that time Lieutenant Loren Decker came over to see what was going on. "Is everything all right?"

Doc chuckled and said, "Yessir. Everything is fine. Smitty only broke his leg. All he needs is a couple of aspirin and an ice-cold beer."

"Where have I heard that before?" I mumbled to myself. Sure enough, my good friend Doc handed me an ice-cold beer after they helped me into the back of the ambulance. No placebos for me, I thought as I shivered from the cool, damp night. While Doc drove the ambulance over incredibly rough terrain, he managed to hit a huge pothole, throwing me up into the air and crashing down onto the floor, banging my right leg against the side of the seating area and spilling beer all over my head, face, and chest. Some days you eat the bear and some days the bear eats you, I thought as I crawled back up on the padded seating area.

Doc yelled back and asked, "Are you all right back there?"

"Yeah, hand me another beer, you spilled the last one," I replied while trying to maintain my sense of humor.

Because we were the last of the jumpers for that night, Doc and Lieutenant Decker soon had me back on the Strand and over to the NAB's (Naval Amphibious Base) dispensary. Once I got into the well-lighted building, I noticed that my right foot hung at a strange angle from my leg. At least the bone hadn't stuck through the skin, I thought. One of the best XOs that SEAL team ever had, Lt. Comdr. Paul D. Plumb, came by for a few minutes to see how I was doing. He looked at my crooked leg, shook his head, and left. The X ray soon confirmed that my fibula was indeed broken and would have to be screwed together. Speaking of getting screwed, the doctor told me to go home and to report to the Naval Hospital at Balboa the following morning. That was easier said than done. I had a devil of a time driving my standard-shift pickup home with that broken leg, and a worse time while I was attempting to take a bath. The next morning my leg was so swollen that I couldn't drive. I had to call Doc Bryant to send one of the guys to my house to take me to the hospital.

Once the doctors got me into the operating room, they gave me a spinal, screwed my lower fibula together with two stainless-steel screws, and put a full-length cast on my right leg. A couple of hours later I was rolled into a large dorm filled with Navy and Marine personnel. After the spinal began to wear off, my lower leg caused me great pain. It was the most intense pain that I had ever endured. I eventually had to get rough with the nurse to get something done. Finally, I was taken into a small room where a hospital corpsman sawed off the cast and carefully constructed another one. The corpsman told me that the young and inexperienced doctors hadn't allowed for any swelling—hence the extreme pain.

During the next two months, our SpecWar doctor put me in the recompression chamber on oxygen for thirty minutes at sixty feet three times a week to speed the healing. Two months later the cast was finally removed and I was able to begin the early phases of specialized exercising at Balboa. Within another couple of months I was back to running four miles a day. Until I broke my leg, I had arrogantly assumed that I was infallible as an operator. It was good to be humbled.

By November, I was assigned to Bravo Platoon as the platoon chief. In December, I was tasked to attend a special demolition course at the Harvey Point Defense Testing Activity near Hertford, North Carolina. A dozen or so of SEAL 1 and 2 personnel attended. I missed getting to see Big John T. by only a few days. The course was one of the most interesting that I had ever attended. The instructors were incredibly experienced, highly motivated, and a delight to study under.

The FTX phase was the most exciting that I had ever participated in. Chief R. R. Schamberger and I were assigned to blow up a large three-thousand-gallon tank of diesel. (Schamberger and two others were later to disappear on a stormy night during a water combat equipment jump a few miles off the island of Grenada. Their bodies were never recovered.) Carrying carefully calculated and prepared incendiary charges, the two of us successfully avoided the security forces, placed the dual-primed, multiple charges at the fuel level, pulled the fuse lighters, set the timers, and departed the area in well under a minute. The best part of the mission was watching the tank explode into a huge fireball. Saboteurs get all of the fun while EOD technicians have all of the work. It's good to be cross-trained—when you get tired of one profession, the other can be a breath of fresh air.

On February 8, 1977, Bravo Platoon was riding aboard a Combat Talon C-130 on a nonstop flight to Subic Bay. Our mission was to jump into Green Beach and destroy an enemy target. It was a very long three-day ride. Because the C-130 was refueled in the air, we were required to suit up with our parachutes in case there was a snafu. In an emergency, we were to run off the loading ramp ASAP and rendezvous in the water for eventual rescue. Fortunately for everyone, there were no hitches. On the night of the tenth we prepared to make our combat (training) equipment jump into Green Beach. HT1 Terrie McCullah and I were the jump master and assistant jump master. Terrie would lead the 1st Squad out the port door while I would lead the 2nd Squad out the starboard door.

The aircraft's computer had been programmed with the eight-digit coordinates of the DZ, and Combat Talon's goal was to test the accuracy of the computer and, more important, U.S. charts by dropping us without the guidance of a jump master. I had previously jumped into Green Beach, had traveled over much of the area, and was aware of the many dangerous ground obstacles. I told Terrie that I expected casualties and worse if the spot let us out over the boulder-strewn river bottom with its high banks. Terrie and I both knew that the drop zone would have at least a fire marking its center and had agreed that if the aircraft's green lights flashed on too early or too late, we would preempt the spot and jump at our own discretion.

At approximately 0230 hours both squads of Bravo Platoon were hooked up and waiting anxiously for the green lights to flash on. It had been a long and boring eight-thousand-mile trip. The night was moonless and dark. We had started across the Subic Bay and were rapidly approaching Green Beach, located at the foot of a mountain range. As I stood in the door, I strained to look ahead of the aircraft and watched intently for the DZ fire to appear in the blackness as we flew along at 130 knots. As soon as I spotted the DZ fire, I was able to judge the accuracy of the computer's spot. Amazingly, the approach to the DZ light was right on. Still unknown was whether the green light would flash on just prior to our flying over the center of the DZ. I needn't have worried.

Just when I was about to exit and lead 2nd Squad out of the aircraft, the green light flashed on. In a matter of seconds all fourteen of us had exited the C-130 at an altitude of three hundred feet. As soon as my canopy opened, I dropped my equipment bag and hit the ground hard. The only reason I didn't break my leg again was that I had worn a pair of French jump boots, one of the best investments that I had ever made. Maybe I'm getting a little smarter after all, I thought.

As luck would have it, MM2 Frank Wilson landed on the edge of the twenty-foot river bank. After landing in the midst of a few brushy trees, he started crawling out from underneath the canopy when one of his hands reached out into space. He carefully got out of his parachute harness and crawled in the opposite direction into the pitch-black night. Once Frank found his red-lensed penlite, he managed to get his weapon and gear and reported for head count.

Amazingly, no one was hurt other than the normal scrapes and bruises. After our muster, we spent the remainder of the night patrolling to our target, which we successfully destroyed. The following day we found out that the Combat Talon C-130 commander had decided that he would not rely on the computer but spot visually. Sound wisdom, I thought.

We spent the next few months training a group of Filipinos in an exercise called Palah, diving and getting in quite a few free falls. Chief W. D. Powers, previously with SEAL Team 2, was SpecWar's REMF for all air operations. Shortly after Bravo Platoon's arrival, I bought WD's Para Commander parachute and steerable reserve. I hadn't jumped with a Para Commander in over a year, since my trip to Yuma, Arizona. The Para Commander was one of the first civilian high-performance canopies, made in about 1960.

It wasn't long before WD and I organized a group of guys to go free-falling whenever possible. On one particular day, WD had me jump first as the base man while he moved in from above as the pin man. The idea was for the pin man to come in slowly, face-to-face with the base man, until we grasped hands. As the base man, I had to be patient and not look upward because I would tend to slide backward and force WD to chase after me—so I just waited. Suddenly, WD hit me hard from behind and grabbed onto one of my legs, causing us to spiral out of control. WD had inadvertently come in too fast and certainly too hard. However, neither of us was hurt and, in spite of our tumbling, WD managed to hang on and pull himself up my flying suit pants leg toward my shoulders. We flipped through the air for a couple thousand feet before we managed to grab each other's hands and stabilize. The number three, four, and five men moved in quickly for a linkup before we had to separate at 3,500 feet. When our altimeters indicated that we had reached 3,500 feet altitude, we each made a 180-degree turn and moved away from each other with the use of our hands and feet, followed by the standard wave off. For safety reasons, each jumper was required to wave his hands back and forth three times prior to pulling his rip cord. This would give warning to any daydreaming jumpers who might be directly above to get out of the way. At three thousand feet, all hands pulled their rip cords and were in the saddle usually no lower than 2,500 feet. For those of us who were fortunate enough to own our own personal Para Commander, we were soon flying circles around the rest of those who had the military-issue 7-TU thirty-five-foot conical canopies. All of us enjoyed a nice ride down to the old World War II Japanese runway near the Philippine village called Castillejos. After the day's last jump— some days we had Marine CH-53s long enough to make three jumps—we traditionally stopped by a small Filipino open-fronted palm frond refreshment stand where we each purchased a couple of San Miguel cool ones before our hot trip by truck back to Subic Bay. Those were exciting and euphoric times.

In March and April we deployed to Korea, where we participated in the Foul Eagle-77 FTX with the ROKN's UDU (Republic of Korea Navy, Underwater Demolition Unit). The Korean UDU, unlike the Korean UDT, is closely associated with the Korean CIA. Their CO was a very handsome, dynamic, and charismatic individual, of heavy muscular build, five feet eight inches tall and 180 pounds. He reminded me very much of the Republic of China's Navy UDT/EOD commanding officer, Captain Feng Chien.

We spent the better part of our visit on the island of Che Ju Do—located a short distance off the southern coast of Korea—doing what we normally do—raping, pillaging, and burning, symbolically speaking. One particular day we watched the indigenous women free-diving down to one hundred feet for small abalone, octopus, urchins, and a variety of mollusks. They usually swam for four to five hours and earned up to forty dollars a day. Some of them wore dry suits versus wet suits, as did some of the UDU divers. As long as one didn't get a hole in his dry suit, it was superior to a wet suit because the diver could wear multiple layers of dry underwear and heavy socks. However, I generally preferred wet suits in combat situations, except in extremely cold weather.

Interestingly, UDT was issued green, lightweight, rubber dry suits for extremely cold water swimming during the Korean War. While we were aboard the USS *Diachenko*, APD-123, off Vietnam during my tour with UDT-12's Fourth Platoon in 1965–67, SF1 Ronald E. Saillant told us about some of his experiences during the

Korean War while he, as a member of UDT-3 (later changed to UDT-12 in 1953) was aboard the USS *Diachenko*. During the winter of 1952–53 they were tasked to destroy or take North Korean fishing nets at night during "Operation Starvation." During those frigid nights, they worked out of LCPRs (Landing Craft Personnel Ramps) and IBSs when possible, cutting and rolling up the fishing nets, which were later given or traded to South Korean fishermen. All that the swimmers had available were dry suits similar to the old Jack Brown surface-tended diving suits, but made instead from a lightweight rubberized fabric. While the guys were working on the fishing nets, several of them unfortunately tore holes in their dry suits and suffered severely from hypothermia. RE's final comment was, "A dry suit isn't worth a damn after it gets a hole in it. I'll take a wet suit any day." He should know; he was one of the guys that inadvertently tore a hole in his dry suit.

In late March, Bravo Platoon and a few Korean UDU men were dropped off with four motorized Zodiac boats approximately ten miles off the coast of a supposed Marxist country (Che Ju Do Island) from a South Korean PT boat on a cold, black night. Our two-day-and-three-night training mission's objective was to rescue a group of U.S. and allied civilian political hostages held inside the Marxist country's international airport terminal by members of a notorious terrorist organization. Our intelligence briefing told us that the terrorists were a well-trained and disciplined force and they were holding the seventy-odd hostages within a specified area of the terminal. We were also told that the tyrannical leader of that country had added an additional battalion of crack infantry troops to the airport's security forces to respond to and discourage any rescue attempts.

The Zodiac coxswains took us to within 1½ miles of the beach. From that point, we entered the water with our gear and weapons attached to flotation bladders and swam for over an hour until we could hear the surf pounding on the beach. One UDU man and I had been assigned as the points. Then Lieutenant Keith, who was a very powerful swimmer, towed my gear in addition to his own, while my Korean mate passed his gear to one of his UDU teammates. The two of us swam on to the beach with only our weapons and basic web gear. Once there, we scouted the right and left flanks and a short distance into the hinterland above the high-water mark for any signs of recent enemy activity. Finding none, the two of us set security and signaled with red-lens flashlights for the remainder of our force to swim in. After everyone arrived, we split into two groups, with one changing from their wet suits to dry clothing while the other set security, and vice versa. Once everyone had changed into his longhandles, cammies, heavy coat, and gloves, and had concealed his swim gear, our Korean point guided us toward our bivouac.

Because we were carrying a lot of ammo, munitions, grenades and artillery simulators, food and water, our gear was very heavy. As an example, my personal rucksack and web gear weighed 105 pounds before we entered the water. It was a long night for all of us until we finally reached our clandestine bivouac, which was located in the midst of a reproduction pine tree grove and brush. For the remainder of the night and during the next day, we set observation and listening posts and lay low because of the intense farming activities that surrounded us.

The second night, we split up into small elements: one to reconnoiter for potential vehicles to be used on the third night, others to surveil the airport's terminal for any activity patterns, and the remainder assigned to covertly probe the airport's security forces for strength and response time.

On the third and final night, the consensus was to frontally assault the airport terminal with all hands loaded aboard two vehicles. We had learned that the security forces preferred staying around a warm stove to responding to false alarms. The only hitch was the narrow gateway into the main entrance of the airport. The gate stanchions appeared to be made of reinforced cement and volcanic rock and were judged too narrow to admit a 2 1/2-ton truck. Because the recon element of the previous night had located one 2 1/2-ton truck and a weapons carrier that could be easily stolen, the plan was for the weapons carrier, loaded with the initial assault element, to drive through the gate and get as close to the front doors of the terminal as possible. The 2 1/2-ton truck would have to stop just outside the gate, and the remainder of the guys would assault from approximately seventy-five meters to the rear.

The initial assault element's objective was to gain access to the hostages within a matter of seconds, eliminate the terrorist guards, and secure the safety of the political prisoners—tactical surprise, speed, and execution would be crucial. The second assault element's objective was to eliminate or neutralize the security guards at strategic areas of the terminal with speed and maneuver, and set blocking subelements against any counterattacks.

At 0215 hours on our third night, both assault elements were aboard the two borrowed vehicles and driving at normal speed to the airport gate. BM2 C. J. Dunn, who was driving the weapons carrier, drove the vehicle perfectly between the narrow gate and its cement and lava pillars, where it came to a sudden, screeching halt with a loud crash. Our weapons carrier was stuck solidly between the gate pillars! At that moment, the gate's immovable stanchions reminded me of the courageous Macedonian warriors who were renowned for their frontal attack in the form of a massive wedge.

Once the element of surprise was lost, our tactics boiled down to two main principles—speed and execution. Simply put, it was all or nothing. All of us immediately started sprinting for the terminal doors for all we were worth, firing our M-16s, M-203s, and M-60s. Those of us who were carrying M-203s attached to our M-16s were firing 37mm Vari flare cartridges to simulate 40mm HE rounds. Just before I reached the terminal glass doors, I noticed that when the 37mm flare projectiles coming from behind me hit the large, one-inch-thick, plate-glass windows, they created two-inch holes through them. I bet the Korean authorities will love that, I thought, as several of us continued topside to the roof to eliminate any security forces and maintain a vantage point to frustrate any counterattacking forces. Within a couple of minutes our objectives had been achieved—the political hostages were rescued and the remainder of the enemy forces had been held at bay long enough for all of us to be airlifted to safety. The Australian SAS motto says it best: "Who Dares Wins."

Several days later, after we had returned to Subic Bay, Philippines, we were notified that it cost over $35,000 to replace the plate-glass windows in the Che Ju Do Island's airport terminal.

The members of Bravo Platoon were: Lt. J. S. Keith, ENS Unknown, RMCS G. R. Smith, HT1 T. L. McCullah, SM2 T. K. Davis, BM2 C. J. Dunn, GMG2 S. R. Ellis, QM2 R. W. Kennedy, RM2 W. W. Nehl, BM2 H. R. Nush, HM2 J. L. Shoemate, EN2 J. C. West, MM2 F. W. Wilson, and SM3 R. T. Quinnett. Bravo Platoon returned to CONUS and reported onboard SEAL Team 1 June 28, 1977.

By July, I was assigned to Cadre, and spent most of the

following eight months at our training camp near Niland. During those months we trained multiple platoons, one class of U.S. Customs Patrol officers, and supported a desert exercise with a contingent of Australian SAS troopers and a SEAL platoon near the Salton Sea during December, when the ambient temperature reached an official 100 degrees.

When I first returned to our training camp located on the Navy's Chocolate Mountains Bombing Range, I found an eight-by-eight-foot, screened-in cage that contained approximately thirty rattlesnakes and several non-poisonous snakes. The cold-blooded reptiles were generally rattling and striking at the screen wire because the guys agitated them every time they passed by the pit. During that summer, the area had received an unusual amount of rain in a short period of time. As a result, snakes had become more common because of the temporarily flooded low areas. When the camp guards or platoon members were returning to the camp from Niland, they would stop and capture the snakes lying on the dirt road and later place them in the camp's snake pit.

On a Thursday evening, at the end of one of SEAL platoon's training phases at the camp, I decided to take one of the small eighteen-inch sidewinder rattlesnakes home with me and keep him in one of my large aquariums as a pet. I had gotten a broomstick and was maneuvering Bolivar II—the snake's new name—to the edge of the cage, intending to carefully place the end of the stick directly behind his plated head, when GM3 Andy Nelson came over.

"What are you gonna do, Senior Chief?" he asked.

Continuing to concentrate on my task, I gently pressed the stick downward just behind the snake's head without hurting him, but without success. The varmint was feisty and wiggled from under my stick. I looked at Nelson and replied, "I'm tryin' to catch this sidewinder so that I can take him home for a pet."

Andy was young, motivated, enthusiastic, and full of energy, like all of the guys, but a little short on discernment. "Let me do it, Senior Chief. Let me do it," Andy begged.

I just didn't have it in me to say no, and replied, "Okay. But you've got to get the flat end of that stick directly behind his head and press hard enough without hurting him. And remember," I admonished, "place your index finger and thumb directly behind his head so he can't turn and bite you."

Nelson shook his head and replied, "Yeah, I know, Chief. I know how."

I handed Andy the stick and watched closely as he placed the flat bottom of it approximately one inch behind the rattler's head. I warned him that the stick was too far behind it, and that he was going to get bit, but I was too late.

Andy had already reached down and grabbed the little serpent just aft of the stick. When he let up on the stick, the snake quickly turned his head to the left and buried his left fang in Andy's left index finger. Andy dropped that snake like a bad habit.

"I'm bit! I'm bit!" he cried.

Lord, I'm in trouble now, I thought. Naturally, his platoon officer wasn't pleased, and neither was I. In a matter of minutes Andy's left forearm started swelling and was becoming increasingly painful. Consequently, Andy and the corpsman immediately headed south for the small community hospital in the little town of Westmoreland for rattlesnake antivenin—there was none. They continued south toward El Centro and its hospital, where they were told that they didn't have any antivenin either. From there Andy and Doc drove all the way back to San Diego—160 miles from Camp Kerrey—to the Navy's

Balboa Hospital, where they did have the antivenin on hand. Later, Andy Nelson told me that after he received the antivenin, he had a serious reaction to it. The doctors were forced to give him shots to counter its effects.

Approximately one year later, I noticed that Andy's left index finger was still somewhat black, and I asked him how his finger was doing. He explained that the first joint had a tendency to peel two to three times a year and remained numb, but other than that, it gave him no trouble.

I laughed and said, "Because your index finger sheds two to three times a year like a snake, I'm going to start calling you 'Snake Man' after the famous snake-catcher extraordinaire, C. J. P. Ionides."

However, Andy Nelson thought poorly of his new nom de guerre, and seemed to dislike me thereafter. In some ways, I suppose I really couldn't blame him. The sidewinder only lived a year after his captivity. Bolivar II didn't seem to like his new coastal environment, unlike my Bolivar I—boa constrictor—from Panama (see *Death in the Jungle*).

During some of my time as a member of Cadre, I wrote and constructed live-fire combat pistol and rifle courses, using M-26 fragmentation grenades and foxholes. The courses tested individual marksmanship while rapidly moving from target to target. Both courses were timed and proved to be a lot of fun, and most important, confidence builders.

During those months, I also created, wrote, and started teaching SEAL Team 1's first one-week, day-and-night sniper course, which included a one-day-and-one-night FTX that took place in the pass between Lion Head and Beal Well in the Chocolate Mountains. With the help of others, it took me several months of range, equipment, and lesson-plan preparation before I was ready to teach the first two-man class. The purpose of the course was to prepare at least two members of each SEAL platoon in the basics of sniping and weapons care before their deployment overseas. Unfortunately, prior to this basic course, there had been no in-house sniper training per se in SEAL Team 1. It was rare, at that time, for anyone to be sent to the Army sniper course, and never, to the best of my knowledge, was anyone sent to the Marine Corps sniper course at Camp Pendleton.

However, before I could teach the mathematical portion of the course, my good friend Lt. Loren Decker—UDT-12's training officer—had to give me instructions in basic trigonometry and calculus so I could competently teach uphill/downhill trajectory curves, moving and moving oblique target leads, vertical adjustments relative to wind direction, and so on.

Next, I had to overhaul each M-40A1 Sniper rifle, a Remington M-700 with 7.62×51mm caliber, heavy barrel, parkerized finish, glass-bedded with free-floating barrel. I removed the accumulated copper deposits from the bores, then I recrowned each muzzle of every barrel, reset the Redfield scope rings and mount properly on the action, had damaged Redfield 3–9× Accurange scopes repaired at the factory, cleaned scope lenses properly, and purchased one-piece cleaning rods, among other things.

The only prerequisite for the course was that both men represent the best marksmen from each platoon. Because SEAL Team 1 lacked funding—during the Carter years and prior to the Delta Force's special funding—to acquire all of the equipment needed, I allowed both men of the second class to use my personal M-1A in competition, heavy barrel, Match rifle, which is similar to the military M-14, but semiautomatic only. For myself, the highlight of that class was when MM2 Frank Wilson fired a five-shot group of just under five inches into the center of a green silhouette at five hundred yards with issue M-118

7.62×51mm NM ammo while he lay on a limb of a desert ironwood tree. Wilson rightly decided to take that silhouette home for a souvenir. I was very proud of his fine achievement under field conditions and with minimal training.

During the Carter White House years the operational and training programs of the Department of Defense, and SEAL Team 1, were severely cut back because of a reduction in military funding. As an example, at one time, most of the Navy's F-14s at the Miramar Naval Air Station were grounded for lack of funds for fuel and replacement parts. The imprisonment of the U.S. Embassy personnel in Tehran for over a year and the failed rescue attempt added insult to injury. Those folks paid a terrible price for indecisive and incompetent leadership. Those were dark days for the U.S. military personnel.

CHAPTER FIFTEEN

The individual who refuses to defend his rights
when called by his government, deserves to be a
slave, and must be punished as an enemy of his
country and friend to his foe.
— Major General Andrew Jackson

By March 1978, I was transferred to UDT-12 as the
assistant training officer. My immediate superior was my
good friend Lt. Loren E. Decker, the training officer. Lt.
Comdr. Ray Smith was the XO, and Comdr. Al Winters
was the CO. Lieutenant Decker had originally served as an
enlisted man as a member of SEAL Team 1's Mike Platoon with Lt. (jg) Sandy Prouty (the OIC) and ENS Roger
Clapp (the AOIC). GMG2 Decker's platoon spent most of
their 1969–70 tour at the U.S. Navy's new Sea Float located near the southern tip of South Vietnam in An Xuyen
province. By September 1970, Loren had gotten out of the
Navy and was attending Kearney State College in Ne-
braska, where he completed his bachelor's degree in political science. After his graduation, Decker applied for the
Navy's Officer's Candidate School and was granted a
commission. ENS Decker promptly returned to SEAL
Team 1 in May 1973, and was assigned to Bravo Platoon
as the AOIC under Jon Wright, the platoon commander.
Bravo Platoon deployed to WESTPAC in '74 to Korea

and the Philippines. By August '74, Lieutenant (jg) Decker was reassigned as the platoon commander of Hotel Platoon with his AOIC, ENS Paul Salerni and the platoon chief, S. Sgt. Frank Cashmore—an Australian army SAS participating in the Personnel Exchange Program. Decker's platoon deployed to WESTPAC from August 1975 to April '76. Upon return to CONUS, he was transferred from SEAL Team 1 to UDT-12, where he was eventually assigned as the command training officer.

Within a couple of weeks, Lieutenant Decker and I were back at the SEAL training camp six miles west of Niland, teaching one of UDT-12's platoons about small-unit tactics and weapons. Shortly after that trip, the two of us accompanied another UDT-12 platoon to San Clemente Island for diving training and wild Spanish goat hunting during our off time. In between our arduous trips, the two of us managed to make a few free-fall jumps and dives for lobster and abalone near Point Loma.

It was during those good times while back on the Strand that I came to know a couple of ex–East Coast guys, MCPOs Hershel Davis and Roy Dean Matthews. They were two of the best natural comedians that I had ever known, especially Hershel. I had first met them during my tour with the PRU in '69 when they were members of a SEAL Team 2 platoon operating out of My Tho, Vietnam. However, I didn't have much of a chance to get to know either one of them before they had to leave the country quite suddenly. The reason for their untimely departure was that they had injudiciously targeted and killed a legal VCI on VC island in the My Tho River. Colonel Dao, the province chief, and his U.S. counterpart—the province senior adviser—and the Company province officer in charge raised hell about the incident to the Navy. Apparently, the VCI was a double agent and was working for agencies/intel organizations on both sides of the fence. In that light, the SEAL 2 platoon was swiftly judged and punished by expelling Davis's and Matthew's platoon immediately from the Republic of South Vietnam. There's no doubt in my mind that Roy Dean and Hershel had something to do with the death of that double-dealing, VCI pig.

Usually, during the noon hour, Lieutenant Decker and I stayed in the training office and ate our lunch together while discussing two of our favorite subjects: firearms and hunting. Loren's wife, Melanie, always fixed him a large lunch, which was placed carefully in a brightly colored Bugs Bunny and Mickey Mouse–type metal lunch box. For some strange reason, Roy Dean was drawn to that lunch pail and started sneaking into the training office and stealing one of Decker's two delicious sandwiches from it. Roy Dean would surreptitiously steal the sandwiches, while Lieutenant Decker and I were suffering under Senior Chief Frank Perry's butt-bustin' PT and run/swim/run or burnout PT on Fridays. Neither Lieutenant Decker nor I had any idea who was stealing the sandwiches until a week or so later when Roy Dean, short on discernment but long on cunning, stuck his balding head into the training office, smacked his lips with obvious satisfaction, and asked, "Mr. Decker, what is your wife's name?"

Loren, being a bit puzzled, answered, "Melanie. Why?"

"Tell Melanie to use sweet pickles rather than those dill ones. . . . I hate dill pickles," Roy Dean replied.

Decker wisely revealed no emotion and didn't comment. After Roy Dean had left, laughing arrogantly as he walked toward the quarterdeck, Decker smiled and said, "Tomorrow I'll have a surprise package waiting for Master Chief Roy Dean Matthews."

For several weeks Lieutenant Decker placed a variety of sordid items inside each sandwich for Roy Dean's indiscriminating palate. Strangely, Matthews never did catch on to Decker's covert sandwiches and continued to unwittingly consume their contaminated contents with relish.

By the fall of '78, Lieutenant Decker had been reassigned as NavSpecWar Group's Air Operations officer, and I was reassigned TAD as the assistant Air Operations officer of the combined UDT/SEAL parachute loft located just behind the SEAL Team 1's administrative spaces.

Continuing in my REMF (Rear Echelon Matriarchal Facade) responsibilities, I was tasked to aid and partake in the training of jump masters, rappel/McGuire and cast masters. I enjoyed my new assignment and especially enjoyed working for Lieutenant Decker. However, I was forced to adjust to those administrative tasks of aircraft scheduling, maintenance of filing systems, and many other mundane tasks that REMFs have to take care of.

In January and February 1979, Lieutenant Decker and I were tasked as the logistics officer and the assistant logistics officer for SpecWar units while participating in the Joint Readiness Exercise Jack Frost '79, based out of Camp Carrol, Fort Richardson, Alaska. It was a new experience and gave me greater insight and appreciation for the admin'er types, considering that I had become one. We worked long hours, including a surprising amount of hard physical labor to support the SEAL platoons and the SpecWar Air Department; however, we did have time to get in a fair amount of cross-country skiing on Fort Richardson's excellent ski trails.

After our return to the Silver Strand, SEAL Team 1 requested me to teach two more two-man sniper classes. Lieutenant Decker was very tolerant in allowing me to leave the Strand and head for the bush for short periods of time. PO2 Bob Keene of UDT-12, who was an invaluable assistant, was a graduate of the U.S. Army's sniper course. Blue-Eyed Bob was a delight to work with. As usual, both of us learned more than the students, and between the two of us, we gradually perfected the short, no cost to the government, one-week course.

During May 1979, my good friend Senior Chief Radioman John Bagos, a member of Beach Jumper Unit 1 and TAD to SpecWar's sensor program, was at my home one evening discussing his upcoming retirement after twenty-four years of service. John was telling me that he wasn't looking forward to retiring from the Navy, but he didn't want to remain in it either. John was worried about his ability to make enough money as a civilian to support his wife and two small kids and make payments on his home. I could tell that John was battling with his decision to muster out within a month, and thinking that the jumps would raise his morale, I suggested to him that he come with Lieutenant Decker and me to make a couple of jumps that Friday at Rolls Farm as a going-away present. John reluctantly agreed.

May seventeenth was a beautifully clear day, with little or no wind. SEAL Team 1 had several platoons scheduled to make multiple combat equipment jumps from our CH-46 helo that morning prior to any free falls, which was SEAL team's policy. During the first two helo loads, Lieutenant Decker and I alternated as the jump master while the other made the mandatory static-line combat equipment jump.

One of the SEAL platoons had a young corpsman who had recently graduated from the Army's airborne school at Fort Benning, Georgia, where they had made five jumps from the large, C-141 jet aircraft. During my turn as jump master, Doc was to make his sixth jump and his first ever from the ramp of the slow-flying helicopter. Because of the helo's slow forward speed and downward main rotor wash, the jumpers' parachutes were slow to open. Poor Doc dreaded that long falling sensation before his canopy deployed.

Once the CH-46 had reached 2,500 feet altitude and approached the exit point, I gave the hand signal to the assistant jump master for the jumpers to begin their two or three steps down the aircraft's ramp, where they stepped off into space and fell rapidly out of sight toward the ground as their parachutes slowly opened. Doc, the last jumper, timidly stepped onto the downward-pitched ramp and stopped—filled with fear and anticipation.

Sympathizing with his dilemma, I yelled, "Go, Doc! Go, Doc!" knowing that he couldn't hear me.

Doc took one more weak-kneed step, fell to his knees and tumbled helmet first off the end of the ramp. His exit was the most unorthodox I had ever seen. In spite of his initial fear, Doc landed on the soft DZ as a conqueror. I was proud of him for having the courage to do something that he desperately didn't want to do.

Shortly afterward, the CH-46 settled to the DZ, where Lieutenant Decker and I gave each other and John Bagos safety checks before our jumps. Once the three of us were loaded, the helo quickly gained altitude until we reached ten thousand feet. When Lieutenant Decker made his final spot, he walked aft to the ramp, where John exited first, followed by me, and then Decker. Because John was wearing a slick jumpsuit and Decker and I were wearing our specially made flying suits, with added material between the arms and legs for catching additional wind, thus slowing our rate of descent, both of us were having a difficult time catching him in the air. I finally had to draw my arms and legs in tight to increase my rate of descent in hopes of gaining on John. In the meantime I noticed that John was spinning slowly to the left. I was gradually getting closer to him, but not soon enough for a hookup—we were to wave off, as briefed, at 3,500 feet. Because John failed to wave off, I decided not to wave off to Lieutenant Decker and continued to gain on John. Strangely, John continued to spin slowly to his left but gave no other signs. Once he passed two thousand feet, he spun to his left and made no effort to pull his rip cord. Naturally, I was confused at John's actions and knew that something was desperately wrong. As I continued trying to get down to him, I caught myself yelling, "Pull, John! Pull, John!" I knew he couldn't hear me. I watched him continue to fall toward the ground at about 160 miles per hour with no attempt to pull his rip cord. Finally, his shadow and body came together on the ground with a cloud of dust flying up, creating a silhouette around his body.

By that time I was in a daze and well under one thousand feet. After I had pulled my rip cord and was in the saddle, I broke into tears. I landed a few feet from John's body, which was lying facedown as if he were still free-falling. I knew he was dead. For some reason, I didn't have the courage to go over to his body, and I simply continued to grieve. Within a short time Lieutenant Decker landed nearby and came over to me, put his arm around my shoulder and comforted me. I kept thinking that I was responsible for losing one of my very best friends. John was also a good friend of Lieutenant Decker's; it was a terrible loss for both of us. Sadly, John would have retired in twenty-four days.

Eventually, a Navy ambulance arrived and took John's body to the morgue. Lieutenant Decker and I returned to the Paraloft, stunned and in silence. I quickly showered, changed into my khakis, and went over to NSWG staff to accompany CDR Irve C. LeMoyne to notify John's wife and children that he was dead. That was one of the hardest things I had ever had to do. Because John had previously asked me to be the executor of his last will and testament, my responsibilities had only begun. Early the following Monday morning, Bob Keene and I were back at Niland teaching another sniper course. I had little time for grieving, which was just as well.

I didn't have the heart to jump again until one day before my thirty-seventh birthday, September twenty-ninth. I was the jump master, and jumped with a great bunch of Team 12 guys from 9,400 feet.

Six weeks after John's death I was called back to UDT-12 to replace Senior Chief Frank Perry as the chief master at arms (CMAA). Frank was a legend in UDT and SEAL team as an athlete, a plank owner of SEAL Team 1, and one of the mildest speaking and nicest individuals that I had ever known within the teams. He was making preparations to retire, and needed several weeks to break me in to my new responsibilities. Once I relieved Senior Chief Frank Perry as the command's CMAA, he retired from active duty with twenty-six years service and returned to his home state of Maine.

My immediate boss was Lt. Comdr. Denny Baber, the command's new executive officer. Commander R. A. Gormly had also relieved Commander Winters as the commanding officer, or captain.

While I was the CMAA and acting command master chief of UDT-12, I had the opportunity—or curse, depending upon how one chooses to look at it—to be the jump master of Coronado's annual Fourth of July celebration in 1980. Every Fourth of July, the Navy took advantage of the opportunity to promote excellent community relations between the Navy and the citizens of Coronado and San Diego.

That year's SpecWar show was basically the standard scenario that we had been using for years. One of the events was the UDT/SEAL helo cast and recovery. Initially, swimmers exited a CH-46's ramp or the helo's deck hatch, as it moved slowly forward at an altitude of twenty-five feet. Once the swimmers had entered the water with their fins on their web belts, their face masks, K-bar knifes, UDT life jackets, and, lest I forget, their UDT swim trunks, the frogmen swam toward an assigned beach in a skirmish line as if performing a combat hydrographic survey. After the swimmers arrived at the beach, they performed crowd-pleasing surprises in one form or another. When the swimmers had accomplished their mission, they returned to the center of the bay, where they lined up twenty-five yards apart. A short time later they were picked up by the CH-46, utilizing a Jacob's ladder hanging down from the center of its deck.

Another event demonstrated the use of the McGuire rig for the emergency extraction of SEALs and downed pilots in a hostile environment, and then a squad of SEALs rappeled off the ramp of the helo from one hundred feet. The McGuire event was demonstrated by two SEALs who were hooked up to a couple of 120-foot rappeling lines that were in turn carefully secured to the CH-46. As the two men held hands, they were lifted by the helo to an altitude of a hundred feet or so, and then they sailed over the watchful crowds as the helo made its racetrack flight pattern around and over Glorietta Bay.

The old World War II swimmer cast and recovery from an LCPL MK-4 or -11 was demonstrated by another UDT squad, which swam to the beach for another form of reconnaissance, and later set off a few small underwater charges. After the recon, the swimmers swam toward the center of Glorietta Bay, where they formed a straight line with twenty-five yards separating each man and awaited pickup. Utilizing the time-proven World War II method, the LCPL with an IBS carrying a UDT recovery man attached to its port side soon came along at a speed of approximately twelve knots and started the recovery of the combat swimmers. The coxswain of the LCPL carefully guided the boat alongside each swimmer as the recovery man placed a pickup loop over each swimmer's upraised left arm and flipped him into the IBS.

Another event included a demonstration of SpecWar's SDVs—Swimmer Delivery Vehicles, or minisubs—and seven or so UDT static-line parachute jumpers exiting from a CH-46 helo at about 1,250 feet, depending upon the wind's direction and speed, over Glorietta Bay, where the jumpers splashed into its center. And, finally, the Navy's Leap Frogs (UDT/SEAL skydivers) exited the CH-46 from twelve thousand feet with smoke grenades attached to their jump boots to enable the crowd to see all of the jumpers as they performed synchronous movements and created six- or eight-man stars. Eventually, the SpecWar jump team landed with their five- and seven-cell "squares" (parachutes) on the Coronado Golf Course, in the midst of the awed and pleased crowd, concluding the SpecWar demonstration.

During all of this activity, a SEAL squad, dressed in their combat gear with cammi paint on their faces and weapons, had quietly patrolled into the crowd as if on a combat mission. The squad's mission was to capture another SEAL dressed as a civilian from the center of the unwitting crowd. Once the abduction began, the targeted individual made a good fight of it, which eventually required the SEALs to fire their blank-adapted M-16's to simulate the wounding of the supposed Communist pig. Before the fight was over, pandemonium broke out—terrified women screamed, rug rats bawled, and old women fainted. In short order, one of BSU's high-speed boats arrived to spirit off the SEAL squad and their prisoner from the confused crowd. These shows were greatly enjoyed by the public; however, detailed rehearsals had to take place before each July fourth.

On the morning of July second, after several days of preparation by all departments, I briefed the helo swimmer cast and recovery personnel first in the UDT briefing room. Shortly afterward, when I started briefing the parachute jumpers, I discovered that my request of the UDT-12 training officer to select only experienced jumpers had fallen on deaf ears. I needed experienced jumpers because the very narrow Glorietta Bay was no more than 150 meters in width and had a hundred or so yachts that lined the golf course side of the bay. Because time was short, I accepted my lot in life and the very real possibility that some of the jumpers would get hurt or worse.

With that in mind, I began my briefing with a few solemn statements. "I know that some of you guys have recently graduated from Airborne School and are looking forward to today's jump. However, you are about to make your first water jump under adverse conditions. The bay is narrow and filled with obstacles, and the wind seems to be gradually increasing from offshore. My spot as the jump master must be exact—there is no room for error. You must do exactly as I tell you. I may have to give you last minute instructions just prior to the exit point due to changes in the wind. Now let's get on with the briefing."

Within another two hours, all of us were in the helo at an altitude of 1,250 feet circling Glorietta Bay in a clockwise, racetrack flight pattern. I threw out two streamers—the streamers have the same rate of descent as a jumper using a T-10 nonsteerable canopy—to check for drift. Not surprisingly, the streamers drifted to the far side of the Coronado Golf Course due to the wind having increased to a steady fifteen knots. Using one of SpecWar's PRC-77 radios that I kept in the helo, I called the SpecWar demonstration director, who was on the western edge of Glorietta Bay, and asked him if he wished to cancel the jump due to the borderline wind conditions. His answer was empathic. "No problem. Put the jumpers out as scheduled."

As the jump master, I had the authority, according to SpecWar's guidelines, to cancel the noncombat jump if I felt that the conditions were unsafe. In spite of my dislike of the situation, I decided not to cancel, and had the pilot adjust his racetrack pattern out just past the surf zone, which was approximately 150 meters seaward of the beach, across the highway and on the seaward side of the Coronado Condominiums. Using good Kentucky windage, I dropped two more streamers to recheck the spot where I wanted the jumpers to exit the helo. With satisfaction, I watched both of them land in the center of the bay. I decided that I would spot long so that the inexperienced jumpers would only have to steer directly for the center of the bay. I quickly passed the word to each jumper to exit closely together and to steer directly for the center of the bay as our helo swung around and started its approach to the exit point. I couldn't help but feel a bit sorry for PO3 Douglas B. Smith and the other guys. They knew they would be drifting directly over the new, tall Coronado Condominiums on their way to the bay. They also knew that if anything went wrong, they would be the ones paying the consequences.

As we approached the exit point, I did my spotting from the side of the starboard door of the CH-46. Once we had reached the exit point, which was outboard of the surf zone and above the Pacific Ocean, I gave the hand signal for the seven jumpers to jump off the end of the ramp. Within three to four seconds all jumpers had exited. Unfortunately, one of the jumpers went through several suspension lines of the previous jumper's parachute, resulting in their entanglement. As they were slowly spinning their way toward the bay, I told the pilot to stand by for casualties and had him circle well above the entangled jumpers. Fortunately, my spot was a good one, and the entangled jumpers cleared the Coronado Condos with room to spare and splashed safely into the water, missing the end of a small pier—on the Silver Strand, or west side of Glorietta Bay—by ten feet. The remaining jumpers landed in the center of the bay with no injuries or problems. I was relieved, to say the least. As Ian S., the Company POIC at the Embassy House in My Tho in '69, was fond of saying, "All's well that ends well." My feelings exactly, I thought as I returned to the North Island Naval Air Station with the helo and crew.

As in the past, SpecWar's Fourth of July demonstration and all of its events went exactly as planned with no hitches or casualties.

For the remainder of that year, I served under two of the best XOs—Lt. Comdr. Denny Baber and Lt. Comdr. Dale L. McLeskey—and the best CO of my career—Comdr. Robert A. Gormly. I was also selected to attend the prestigious Sergeants Major Academy located at Fort Bliss, El Paso, Texas.

Prior to my departure for the Sergeants Major Academy, I decided to have a going-away party at my house with two of my best friends, Randy Bryant and Jim Thompson, both ex-Marines. I had promised them refreshments, hors d'oeuvres, a barbecued venison hindquarter, and other forms of fine victuals as enticements. What I didn't tell them was that the "venison hindquarter" had actually come from a large, male, German shepherd. For entertainment, I told them we would have pellet pistol and pellet rifle matches between the three of us, and the loser would wash the dishes and serve the other two. Neither hesitated in accepting my invitation. Because Jim had shot competition in the Marine Corps, he was especially eager to challenge me in the pistol and rifle matches. In some ways we were alike—Jim had to justify his pride and I had to protect my image.

A week before the party, I had been awakened at 0130 hours with whining and growling that seemed to be coming from Lady, my black Labrador bitch. I went to my back door and saw that a German shepherd had crawled over my six-foot backyard fence and was hung up with my prized bird dog. I was infuriated! I didn't want another batch of puppies. Lady had a nasty habit of having nine puppies per litter, which resulted in over one hundred dollars per month increase in 1980–81 dog-food dollars. I got my .22 pistol, walked up to the two lovers, and let fly a projectile into the preoccupied German shepherd's ear. Within seconds I was dragging the dehorned dog to my shop, where I strung him up from the rafters. I gutted and skinned him like a deer and put his four quarters into my freezer. That's justice—that'll teach you to screw around with my dog, you Communist pig, I thought.

The next day, I called a Filipino friend over and gave him three of the quarters. He told me to be sure to rinse the hindquarter with vinegar before cooking to eliminate the "doggie" flavor. However, I knew better. I had eaten dog meat fresh cooked out of a wok within minutes after a dog's death. While I was a PRU adviser in 1969, a few of us had passed through a Vietnamese hamlet on our way back to Rach Gia. It had been a long day and everyone was absolutely famished. With that in mind, one of the PRU commandeered a dog for our dinner and was leading the young and tender canine from the village with a bit of twine that had been tied around his nearly hairless neck. He justifiably received a severe tongue-lashing from the dog's owner, a young mother. Apparently, the dog was a coveted pet of the lady's family, for, as we departed, the dog and the kids were protesting and crying. Once we reached the bush, the PRUs butchered and cooked the dog, broken bones and all, in an aluminum wok over a small fire. Because we had no water, we chased the delicacy down with Vietnamese *ba xi de* rice whiskey. It was an experience I shall never forget.

On the day of the party, Randy, Jim, and I had a blast competing with my target air pistol and air rifle. Randy did well, but eventually lost to Jim and me. However, the matches between Jim and me were tough. We continually had ties until, luckily, I won out. Shortly afterward, the main dish was served. All three of us agreed that I had cooked the best "venison" that any of us had ever eaten anytime or anyplace. At the end of the meal there was only the bone left to give to Lady, my Lab. Like my two mates, Lady unwittingly enjoyed the thigh bone of her lover—the eighty-pound German shepherd. Approximately one month later, I told Randy and Jim the truth about the fait accompli. However, to this day, neither of them has accepted the fact that they had enjoyed eating a two-year-old German shepherd's hindquarter.

By January 1981 I had moved into the BEQ (Bachelor Enlisted Quarters) and was attending the U.S. Army's Sergeants Major Academy's Class 17 with approximately 250 men and women from the Army and Marine Corps and fifteen other squids. Before I graduated in July, I was forced to burn a lot of coal oil during the evening hours studying for and attending two mandatory college courses. However, life was not always mundane—we usually found time to have fun, even during class.

Surprisingly, the academy's policy toward physical exercise and activity was very good, and required all students to partake of it in one form or another. I had volunteered to lead the biweekly PT and run simply because I preferred that to riding bicycles or playing tennis. Eventually, there was a group of us, including an Army Airborne Ranger (M.Sgt. Thomas M. Cruise), a very good male Marine 1st Sgt. (David R. Robles), a female Marine (1st Sgt. Dolores D. Johnson), and one Navy master chief (Jimmy E. Cox), who attended, plus others. All of us had a good time, and occasionally, after our PT and run, we retired from the 100-degree-plus heat to the club, where we enjoyed a couple of ice-cold ones to normalize our metabolisms.

In February, while I was in the First Group Life, I and all of Class 17 had the privilege and honor of shaking General Omar Nelson Bradley's hand. Prior to his death on April 8, 1981, it had been the general's policy to give a "Welcome Aboard" speech to each class and shake every student's hand. We were the last academy class to have that great privilege. General Bradley had truly dedicated his life to serving his country, and did so with great character, diligence, and honor. While I was attending the First Group Life, I gained two good friends: M.Sgt. Charles E. McCain and M.Sgt. "Deacon" Exnelianle Holmes.

Later that month, I was promoted to master chief petty officer (E-9) and became the senior student during my Second Group Life. Sgt. Maj. Robert W. Hale was an outstanding admin'er/staffer and group leader, with a unique sense of humor. M.Sgt. James A. Robertson (MOS: 11 Bravo), a large, powerful man who called himself "Whop-a-Ho" and claimed to be half Italian and half Arapaho, had been the senior man until I was promoted to master chief. We had a hilarious special ceremony, in which SGM Hale ensured that Robertson passed his symbolic hat to me as the group's newest senior man.

It was during the Second Group Life that one of our multitalented classmates, M.Sgt. Adrian Garcia, demonstrated his specialty of dry humor. One Monday morning, shortly after Adrian had arrived at our classroom, he made a comment to the group that he had observed a phenomenon that appeared to happen regularly on the El Paso freeways on Sunday mornings. "You know, I have noticed during the last several Sunday mornings that while the whites are going to church, the Mexicans and their jalopies are broken down on the freeways, and the blacks are being taken to jail!" Everyone laughed at Adrian's insightful observations; but no one volunteered any comments.

Another morning just before class started, Adrian offered me some beef jerky to go with my hot cup of coffee. I gratefully accepted. After I had finished eating it, Adrian pulled out another that was still in its wrapper and handed it to me. Without saying a word, Adrian pointed at the labeling. I read the small print and discovered that I had been eating dog food. With a deceitful heart and evil motives, I leaned over to my amigo and whispered, "Let's not be selfish. This unique jerky must be shared with our classmates."

Adrian chuckled, and with a gleam in his eye, pulled out a handful of jerky from his khaki pocket. It then dawned on me that my amigo had planned this ruse. I could see that Adrian had learned his Intelligence Specialist trade well. While eating the jerky ourselves for bona fides, the two of us cunningly passed out the left-handed jerky. Within a few minutes the whole class, including Sergeant Major Hale, was busily chewing away at the dog food and chasing it down with our typically weak, aluminum-flavored, military coffee.

During the next class break, Adrian and I broke the news to them that we had easily manipulated them into eating dog food. Naturally, they all denied our revelation until we told them to read the jerky's wrapping for themselves. A couple of the guys stopped chewing and started lip-synching the words of the label as they read silently. Gradually, as the truth revealed itself, some of our classmates started having stomach problems. While the better part of the Second Group Life lamented, my amigo and I openly rejoiced and cheered at the success of our ignoble ruse.

"Nonhackers," Adrian teased as a couple of the guys,

who seemed to be suffering from a form of male morning sickness, spit out the remnants of the substance into the trash can.

All went well until I noticed that the large master sergeant, Robertson, wasn't laughing, and had started giving both of us the evil eye. Our timing must have been wrong, I thought as I moved closer to my escape route—the classroom door.

Robbie commented satirically, "You two guys have gone to the dogs."

There was some truth in what he said. I had begun to perceive that Robbie was contemplating grabbing us by our stacking swivels and thrashing the thunder out of us both. With a sense of urgency, I nudged Adrian and said, "Avast! It's time to cut the moorings of our dinghy and catch the rising tide to get beyond the harbor bar and into deeper waters. The strong winds of revenge are drawing ominously near."

Adrian nodded and mumbled, "You're right, my friend, the water under our keel is too shallow and it promises to get much rougher. I must do something quickly," indicating that he had accurately interpreted the savage's body language. With that, Adrian lost no time offering an apology that was intended to create sympathy and give us additional time to maneuver and to collect our thoughts. Initially, my amigo tried to justify our deceitful ruse inthe minds of our classmates, especially the big chief, with the following reasoning:

"It's okay guys. . . . This jerky is good and safe to eat. I'll give you four good reasons why. Reason number one, some of my kinfolks are from Mexico and we eat this jerky all the time. I bought a whole box of it for my family in Juarez the other day while it was on special. Reason number two: dog meat is cheap. Reason number three: it's not so bad after you get used to it." Pointing to me, Adrian continued, "And finally, reason number four: just ask Smitty, he's eaten dog meat in Vietnam and in California several times and swears that German shepherd is the best meat he's ever eaten. How do you like us so far, amigos?"

The choleric Master Sergeant Whop-a-Ho Robertson saw through our duplicity, recognized us as rattlesnake liars, and started toward the then-defunct Garcia/Smitty duet with body language that left no doubt as to the outcome—scalpings, boiling in a pot, and cannibalism. I tried subterfuge by offering Robbie the token position of "Senior Man" of the group, but got no response other than the stink-eye.

Suddenly, I remembered what Sir Walter Scott had said: "Oh, what a tangled web we weave, when first we practice to deceive!" The truth of our humorous scheme had been received with scorn, we had failed in our professional fields of cunning and deception, and worst of all, we were undone by a mere Neanderthal.

Fortunately, our omniscient Sergeant Major Hale recognized that we were hors de combat and came to our rescue by putting on his genuine general's hat, which represented his sovereignty, and reconvened the class in a timely fashion. Actually, there was a second reason we were thankful that Sergeant Major Hale had placed the general's hat over his balding pate: the reflection of the sun's rays off his slick dome had forced most of us to wear sunshades in the classroom to filter out the worst of the glare.

The dog-food incident and other occasions that revealed defective traits of specific members of the Second Group Life soon earned us the sobriquet of "Hale's Warthogs."

Prior to Class 17's graduation in July, I had to reenlist again for the final time of my career. Colonel Joseph Ostrowidzki, commandant of the academy, performed the ceremony in his office.

CHAPTER SIXTEEN

What a society gets in its armed services is exactly what it asks for, no more or less. What it asks for tends to be a reflection of what it is. When a country looks at its fighting forces it is looking in a mirror; the mirror is a true one and the face that it sees will be its own.

—General Sir John Hackett

Once I had reported aboard EOD School at Indian Head, Maryland, for additional diving training, EOD refresher, and basic nuclear weapons disposal training, I was immediately placed in a student diving class. For the next few weeks I found myself back in the old MK-V deep sea diving rig, crawling around on the bottom of the Potomac River performing a variety of tasks.

When I completed my MK-V refresher training, I was instructed in the use of the new MK-1 surface supplied diving apparatus that was replacing the old Jack Brown shallow water system. The main difference between the two was that the Jack Brown system was limited to a maximum depth of sixty feet, versus 130 feet—extended to 190 feet with a bail-out bottle—for the MK-1. Also, an optional advantage of the MK-1 was that it could be used with mixed gas.

After the MK-1 training, I was instructed in the use of the new MK-12 surface supplied deep sea diving apparatus that was replacing the old MK-V (Hard Hat) system. I especially appreciated that the MK-12 designers had engineered a new deep sea diving apparatus that was much lighter, the MK-12 weighing approximately thirty-five pounds total, including the hat, boots, and lead weights. The old MK-V's basic weight was 190 pounds, and the mixed-gas version weighed 290 pounds. Lastly, I received refresher training in the MK-VI mixed-gas scuba diving apparatus.

During the EOD refresher training, my Navy class reviewed aircraft explosive hazards, conventional ground and air munitions, nuclear weapons, improvised explosive devices, and underwater ordnance. We also received a special training section that was dedicated to improvised nuclear devices: their identification, location, access and interface with other military, federal, and civilian agencies involved in INDs.

After I graduated from the difficult eight-week basic nuclear weapons disposal phase in October and November, I was again on the road to EOD Group 1's Detachment Whidbey Island, located at the upper end of Puget Sound on the Naval Air Station, Whidbey Island, Washington.

The EOD (Airborne) Detachment consisted of CWO3 Clark L. George (Gunner), who was the OIC, with BMCM Jim R. Collins as the AOIC, ABH1 Tony C. Tennyson, and I.

In December 1981, EOD Detachment Whidbey and Detachment Keyport (Indian Island) were called to support the Sheriff's Department of King County in locating a downed aircraft suspected of being in Lake Youngs, one of the more important reservoirs for the city of Seattle. The Seattle officials were especially concerned about the potential pollution to their reservoir.

The Naval Undersea Warfare Engineering Station's

December 18, 1981, *Keynotes* semimonthly newspaper told the events of the story as follows:

Neil Brown, 43, of Seattle, and his 15-year-old son, Michael, took off from Boeing Field in a Cessna 150 about 9:15 A.M. Thanksgiving day intending to practice touch-and-go landings. They had done so often in the past, and that particular Thanksgiving day flight was not unusual.

A while later, 16-year-old Dianne Vale of the south Seattle area saw what she took to be a model airplane diving low over the trees near her house about three miles from Lake Youngs, a major reservoir for the Seattle area.

Dianne thought nothing more of the incident and didn't connect the supposed model airplane with later reports of Brown and his son being missing on their flight.

But on December 6, she put together news reports of aircraft fragments and pages from a pilot's log being found in the nearby lake with the sighting she had made and called the King County Sheriff's Department. The sheriff sent a team of investigators to question her.

The team took Dianne into her yard and had her stand exactly where she had been when she saw the plane go down. Taking a compass reading based on her observations, sheriff's people laid out a swath on a map of probable crash locations.

The swath ran directly across one of the deepest parts of Lake Youngs.

Confronted with the task of searching through the dark waters looking for the wreckage, the Sheriff's Department called the Explosive Ordnance Disposal (EOD) Unit at NAS Whidbey Island and asked CWO3

Clark George for help. CWO3 George then called Lt. (jg) David Bodkin of the EOD Unit at Indian Island. Lt. (jg) Bodkin is the EOD coordinator for the ComNavBaseSeattle area and had access to the hand-held sonar unit at the NUWES Diving Locker.

Without the sonar unit, divers could search the bottom of the lake for weeks and still not find any wreckage. Sheriff's divers had already spent many futile hours probing its bottom.

Lt. (jg) Bodkin detailed AO1 James Tomiko and MM1 Timothy Pierce to assist CWO3 George in the search for the wreckage.

AO1 Tomiko said the first order of business was to establish a search pattern. AO1 Tomiko said searchers agreed to divide the search swath into two parts; starting from the middle of the lake and working toward each shore separately. Each part of the search would cover an area about a quarter mile long by about 200 yards wide.

The first dive produced nothing. AO1 Tomiko dove with Lt. Larry Zimnisky of the King County Sheriff's Department, searched the bottom with the sonar, and got nothing indicating a sunken mass of metal.

Their next dive was right on the mark. AO1 Tomiko said he and Zimnisky found the aircraft practically right in the middle of the search swath. But by then, he and Zimnisky were out of time. Divers working water as deep and cold as Lake Youngs are limited to about a half hour a day. AO1 Tomiko and Zimnisky marked their location with a buoy, returned to the surface, and turned the sonar over to ABH1 Tony Tennyson of NAS Whidbey and Patrolman Joe Lane of the Sheriff's Department.

ABH1 Tennyson and Lane took the sonar unit and dove to the wreckage. Tennyson said the aircraft was right side up on the lake bottom in about 90 feet of water. Both Neil and his son were still in the cockpit of the badly damaged aircraft.

ABH1 Tennyson and Lane attached a buoy to mark the aircraft's location and returned to the surface. Evening was falling and any recovery attempt would have to wait for morning.

Early Wednesday morning, two divers from the Sheriff's Department dove to the wreckage and recovered Neil Brown's body. His son's body was tightly wedged into the wreckage and could not be easily removed.

BMCM James Collins and RMCM Gary Smith of NAS Whidbey took a large pry bar and dove to the wreckage about 9:30 A.M. that morning and, after some work on the twisted fuselage of the aircraft, freed the boy's body and returned it to the surface.

Then MM1 Pierce and CWO3 George returned to the sunken aircraft and attached a large lifting balloon (Mark 2 Mod 1) to the wreck. The balloon, which can be inflated on command from the surface, brought the aircraft to within about ten feet of the water's surface. It was towed to shore and recovered by a crane.

Officer Mike Hagan of the King County Sheriff's Department said he was "very grateful for the help his department received from the Navy." He added that the sonar unit was the key to finding the sunken aircraft.

"If we hadn't been able to get that sonar unit, we would still be looking for the wreckage next week," he said.

In early February, while we were preparing for our upcoming mine readiness certification inspection, Gunner George got a case of the bends while diving the MK-VI scuba rig with a mixture of sixty-eight percent helium and thirty-two percent oxygen at a depth of ninety feet.*

Gunner, like the rest of us, had remained well within his allowed bottom time. Sometimes those things happen, especially after years of diving. Fortunately, we were located only a little more than three-quarters of a mile out in the Saratoga Passage just southeast of Forbes Point, Whidbey Island. Once we notified the NAS duty officer, a helicopter picked us up and took all four of us at about fifty feet altitude south to the Navy's recompression chamber located near Bremerton at Naval Undersea Warfare Engineering Station. After the Navy's diving-specialist doctor asked Gunner a few questions and examined him, Gunner was placed into the recompression chamber table with an attendant for two hours and fifteen minutes. After his treatment, Gunner said, "Man, I feel fit as a fiddle. Let's pick up a case of beer for the road."

In late February our detachment was required to undergo a mine recovery certification inspection. The inspection team were all EOD personnel assigned to the Mine Counter Measures Inspection Group located at Charleston, South Carolina. Their primary responsibility wasto inspect Navy EOD Detachment's operational capabilities in the location, destruction, or RSP (Render Safe Procedures) and recovery of underwater mines in a variety of tactical situations using regular air and the MK-VI mixed-gas scuba rigs. Gunner George had all of us busily preparing for the inspection. As was normal for

---

*The bends is a diver's disease commonly called decompression sickness, or caisson disease. It is a condition resulting from inadequate decompression following exposure to any inert gas (e.g., nitrogen, helium, etc.) at a critical depth and for a critical time. Bubbles of nitrogen are formed in the tissue and blood stream and by mechanical obstruction cause pain, paralysis, asphyxia, and, if large or numerous enough, can be fatal. (From "The Hazards of SCUBA Diving," prepared by U.S. Naval Safety Center.)

that time of the year, an Arctic storm came down through the Gulf of Alaska and struck the Northwest. In spite of the storm and the accompanying rough seas, we continued with our mine recovery rehearsals by diving in the somewhat sheltered Crescent Harbor, just west of Oak Harbor Bay near Polnell Point. Our diving platform was our outboard-motor-powered Zodiac—a rubber boat with a plywood deck and stern—which was soon coated with a thick layer of ice. Because we were diving with rubber wet suits and rubber gloves, our maximum diving time was no more than thirty-five to forty-five minutes. If we extended our bottom time, our minds, bodies, and especially our hands began freezing up from the effects of hypothermia.

Later, Gunner managed to convince the Whidbey Naval Air Station to purchase dry suits for the four of us, extending our time to well over an hour in the water during extremely adverse conditions. We also put on several layers of woolen longhandles and socks under our dry suits to extend our diving time.

Once the inspection team arrived, we worked fourteen to sixteen hours a day for six days searching for, destroying, or recovering rendered safe mines of one form or another on land, in the surf, and in black, muddy Puget Sound waters. All four of us made as many as four dives per day. Because of the weather, tight schedules, and long hours, we were very tired by the end of the sixth day and relieved that the inspection was over. Not surprisingly, the inspection team gave us very high marks for all of the MRCI scenarios.

On March 15, 1982, we flew to Honolulu and reported aboard EOD Group 1, Barbers Point, Hawaii, for five weeks of detachment/team training.

The worst part of the training was having to wear the chemical warfare Butyl rubber suit, M-3 TAP

(Toxicological Agent Protective) with the M-9A1 protective mask during surprisingly hot and humid weather. The experience reminded me of the summer I worked for the Bridwell Hereford Ranch. When we weren't hauling hay and alfalfa bales from the fields, I was stacking them in an incredibly hot metal barn's second-story hayloft. The only difference was that the Butyl rubber suit and mask were worse—I couldn't even chew my Skol.

The most enjoyable portion of the training was parachute operations: four day water jumps that included one equipment jump and one night, water jump. Because of my past experience in airborne operations, Gunner George graciously allowed me to jump-master all five jumps. The first four day jumps took place from Marine CH-46 helicopters into the West Loch of Pearl Harbor. Interestingly, an honest-to-goodness fifteen-foot—some claimed it to be at least twenty—hammerhead shark was often seen cruising about the West Loch seeking tasty EOD divers and jumpers for dinner. Fortunately, we never saw the man-eater during our stay. (I didn't watch the movie *Jaws* until after I had retired from the Navy.)

Our last jump took place outside of Pearl Harbor near Po Kai. On that particular night I had to drop Gunner, Jim, and Tony off first, then have the helo swing around and jump when the pilot gave me thumbs-up. All of us enjoyed our week of parachute operations—it beat the thunder out of walking around in hot, humid weather trying to view a chemical piece of ordnance from a fogged-up gas mask and fighting off a heat stroke in a Butyl rubber suit.

Because of the shortage of berthing at Barbers Point, we were "forced" to reside in individual rooms at the Holiday Isla Hotel in the heart of Waikiki on Kalakaua Avenue and Lewers Road, only a couple of blocks from the beach. We were also "forced" to eat at the many fine restaurants in the area. I even had time to visit the Davy

Jones Locker for a couple of cool ones one evening for old times' sake. While there, I gave a toast to the memory of my UDT teammates and my very good regular Navy friend John Bagos. I couldn't help but reflect on the good times John and I had had together over the years, and especially when I visited his home for a couple of days while he was stationed at Pearl Harbor's communications center. That visit took place when I was chief of Alfa Platoon in September of 1974 while traveling on board the USS *DuBuque* on our way to Subic Bay.

Our detachment/team training was generally enjoyable, but after five weeks it was time to return to Whidbey Island and cooler weather.

In July 1982 Detachment Whidbey spent two weeks aboard the USS *Constellation* (CV-64) in support of the Third Fleet exercises. It was my first time aboard an aircraft carrier, and my last. During the F-14, F-8, and A-6 aircraft launches, I learned the value of using ear plugs and the Navy Mickey Mouse ear protectors to reduce the incredible jet blast reverberations that seemed to penetrate all of my body. The blast was especially severe just before the steam-powered cable jerked the jet forward at a tremendous rate until the aircraft gained enough speed to shoot off the ship's bow under its own power. More important, I also learned that during the frantic activities of men and aircraft moving about the flight deck in preparation for individual aircraft launching, it was easy to get sucked into jet engine intakes or get blown over the side. It was a simple matter of being in the wrong place at the right time or, on the other side of the coin, the right place at the wrong time. Fortunately, everyone watched out for each other. Even so, fatal accidents were fairly common during launch and recovery operations. Those flight deck airdales and pilots don't get hazardous-duty pay for nothing.

In October 1982 Detachment Whidbey had to endure EOD Group 1's ORI (Operational Readiness Inspection) for a period of six days. The purpose of the ORI was to examine every facet of our detachment's administrative and operational capabilities in airborne and diving, conventional, unconventional, chemical and nuclear ordnance, and so on. When the inspection team arrived, I was delighted to discover that my old Alfa Platoon commander (1973–74 with SEAL Team 1), Lt. Jim Lake, was the OIC. After six days of intense and arduous administrative and operational activities under the watchful eyes of the inspection team, Detachment Whidbey had been judged very capable of performing our mission area responsibilities with ratings high above the norm.

During March 1983 Detachment Whidbey was tasked to support the Secret Service in Seattle during Queen Elizabeth's visit aboard the royal yacht for the better part of a week. We were required to swim underneath the dark piers and inspect all spaces with flashlights for any signs of terrorist activities or bombs. We also inspected the bottom of Puget Sound within a hundred meters or so of Her Majesty's yacht. Interestingly, a SEAL Team 1 platoon was hidden in a structure near the yacht. The platoon's tactical objective was to immediately neutralize any terrorist attack against the queen and/or the royal yacht.

After our waterborne search activities, Detachment Whidbey was utilized by the Secret Service to inspect all cameras and baggage in the lobby of the Westin Hotel, plus all of the rooms that were visited by the queen and her entourage for every type, design, and form of bomb. It was an awesome responsibility and required long, tiring hours of searching under beds, inside closets, commodes, under carpets, and in all areas that could possibly conceal a bomb and its supporting or diversionary devices.

Some of the more sophisticated terrorist bombs, which

had generally come out of Ireland and Libya, had a combination of collapsing circuits, photoelectric cells, magnetic, mercury, trembler, and pressure switches as the primary and/or secondary modes of triggering the detonation. Also, infrared and laser beam systems were sometimes used, alone or in combination with radio firing devices. It was a game of schemes and psychology when dealing with terrorists. The EOD profession was not an easy one, as was well-demonstrated in the movie *Juggernaut* with Richard Harris and Omar Sharif. However, an EOD technician never had to worry about finding a job after leaving the military.

During one of the days that we were working in the hotel lobby inspecting baggage and cameras, I ran into Captain Gormly, my past CO of UDT-12, and a friend. He was at that time the command staff officer of Naval Special Warfare Group 1. Captain Gormly told me that two of my old teammates, R. E. Saliant and Chief Paul McNally, had recently died of heart attacks, and that Capt. Maxi Stevenson had drowned.

Maxi Stevenson was the XO of UDT-12 when I first reported aboard after graduating from UDT Training Class 36 on December 3, 1965. Maxi stood about six feet tall, and weighed approximately 230 pounds the last time that I had seen him in 1980. Captain Gormly went on to explain that Maxi had been scuba diving with two friends in Hawaii when he made a slashing motion across his throat with his hand, indicating that he was out of air, followed by pointing toward the surface, indicating that he was going to return to the surface. Because Maxi's signals didn't indicate an emergency, they acknowledged and continued on their dive. Later, when they returned to the boat, they discovered that there were no signs of Maxi having returned from his aborted dive. The two men dove back to the vicinity where they had last seen him, and found his body a short distance from his scuba tanks. Obviously, Captain Stevenson had ditched his tanks and weight belt and tried to free-ascent to the surface, but apparently he blacked out before he could reach the surface.

Chief Paul McNally was one of the true legends of the West Coast UDT teams. Chief McNally had been one of my instructors while I was a member of UDT Training Class 36. Over the years, Paul and I had developed a type of a father/son relationship and were very close. Paul had always been a legendary long-distance swimmer, and delighted in competing with the occasional UDT line officers who competed as collegiate and Olympic swimmers. Much to their chagrin, Paul never failed to soundly defeat all of them until he was well into his forties.

Capt. Maxi Stevenson, Chief Paul McNally, and Petty Officer 1st Class R. E. Saliant were some of the last and best of the old-timers. In accordance with naval tradition, they had been piped over the side for the last time and passed over the bar for eternity.

In parting, Captain Gormly also told me that UDT-11 would become SEAL Team 5, and UDT-12 the new SDV (Swimmer Delivery Vehicle) Team 1 effective May 1983. On the East Coast at Little Creek, Virginia, UDT-20 would become SEAL Team 4, and UDT-22 the new SDV Team 2. Somehow I felt some sadness at the change—the UDTs were now history.

In August 1983 EOD Detachment Whidbey was tasked to support the Secret Service during Vice President Bush's visit to Glacier National Park during the national "Outdoors Week." Surprisingly, for us, the ambient temperature reached over 100 degrees throughout the week; however, the temperature dropped down into the fifties during the night.

That week, the four of us worked sixteen to eighteen hours a day crawling under beds, searching closets, the basement, and all of the other nooks and crannies of the old Lake McDonald Lodge and Apgar campground. We also donned our scuba gear—because the water's temperature was about 40 degrees, we naturally elected to wear our wet suits—and dove under and around the pier in back of the lodge, searching for any form of bombs or terrorist activities before the vice president and his wife toured the lake by boat. We were also utilized by the Secret Service to search under small bridges and the surrounding terrain prior to Vice President Bush's and Senator Alan Simpson's (Wyoming) fly-fishing trip by canoe down the McDonald Creek toward the middle fork of the Flathead River. I didn't have the time or opportunity to speak with the vice president, but I did get to speak with Senator Simpson for a few minutes about trout fishing, hunting, and backpacking. It didn't take me long to realize that Mr. Simpson—slender of build and about six feet four inches tall—was a knowledgeable fisherman and outdoorsman, and, most important to me, he was never condescending in tone or vocabulary and very enjoyable to talk to.

On two other occasions, Detachment Whidbey supported the Secret Service: during Mrs. Nancy Reagan's visit to Seattle in support of that administration's "War Against Drugs," and during Senator Gary Hart's visit to the Seattle area during his run for the Democratic candidacy for president. Fortunately, we never encountered any terrorist problems during any of the occasions that we supported the Secret Service.

In October 1983 Detachment Whidbey spent a few days at the U.S. Army's Yakima Firing Range to dispose of a large amount of retrograde munitions. While there, we had the opportunity to hunt for Hungarian partridge (called Huns) and prairie chickens for the better part of one day. It was a great day for varmint hunting, too.

The next morning, Gunner, Jim, and I waited and waited for Tony at our vehicles. The previous day, we had all agreed that we would muster at 0700 hours sharp at our vehicles and depart for the Yakima Firing Range. Because we were anxious to go hunting, Gunner George went to Tony's motel room and knocked on the door. After a minute or so the always garrulous Tony opened the door with a toothbrush in his mouth and nary a stitch of clothes on and asked, "Aren't you guys ready to go?"

Later that morning, Gunner George, Jim, Tony, and I began our hunt with Lady, my black Labrador retriever. As luck would have it, we blundered into a large flock of prairie chickens atop a barren knoll. The large birds slowly took flight and flew just out of range of everyone's shot. As we proceeded to the other side of the knoll, we ran into another flock that was too stupid to fly or run away. Tony and I, being practical men and meat hunters, each shot one on the ground (that was the limit per hunter), but Gunner and Jim missed cleanly. Tony's cock appeared to weigh nearly five pounds, and my hen approximately three. Later, Gunner and Jim decided to return to the Mesa Motel in Yakima while Tony and I continued to hunt for Hungarian partridge.

About two hours before sundown, with the sun and wind at our backs, Tony, Lady, and I had started back toward the EOD vehicle with our six Hun limits in our game bags when we saw a large badger lumbering along, approximately fifty meters at twelve o'clock. Because I had trained Lady to retrieve, I knew that I had best slip a couple of number-four buckshot into both barrels of my Winchester Model 23 side-by-side twelve-gauge shotgun before she spotted the badger and took off after him. I had barely gotten the cartridges into my shotgun's chambers when I noticed that Lady had seen the badger, which was then running to beat hell. Lady and I took off neck and neck toward the large member of the weasel family. I knew I had to get close enough to put some number-four buckshot into the badger before Lady got to him or else I would have a large veterinarian bill, a dead retriever, or both. Because Lady was nine years old, a little overweight, and somewhat slow, I knew I had to maintain my small lead on her and get near enough to the badger to fill him with at least one and a quarter ounces of buckshot—and did by a narrow margin. In an instant after the shot, Lady grabbed the badger's chest, but in the next the dying badger grabbed Lady by the nose. The badger was pulling revengefully from his end while Lady was bearing down and howling from hers. I ended the tug-of-war with a swift kick to the badger's head, stopping the tussle and resulting in Lady's nose suffering a neat slit through her left nostril. I turned around and noticed Tony laughing out of control with tears streaming down his cheeks. It was then that I realized it was time for both of us to have a good laugh.

However, the story was not over. Continuing toward our vehicle, we encountered a huge, well-endowed porcupine that must have weighed twenty-five to thirty pounds. Again I knew that if I didn't grab Lady in time, I would have a useless, blind retriever, or worse. I managed to grab her choke-chain collar just as she was headed for the porcupine. Once I got her under control, I guided her closer to the critter and gave her instructions to never, ever tangle with such a varmint in the future. That encounter was a good one in that both of us satisfied our curiosity and were none the worse for it.

Throughout that winter, while Lady was sleeping on my living room floor, she did have problems with nightmares. Occasionally she would whine and snort with her front feet twitching as if running from something. There was no doubt that she was reliving her terrifying and humbling experience with that mortally wounded badger. It would be a long time before we could forget about the events of that hunt. Lady eventually died at the ripe old age of fifteen. The wonderful thing about a Labrador is that the dog is always loyal, and returns a person's love, affection, and faithfulness, no matter what.

During the early summer of '83 we spent the better part of two weeks on Kodiak Island, Alaska, riding a Navy minesweeper during a minesweeping exercise, and we encountered a nasty storm in the Shelikof Strait and the Cook Inlet.

During our stay at the fishing village of Kodiak before the minesweeper picked us up, we fished for red salmon with flies in the Buskin River and toured the island.

Once the four of us and our diving gear were aboard, Jim Collins and I slept in the line locker on makeshift bunks, hastily fabricated from plywood and two-by-fours, that were located all the way forward in the bow. Because the seas were rough and our boat was small, it was like riding a wild bronco in slow motion, and difficult to keep from rolling out of our racks during the night. In spite of my past record, I came perilously close to getting seasick and ruining my "sea daddy" image. The last couple of days that I was on that minesweeper, I felt little better than flotsam. I was one happy squid when I finally walked over the gangway and onto terra firma.

On the morning of February 10, 1984, my retirement ceremony took place at the Whidbey Island EOD Detachment office building on the old seaplane base. It was a very sobering occasion for me.

After the ceremony, approximately seventy-five EOD/UDT/SEALs and retirees attended a party at the home of my relief, Chief Tim Herron. It was quite a blow-out and was the first meeting of the Navy EOD Association's Northwest Chapter. I had finally gotten the opportunity to meet many of the famous old-timers, whose military service dated back to World War II. By 2200 hours I was asleep in my camper, dead to the world and feeling absolutely no pain.

By February sixteenth I had my truck and my camper filled to the gills and headed for Montana, where unknown adventures and tribulations awaited me.

During my twenty years, two months, and ten days in the Navy, I had fought the good fight, I had finished the race. But, I thought, as I drove through Ellensburg, Washington, I'm no longer moored to the Navy—I'm a free man! I had visions of fulfilling my lifelong dreams of trapping, backpacking, hunting, fishing, camping, canoeing, exploring, and doing those things that I thought were never possible before. I really didn't know where I was going until I got there. And, in some ways, it didn't matter as long as it was in the Rocky Mountains in Montana.

EPILOGUE

My career as a Navy radioman, EOD/UDT/SEAL technician reflects, in a small way, many legacies that have been handed down through all generations of American military men—including men of all classes, who, when called to arms, faithfully served and died for their country.

My three books—*Death in the Jungle*, *Death in the Delta*, and *Master Chief*—are dedicated to those men who served this country honorably, who took up arms and died for Old Glory in the fight against tyranny. I'm thankful for those military men who served and fought during my youth. I was never the same after listening to many of those old warriors' experiences during the Normandy invasion and their march to Germany or the sorrows of the Bataan death march on Luzon Island in the Philippines in '42. My good friend Father Webb, Catholic priest at the Coronado NAB chapel, was with the Marines during that cold winter of 1950–51 when they rescued the frozen remnant of one of our Army divisions at the Chosin Reservoir from the Chinese Communists who crossed the Yalu River into North Korea. Father Webb stated that it was a long and bitter battle to the southern tip of South Korea, where the rest of the U.S. and Allied forces finally took a stand.

In the late fifties and sixties it was time for my generation to serve and fight for our country. Sadly, there were a few who refused to serve their country, and tragically, some even served and worked openly for the enemy as informants and saboteurs. "Hanoi Jane" was one of the most infamous during those dark days.

In spite of the traitorous few, I specifically dedicate my books to those of my generation—those who remained true to this country—who served, fought, and gave their life's blood in Vietnam, Grenada, Panama, the Persian Gulf, Central and South America, Somalia, and many other places too secret to mention.

And we should not forget those who fought so long ago before and after our Declaration of Independence in 1776 for our God-given Constitution and its amendments, and for Mom and Dad, family traditions, and apple pie. This nation's independence was purchased and maintained with a high cost of blood through military and public service to God, country, and family. Some of our wise and God-fearing forefathers had this to say:

> We have not a government strong enough to restrain the unbridled passions of men. This constitution was made only for a moral and a religious people. It is wholly inadequate for any other.
> —John Adams

> Reason and experience forbid us to expect public morality in the absence of religious principle.
> —George Washington

> The world will little note, nor long remember what we say here but it can never forget what they did here. It is for us the living, rather, to be dedicated here to the unfinished work which they who fought here have thus far so nobly advanced. It is rather for us to be here dedicated to the great task remaining before us—that from these honored dead we take increased devotion to that cause for which they gave the last full measure of devotion—

that we here highly resolve that these dead shall not have died in vain—that this nation, under God, shall have a new birth of freedom—and that government of the people, by the people, for the people, shall not perish from the earth.

> —Abraham Lincoln, Gettysburg Address, November 19, 1863, at the dedication of the Gettysburg National Cemetery

Finally, I'm especially thankful for my older teammates who were my mentors at one time or another and for those few mates who didn't hesitate to tell me candidly of their experiences of success and, more important, their failures. A teammate who is willing to expose his innermost thoughts relative to his good and bad experiences of military and personal life is a friend indeed. Cherish and hang on to such a man. As we all know, society today is changing rapidly. There are some who have little respect for the blood that has been shed for the freedom that they so readily take for granted. I hope that the sacrifices of my generation of EOD and SpecWar personnel, the lessons learned and the memories of these books, will not be soon forgotten.

It is possible that I have made mistakes in the telling of some of the events of these books; I know that I have failed to record some of the names of the EOD/UDT/SEAL personnel in several chapters simply because I couldn't locate individuals who had the information. I encourage my EOD and SpecWar mates to submit names and dates to me personally for corrections and additions to future editions.

Semper Fi,

Gary R. Smith
June 1994

Find out the whole story about
'Nam—from the swamp warrior
who served five tours in hell.

Death reigned as king in the
jungles of Vietnam. Gary R. Smith
and his teammates gave each other
the courage to attain the unattainable.

DEATH IN THE JUNGLE
Diary of a Navy SEAL

by Gary R. Smith and
Alan Maki

Published by Ivy Books.
Available in bookstores everywhere.

Don't miss the second account of
Gary R. Smith's Vietnam
experience:

DEATH IN THE DELTA

"Mankind is a predator by nature and a
hunter by instinct. I loved to hunt. It was
in my blood. And I was now ready to head
back to the bush, to hunt the biggest
game in the world—man."
—*Death in the Delta*

DEATH IN THE DELTA
Diary of a Navy SEAL

by Gary R. Smith and
Alan Maki

Published by Ivy Books.
Available in your local bookstore.